Mobius *on*

Emerging Markets

Mobius *on*

Emerging Markets

Dr J Mark Mobius

The Second Edition of
The Investor's Guide to Emerging Markets

FT
PITMAN
PUBLISHING

London · Hong Kong · Johannesburg
Melbourne · Singapore · Washington Dc

PITMAN PUBLISHING
128 Long Acre, London WC2E 9AN
Tel: +44 (0)171 447 2000
Fax: +44 (0) 171 240 5771

A Division of Pearson Professional Limited

This book is the second edition of
The Investor's Guide to Emerging Markets, published in 1995.

The Investor's Guide to Emerging Markets was published and distributed in North America
by Irwin Professional Publishing, New York.

© Dr J. Mark Mobius 1996

The right of Dr J. Mark Mobius to be identified as author
of this work has been asserted by him in accordance
with the Copyright, Designs and Patents Act 1988.

ISBN 0 273 62284 6

British Library Cataloguing in Publication Data
A CIP catalogue record for this book can be obtained from the British Library.

10 9 8 7 6 5 4 3 2 1

Typeset by Northern Phototypesetting Co. Ltd, Bolton
Printed and bound in Great Britain by Biddles Ltd, Guildford and King's Lynn

The Publishers' policy is to use paper manufactured from sustainable forests.

About the Author

....

Mark Mobius is Director Emeritus of Templeton Investment Management (Singapore) Pte Ltd., and Director of Templeton Asset Management (Hong Kong) Ltd., Director and Executive Vice President of Templeton Worldwide, Inc. He heads the Emerging Markets Division globally for Franklin/Templeton Group, based in the United States, with offices in Argentina, Hong Kong, India, Poland, Russia, Singapore, South Africa, and Vietnam.

He is the coordinating manager of over 34 funds, with funds under management totalling over US$9 billion. The funds include the Templeton Emerging Markets Investment Trust PLC listed on the London Stock Exchange; the Templeton Emerging Markets Fund, Inc., the Templeton Russia Fund, the Templeton Dragon Fund, and the Templeton China World Fund listed on the New York Stock Exchange; the Indonesia Development Fund Ltd listed on the Singapore Stock Exchange; and numerous private funds managed for institutional clients in the United States, Canada, Australia, and Europe. Templeton emerging market funds under Dr Mobius's management have won numerous awards, from organizations such as Lipper International Closed-End Funds Service, USA Today, and Micropal among others.

Dr Mobius has spent 30 years living in Asia and working in emerging markets, with extensive experience in economic research and analysis. He holds a PhD in economics and politics from MIT in the United States and currently resides in Hong Kong, Singapore and other parts of the world.

Contents

Part Three
INVESTMENT

A note on statistics and sources

Please note that many statistics are used in the text of this book but are not cited. This is because of the sheer volume of research that we receive in our offices, the frequency of recycling this data, and the rapidity with which it changes. The figures are most often presented as representative only, and are subject to change with market developments. I would like to thank collectively the research staff of all the brokers and securities companies that we deal with around the world for their diligence in consistently supplying us with up-to-date market information on a regular basis.

Preface and Acknowledgements

This book grew out of the desire to introduce investors to the exciting, and rewarding, realm of emerging markets. I hope that both laymen and professionals will find the subject of interest. For the layman the book gives an introduction to one of the most interesting investment arenas in the world today. For the professional, it gives an insight into how one emerging markets investment manager views these markets and the philosophy he applies when investing in such markets.

In this book I try to define emerging markets, review their history, provide profiles of investors who should invest in emerging markets and reasons why; a description of specific emerging market regions and some individual markets; an outline of techniques and strategies that can be used by emerging markets investors; and finally, insights into what I believe is necessary to be a successful emerging market investor. As much as possible, I have tried to give a comprehensive view, but the rapid changes taking place in the developing world could make each sentence obsolete the day it is written.

The most significant challenge facing emerging markets today is fluctuating levels of investor confidence. When emerging markets were being pushed to new highs around 1993, investors were willing to ignore all the problems inherent in such markets, problems which normally would intimidate investors, such as political instability, lack of infrastructure, and discrimination against foreign investors. Sure enough, once prices reached a plateau and then began declining, the negative news became more salient. In this book, I want to encourage investors to look at emerging markets as more than market index highs and lows. Instead, I want to guide the international investor into a long-term, patient, development-centered view of emerging markets, which takes into account the nature of economic and industrial growth in newly developed countries.

Stock markets in emerging economies are growing dramatically faster than those found in developed countries. The market capitalization of emerging markets constitutes only about one-tenth of the total global market capitalization at this time. But the growth rate of the emerging markets capitalization is double that of the developed markets. Moreover, there is considerable scope for that growth rate to be sustained well into the future. While the ratio of market capitalization to gross domestic product (GDP) in higher income countries typically averages over 90 per cent today, the corresponding average for emerging markets is around half that figure, with the majority of emerging markets falling below the 25 per cent market capitalization to GDP ratio. This means that the stock markets themselves in emerging economies have lots of room for expansion at the current growth rate before they reach any kind of ceiling on that growth. The disparity in growth rates is compelling. Without an appreciation of why it exists, one may miss the importance of emerging markets altogether.

Why are emerging markets growing so rapidly? The reasons include: better investment returns; faster national economic growth; increasing number of listed companies; improved stock market infrastructure; and more disposable income to invest on the part of citizens within emerging markets. All of these factors are working together, creating a dynamic which pushes up the value, the volume and the capitalization of emerging stock markets. So, let's look at them in more detail.

First, faster economic growth. Since, in the long term, stock markets reflect the underlying health and development of the economies in which they reside, the faster growth of the emerging economies means that the whole stock exchange index value is carried upward on the wing of national economic development. Further, the rapidly rising prices of emerging market stocks in real terms have not only been because of overall greater economic performance in these countries, but also because individual companies are able to expand their earnings faster than their developed market counterparts. Greater demand for the limited amount of stock available on emerging counters, fueled by this solid performance, further exerts pressures which lift share prices.

Second, the number of new companies listed on emerging market stock exchanges is growing faster than in the developed nations. Privatization of government enterprises is resulting in many more stock market listings. Former family-run companies have over generations achieved a size, status and change that permit them to become listed public entities. And the sheer number of companies that can be sustained by the burgeoning economies of Asia, Latin America and Eastern Europe means that listings are destined to multiply.

Sources of investment capital in emerging markets are also multiplying. Pension systems in emerging markets, partially as a result of state-owned enterprise privatization, are being reconfigured to permit participation in the domestic equity markets. Higher incomes for workers in emerging economies mean that a greater proportion of take-home pay can be allocated to savings and investment. Add to this pool of domestic money the return of substantial flight capital, once driven away by Draconian government regulations are now attracted by relaxed government regulations and tempting returns on local bourses. Finally, foreign equity investors from the United States, Japan and Europe in search of diversification and higher returns are feeding their funds into the overall demand for emerging market shares.

Technical enhancements in emerging markets are also contributing to market growth. Areas such as stock exchange regulation, settlement and trading systems, and custodial services are all being upgraded. Many emerging stock markets started life as exclusive clubs for the wealthy few – this has been abruptly replaced with egalitarian, open market practices which are attracting a wide audience. These changes have come about often because the old structures and customs did not meet the new and expanded requirements of the growing national economy. Settlement and trading systems have long represented a major bottleneck to developing a capital market. Today, a greater commitment to efficient practices such as central registration, clearing and depository systems is in evidence.

These four forces – surplus investment capital, new listings, generous company earnings and enhanced technical capabilities of local stock exchanges – are the foundation of emerging market growth today. Emerging stock markets represent one of the keys to the development of market economies and thus a vital element necessary for improvement in the lives of people living in the lower-income areas of the world. I hope that this book makes some contribution towards an understanding of this emerging markets phenomenon.

The book may also serve as an introduction to the practice of foreign investing in general. I believe that the better one appreciates the risks inherent in emerging market investments, the more likely one is to benefit from the upside and skirt the danger areas. A large portion of this book is devoted to an explanation of what one is embarking upon when investing in lower income countries. The picture is not all rosy. There are risks of every kind – political risks, currency risks, company or investment risks, broker risks, settlement risks, safekeeping risks and operational risks.

A section of the book has also been reserved for investment strategies and techniques specific to emerging market investing. This area of investing is not as well-documented as is investing in, say, government bonds. Nor are the investment techniques necessarily the same. In emerging markets, the analysis of systemic conditions is of much more importance than in other markets. One may take for granted rules of disclosure, secure custody, or even dispute resolution mechanisms like an impartial judiciary – investors in emerging markets can take no such comfort in the prevailing systemic environment of most emerging markets.

Over the years, there have been many emerging market investment participants each contributing knowledge and experience to the field. Professionals such as Antoine Van Agtmael and David Gill were among the original team at the International Finance Corporation who formulated many of the concepts which nudged the emerging nations towards capital market development. Barton Biggs and his associate Madhav Dhar at Morgan Stanley have done much to foster acceptance of emerging markets investing, particularly among institutional investors all over the world. At Capital International, David Fisher launched the first major privately placed emerging markets fund. As one of the original global investors, John Templeton led the way for US global investors by venturing into the emerging market of Japan in the 1960s. Tom Hansberger at the Templeton organization conceived of the viability of a widely distributed, stock exchange listed, emerging markets fund for global investors.

The Franklin/Templeton Group, under the able leadership of Charlie Johnson, has expanded the scope of emerging markets funds since the original listing of Templeton Emerging Markets Fund, Inc. in New York, the Templeton Emerging Markets Investment Trust Plc in the UK and the open-ended Templeton Developing Markets Trust. Since then, there have been numerous new emerging market fund offerings and growing interest in such investments, with benefits accruing to both investors and the world's emerging market countries.

Additionally, emerging market investing tends to involve a large team of experts. It would not be possible to manage all of the Templeton emerging market funds without the able team of professionals with which I work every day. The image of Mark Mobius as a one-man show is fallacious. I'm not capable of managing all the emerging market funds alone. The Franklin/Templeton organization consists of over 4,500 professionals, many of whom are involved in an entire complex of activities which go into successful emerging market fund management. These activities include not only research and analysis, but also fund accounting, custodial relations, corporate action facilities, pricing, performance tracking, legal monitoring, risk analysis, diversification assessment and a number of other critical activities. Most important is investor service. Every week over 2,000 telephone inquiries arrive at the Franklin/Templeton offices. These calls are important because they give staff an opportunity to explain our investment philosophy.

Although I am the spokesman for the award-winning Templeton Emerging Markets Team, I am supported by a capable group of emerging markets specialists, in addition to many consultants stationed around the world. Of course, in this book, I take upon myself the responsibility for all errors of fact and/or omission.

Much of this book's philosophical leanings and deep conviction in the ultimate value of emerging markets stem from ideas first enunciated by Sir John Templeton. This book is an opportunity to recognize his revolutionary vision and early influence on my approach to investing.

This book deals with my passion, emerging market investing. However, one never works in a vacuum and over the years my efforts have been substantially aided by an army of analysts and researchers. More specifically, I'd like to show my appreciation of their dedication by acknowledging Tom Wu, Allan Lam, Zita Ng, Eddie Chow, Dennis Lim, Ong Tek Khoan and others in our global offices for keeping me on the road and in the right country.

My writing team included Angus Barclay, Alister Hill, Susan Forester and Mervin Lim. Financial Times/Pitman Publishing provided us with a first-rate and accommodating editor, Richard Stagg, who nurtured the process and kept the whole project on track without being obtrusive.

And finally, I'd like to thank the millions of individual investors who have placed their funds with Templeton over the years. Their long-term commitment of investment capital is a key factor in enabling companies to grow, markets to expand, and countries to pull themselves and their citizens out of poverty. Let's keep that virtuous circle turning.

Introduction

by Sir John Templeton

When I started investing overseas in poor countries like Japan in the early 1950s, it wasn't called emerging markets then. Mark's book is the kind of source of knowledge we needed then, to help people see how the world was and where it was heading. That kind of perspective would have helped make wise investment decisions. For example, because I knew that the Japanese were industrious people that saved a lot, and were likely to improve their living standards quickly, I could tell that Japan's economy and businesses were going to get better. Japan was the perfect example of how emerging economies can transform over time.

Now, I'm 83 years old but I've still never lost my interest in investing, or in the development of people around the world that makes companies and stock markets grow. When I first started the Templeton Growth Fund in 1954, I already instinctively knew that international investing was the way to find the best bargain stocks with the most appreciation potential, and to protect myself from losses by being diversified. I've stuck with those principles my whole life and they've never served me wrong.

In spite of the arrival of lots of new analytic tools and theories, I'm glad to see that Mark has adopted much the same approach to investing that I have, and that it has also served Templeton investors well. When Mark started out in 1987 with the Templeton Emerging Markets Fund, he had only $87 million to invest in only 6 markets. Look at Templeton today – Mark has $9 billion under management in an array of emerging market funds and has a range of up to 45 countries from which to choose his investments.

Templeton's emerging markets group came along at a good time. Investors were ready to accept three key investment tenets.

First, they were becoming less parochical in their view of the markets and were more willing to try out international markets. Second, investors began to discover the benefits of mutual funds, which are the only one way for a modest investor to obtain professional financial management at a reasonable price. And finally, investors were sophisticated enough to seek ways to reduce their investment risks and protect their portfolios from sudden market swings. Diversification is the answer, and has come to be accepted as one of the best means to reduce portfolio investment risk.

Mark was an early pioneer in emerging markets. He accepted the above concepts early on, and has become a tireless proponent of these fundamental investment principles. His great success in applying them and achieving outstanding returns for his clients over the years has left him in a field of his own when it comes to experience and understanding of emerging markets.

I was born in Winchester, Tennessee, in 1912. Since that time, wages have risen over 10 fold; the federal budget is now almost 300 times as great as at the peak of prosperity in 1929; real consumption per person worldwide has more than quadrupled; 85% of the American people were needed on the farm at that time, but that figure has shrunk to less than 4% and even this number are able to produce a food surplus. Who could have imagined when I was born, the variety of new blessings to come? Today, who can imagine the even greater potential of the next 80 years? Our children and grandchildren are likely to enjoy even more progress than we have. For many reasons, progress may not only continue but may also accelerate.

I think that when the history books are written, the past 20 years will go down as one of the great turning points in history, equivalent almost to the discovery of the New World by Columbus, because up until 20 years ago there were two tremendously depressing influences all over the world. One was the fear of nuclear war; the other one was that the Russians might be right in saying that communism was going to dominate the world. They said it for over 50 years and although I didn't think it could prevail, I had to admit that 23 nations had been captured – never by voting – but captured, and no captured nation ever became free until five years ago.

Now that the influence of communism is gone, the whole world is going to grow more rapidly. There'll be far more international travel, far more investing across international boundaries, far more international trade, less money wasted on armaments, a greater spread of religion and a greater feeling of brotherhood. All of these things will speed up the rate of growth, which is already marvellous. I think it will add greatly to the world's annual growth.

Many people question my unbridled enthusiasm. Sure, I know the world is full of problems. In all of my years, there's never been a year free of problems – big problems, and I never knew how they'd all be solved. In fact, some of them never are solved. You just learn to live with them. But I would say that the problems today are probably no greater, maybe less, than the average of problems throughout my lifetime. But people don't think about problems in the context of history. They think that today's worries will always be there and that existing conditions can't change. I encourage people to try to foresee the future by considering how dramatic have been the changes already, but it's an uphill struggle.

That's why I think it is so important for Mark to have brought out this book now. The book devotes considerable space to reminding readers that the world has changed, that the threats we used to most worry about aren't as prevalent as maybe we still think they are. There is greater world consensus on what it takes to make people healthy, wealthy and to increase living standards. And that changes the profile of the world, changes the way we look at it and should change the way we invest in it.

It's already possible to see that people don't think emerging markets are as exotic and lawless as they once did. Emerging market investing as a frontier sport has made way for international investing, the search for bargains. That's what I started in the 1950s and Mark has taken it to new heights in the 1990s.

Part I

Emerging Markets

*E*merging markets, while a minor global financial force at this time, are expanding rapidly. An understanding of emerging market growth trends is critical to an appreciation of what financial markets will look like in the future.

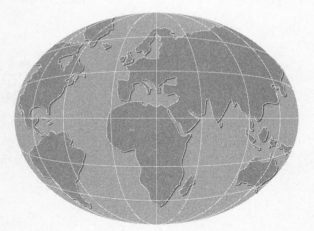

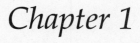

Chapter 1

Origins of Emerging Markets

● THE BIRTH OF EMERGING MARKETS INVESTMENT

The step from international investing to the creation of a specific emerging markets investment funds category has evolved over a long period of time and reflects the evolution of global investing in general. When, in the 1800s, diligent and creative Scottish investors were purchasing farm land in the American West, they probably saw an opportunity to invest in a new frontier, a much less mature market than the European continent. In fact, their conception was probably oriented towards the great potential for wealth appreciation that they saw before them. The 100th Anniversary report of the Alliance Trust of the United Kingdom, established in 1888, relates how that trust invested in what was then a primitive and emerging market: America.

The actual birth of emerging markets as a portfolio investment category had to wait until 1986, when the International Finance Corporation (IFC), the World Bank subsidiary, started its efforts to promote capital market development in the less developed countries. During the tenure of Robert McNamara as President of the World Bank, capital market development began to be taken seriously. This was after a great deal of groundwork was done on the theoretical foundation by economists such as Raymond Goldsmith of Yale University, who wrote about the relationships between real growth and financial intermediation. Robert McNamara established a unit within the IFC in 1971 as the global locus for capital market development theory within the World Bank Group. This group focused the attention of World Bank member countries on the importance of securities markets as a means of mobilizing domestic savings and attracting foreign portfolio capital for productive investment within the context of a competitive market system.

In 1986, at the behest of the World Bank's IFC, 11 institutional investors put US$50 million into an emerging markets fund. At that time, the fund manager was reported to have told investors that it might take the company one year to invest that money. As of 1993 that fund had grown to over US$1 billion, and the fund managers were quoted as saying that if they were given the same US$50 million today, it would take just one month to be fully invested.

It was 1987 when the Templeton organization started the Templeton Emerging Markets Fund, with the specific aim of being the world's first fund listed on a stock exchange with investments in emerging markets. The high returns of that fund, along with the success of other subsequent funds, inspired a considerable amount of excitement in the investment world. The amount of money pouring into emerging markets funds became significant. With the subsequent development of formal securities markets, equity legal structures, and trading systems, international equity portfolio investing was more clearly identified as being compatible with investing in emerging economies around the world.

The purview of international portfolio investors was quite limited in the early days of global portfolio investing. This was so much the case that investing in Japan in the 1960s was considered to be a risky and pioneering adventure. Certainly, had the notion of an "emerging market" existed at that time, Japan would surely have been placed in that category. Japan was perceived in those days to be a land of cheap and shoddy exports, weak currency and an unstable political future. Investors at that time were able to select Japanese stocks at four times price/earnings* ratios: a far cry from the high double-digit price/earnings ratios we have seen in Japan recently.

---

* The ratio of stock price per share and after earnings per share. A lower ratio indicates a cheaper stock since the company earnings are large in relation to its price.

● DEFINITION OF EMERGING MARKETS

This leads us to the point beyond which we should not continue without establishing some working definitions. Confusion persists among investors and readers of the literature of global economics, business and politics because of the loose application of frequently used, but ill-defined terms like "developing" or "markets." The definitions presented below are not definitive, but I'll at least try to be consistent in their usage throughout this book.

"Emerging markets," entered the vocabulary of the investment world only recently. While I was studying economic development at the Massachusetts Institute of Technology (MIT) in the early 1960s, the term "underdeveloped countries" was still in use, while the more palatable euphemisms of "developing countries," "the South" or "the Third World" were just coming into being.

The term "emerging market" as used in reference to stock markets, was first coined by officers at the IFC when they began working on the concept of country funds and capital market development in the less-developed regions of the world. Today, the IFC has a fuller sense of the meaning of this term:

> "Emerging stock markets can be variously defined. On the one hand, 'emerging' implies that change is underway, that a market is growing in size and sophistication in contrast to a market that is relatively small, inactive, and gives little appearance of change. Alternatively, emerging market can refer to a stock market in any developing economy, no matter how well developed the stock market itself may be, with the implication that the stock market's potential to emerge further is strongly linked to the economy's overall development potential."
>
> (IFC, *The IFC Indexes: Methodology, Definitions and Practices*, August 1994)

IFC uses this latter definition.

In this way, then, the IFC links the stock market classification to the country classification. If the country is still categorized as developing, even if the stock market is fully functional and well-regulated, the market will be labeled "emerging."

When the Templeton organization asked me to manage the Templeton Emerging Markets Fund in 1987, a universally accepted operational definition of an "emerging market" did not exist. Intuitively we knew that "emerging" implied "developing" or "underdeveloped," but we could not ascertain what the cutoff point for "emerging" versus "emerged" markets should be. The "low-"

In this way, then, the IFC links the stock market classification to the country classification. If the country is still categorized as developing, even if the stock market is fully functional and well regulated, the market will be labeled 'emerging."

and "middle-"income list of countries fitted into our intuitive definition of what were "emerging markets." These categories are based on per capita GDP figures, and are published annually by the World Bank in its publications *The World Bank Atlas* and *World Development Report*. We found that the World Bank's classification of "high-," "middle-" and "low-"income countries offered us a good starting point, and coincided with the IFC approach.

Since 1987, when the original list of emerging markets, based on per capita GDP, was compiled from World Bank data, there have been a number of changes in the per capita income rankings of countries, with some countries falling out of the "low-" and "middle-"rankings, and others moving down from the "high" income category. Anomalies in these figures have also had to be ironed out. The concept of graduation or demotion from one category to another is still a definitional challenge.

For example, the matter of oil-rich countries in the developing world had to be addressed. Although such countries as Kuwait and Saudi Arabia had per capita incomes clearly higher than the "low-" and "middle-"income countries, the distribution of that income was such that general living standards had not reached developed country status. Also, they were not fully developed in the sense that their economies were not industrialized and did not have the infrastructure or capital market system normally associated with the "developed" or "industrialized" world.

Another question not adequately addressed in this debate was: When does a stock market cease to become an emerging market? As emerging country income levels rise, and emerging stock markets become more developed and easily accessible to all international investors, we will then face the challenge of deciding which countries or markets should be deleted from the list and which should be added. Maybe there is a United Kingdom or United States emerging market in our future!

Some stock markets which continue to be classified as "emerging" are in fact very well-developed and are excluded by some international investors from this category. Hong Kong is a prime example of this, considered by some international investors as one of the world's major stock markets and therefore not included in their list of emerging markets. One pension fund manager said: "I don't consider Hong Kong an emerging market because it's easy to invest there and it's very liquid." However, when one considers the fact that the 1997 reversion makes it part of China, it is clearly in the emerging country category. As noted above, without a defined "graduation point," people are slow to fully appreciate the strides made in economic development, and many markets remain classified as "emerging," in spite of having met mature market standards.

Since those days, numerous attempts have been made to create the conclusive definition of emerging markets. Some investors have defined an emerging stock market as one which represents less than a certain percentage of all the world's stock market capitalization. For example, in one case, an *emerging market* was defined as a market which represents less than 3 percent of the world's stock market capitalization. Some emerging market experts have eliminated certain emerging markets because they either have low security turnover or have very few companies listed. In another case, an analyst included those markets which had less than US$2 billion in market turnover and fewer than 100 listed companies.

The permutations and combinations are numerous and a precise definition, particularly in our changing world, may never be possible. Importantly, the global securities industry itself has not yet defined *emerging markets* in a universally acceptable manner, which means that fund managers and others active in financial matters in this part of the world are likely never to be operating with the same definition of emerging markets. Consensus does seem to converge on the belief that emerging markets require more research and custodial work than normally

As emerging country income levels rise, and emerging stock markets become more developed and easily accessible to all international investors, we will then face the challenge of deciding which countries or markets should be deleted from the list and which should be added.

expected in the developed markets, and that emerging market investment often implies a greater degree of perceived risk.

The recent term "emerging markets" may be a euphemism, but it is also a declaration of hope and faith on the part of those of us who specialize in the study of emerging stock markets. Many believe that although some of the stock markets of the developing nations may sometimes seem to be "submerged," they are generally emerging into better and bigger things. Thus the term *emerging* is perhaps the best description of what we are witnessing.

The low- and middle-income countries list that we use as a base for our investments will continue to change as economic and political situations change around the globe. In 1987, it included all countries in South and Central America; all countries in Asia except Japan, Australia and New Zealand; all countries in Africa; and some countries in Southern Europe, specifically Portugal, Greece and Turkey. Since our original list was compiled, the dissolution of the Soviet Union and a breakaway of Eastern European countries have taken place. These newly independent countries have made more entries to our list of emerging markets possible. That meant that by 1992 all of the East European countries, Russia, Ukraine, and countries which were previously part of the USSR or the former Soviet empire were added to the list. Today the list is 124 countries long. We would consider them to be "emerging" either because they:

- have low or middle per capita incomes;
- have undeveloped capital markets (i.e., the market capitalization of their stock markets represents only a small portion of their gross national product);
- are not industrialized.

At first glance, it may seem that the range of lower-income countries – all 124 of them – is prohibitively diverse for serious investment analysis. But there are many practical factors that have served to reduce the list for us. When we started investing the Templeton Emerging Markets Fund in 1987, we found that most countries were excluded as initial investment possibilities because of a number of barriers. At that time we only had eight countries in which to invest. Even today some barriers remain.

No markets

Many of the emerging countries now do not have stock markets, or even any kind of formal capital market, where investment may be made in an orderly and relatively safe manner. The entire organization of capital markets, in general, and stock markets, in particular, requires a complex infrastructure of settlement procedures, payment systems, custodial or safe-keeping facilities, regulations and a broad range of relationships which are non-existent in most emerging markets today. In fact, one of the defining characteristics of an emerging market is the scarcity of such facilities.

Foreign investment restrictions

Many countries forbid or restrict foreign investment, or impose foreign exchange restrictions which make it impossible to transfer money into or, more importantly, out of the country. In some funds, we therefore enlarged our investment universe to include investments in those companies which are listed in stock markets in major industrialized nations but which attribute more than 50 percent of their sales, profits, or assets to business conducted in specific emerging economies. This provides us with the opportunity to invest indirectly in some emerging market countries which continue to restrict foreign portfolio investment.

For example, early on we invested in companies listed on the London Stock Exchange, whose operations were primarily in Chile. In another case we invested in one excellent company whose operations were primarily in Israel, but which was listed on the New York Stock Exchange. Today there are companies in Australia whose business is primarily Vietnam-based, as no stock market has yet been opened there. In this way, when identifying the entire scope of emerging market investments, companies eligible for investment must be identified on the basis of their primary area of operations and not just on their country of listing.

Taxation

Finally, some countries impose harsh taxation on foreign investors which make such investments unrealistic. Capital gains taxes are the enemy of all equity investors, not to mention the myriad fees levied in some countries, where alternative sources of government revenue are sparse. Prohibitively high taxation and fees have kept us out of many countries in the past, although many governments are now recognizing the damage done to their market development by such policies and are moving to redress the issue.

In 1995, out of the total 124 lower-income countries we listed (Table 1.1 overleaf), over 40 had stock markets but only 24 had actively functioning stock markets in which foreigners could realistically make portfolio investments. Even among the 24 countries there are those which, although open to foreign portfolio investors, continue to place severe restrictions on the entry and exit of foreign investment capital. Such countries include India, Korea, Taiwan and Chile. For reference, most tables in this book cover only those 24 countries in which we can viably invest, as full statistics on the whole range of lower-income countries would be outside the scope of this work.

Table 1.1 Lower income countries

	Population, 1995 (millions)	Area (1,000 sq km)	GNP per capita, 1993 (US$)
Afghanistan	23	652	200
Albania	3	29	340
Algeria	28	2,382	1,780
Angola	11	1,247	600
Argentina	34	2,767	7,220
Armenia	4	30	660
Azerbaijan	8	87	730
Bahrain	1	1	8,030
Bangladesh	121	144	220
Belarus	10	208	2,870
Benin	5	113	430[c]
Bhutan	2	47	180
Bolivia	8	1,099	760[a]
Botswana	1	582	2,790
Brazil	161	8,512	2,930
Bulgaria	8	111	1,140
Burkina Faso	10	274	300
Burundi	6	28	180
Cambodia	10	181	200[c]
Cameroon	13	475	820
Central African Republic	3	623	400
Chad	6	1,284	210
Chile	14	757	3,170
China	1,199	9,561	490
Colombia	35	1,139	1,400[c]
Congo	2	342	950
Costa Rica	3	51	2,150
Cote d'Ivoire	14	322	630
Czech Republic	10	79	2,710
Dominican Republic	8	49	1,230
Ecuador	11	284	1,200
Egypt	58	1,001	660
El Salvador	6	21	1,320
Estonia	2	48	3,080
Ethiopia	57	1,097	100
Gabon	1	268	4,960
Georgia	5	70	580
Ghana	17	239	430
Greece	10	132	7,390[a]
Guatemala	11	109	1,100
Guinea	7	246	500
Haiti	7	28	370
Honduras	6	112	600
Hong Kong	6	1	18,060

Table 1.1 Continued

	Population, 1995 (millions)	Area (1,000 sq km)	GNP per capita, 1993 (US$)
Hungary	10	93	3,350[b]
India	934	3,288	300
Indonesia	193	1,905	740[b]
Iran	65	1,648	2,200
Iraq	21	438	1,940
Israel	6	21	13,920
Jamaica	2	11	1,440
Jordan	4	89	1,190
Kazakhstan	17	2,717	1,560
Kenya	28	580	270
Korea	45	99	7,660[c]
Kuwait	2	18	19,360
Kyrgyz Republic	5	199	850[c]
Laos	5	237	280
Latvia	3	66	2,010
Lebanon	4	10	1,400
Lesotho	2	30	650
Liberia	2	98	395
Libya	5	1,760	5,410
Lithuania	4	65	1,320
Madagascar	13	587	220[b]
Malawi	11	118	200
Malaysia	20	330	3,140
Mali	10	1,240	270
Mauritania	2	1,026	500[c]
Mauritius	1	2	3,030
Mexico	90	1,958	3,610
Moldovia	4	34	1,060
Mongolia	2	1,567	390
Morocco	28	447	1,040
Mozambique	18	802	90
Myanmar	47	677	280[b]
Namibia	2	824	1,820
Nepal	21	141	190
Nicaragua	4	130	340
Niger	9	1,267	270
Nigeria	111	924	300
Oman	2	212	4,850
Pakistan	130	796	430
Panama	3	77	2,600
Papua New Guinea	4	463	1,130
Paraguay	5	407	1,510
Peru	24	1,285	1,490[c]
Philippines	69	300	850

Table 1.1 Continued

	Population, 1995 (millions)	Area (1,000 sq km)	GNP per capita, 1993 (US$)
Poland	38	313	2,260
Portugal	10	92	9,130
Romania	23	238	1,140
Russian Federation	149	17,075	2,340
Rwanda	8	26	210
Saudi Arabia	19	2,150	7,510
Senegal	8	197	750
Sierra Leone	5	72	150
Singapore	3	1	19,850
Slovak Republic	5	49	1,950
Slovenia	2	20	6,490
Somalia	9	638	150
South Africa	43	1,221	2,980
Sri Lanka	18	66	600
Sudan	29	2,506	400[b]
Syrian Arab Rep.	14	185	1,170
Tajikstan	6	143	470
Tanzania	28	945	90
Thailand	60	513	2,110
Togo	4	57	340
Trinidad & Tobago	1	5	3,830
Tunisia	9	164	1,720
Turkey	61	779	2,970
Turkmenistan	4	488	1,230[c]
Uganda	19	236	180
Ukraine	52	604	2,210
United Arab Emirates	2	84	21,430
Uruguay	3	177	3,840
Uzbekistan	23	447	970
Venezuela	22	912	2,840
Vietnam	74	332	170
Yemen, Rep.	14	528	520
Yugoslavia, Fed. Rep.	11	102	3,060
Zaire	73	2,345	220
Zambia	9	753	380
Zimbabwe	11	391	520
Total	4,821	100,672	
Higher-Income Countries			
United States	263	9,809	24,740
Japan	125	378	31,490
Germany	81	357	23,560
United Kingdom	58	245	18,060
Total	527	10,789	

Sources: *World Development Report* 1995, World Bank; *World Almanac* 1993, Pan Books Ltd; and *Britannica World Data*.
Notes: [a] 1992, [b] 1991, [c] 1990

CHARACTERISTICS OF EMERGING MARKETS

Another way to obtain insights into the reality of emerging markets is to create a statistical picture. If one compares markets around the world, the size and liquidity of those markets vary drastically, and it quickly becomes apparent which markets are mature – high trading volume, lots of listings, clear regulatory environment with strict enforcement – and which are not.

Emerging market capitalization

The capitalizations of emerging markets are very small in comparison to those of developed markets. In 1995 Japan had a market capitalization of US$3.7 trillion and the US had a market capitalization of US$6.9 trillion. On the other hand, the largest emerging market, Hong Kong, had a market capitalization of only US$303 billion, while Malaysia, the second largest, had a market capitalization of US$223 billion. The next largest was Taiwan with a market capitalization of US$187 billion and Korea, US$182 billion. The others ranged to as low as US$2 billion for Sri Lanka and US$1 billion for Bangladesh (Table 1.2 overleaf).

Table 1.2 Market capitalization: major emerging and developed markets – 1980 and 1995 (US$ million)

	1980	*1995*	*(%) Change*
Emerging Markets			
Argentina	3,864	37,783	878
Bangladesh	27	1,323	4,800
Brazil	9,160	147,636	1,512
Chile	9,400	73,860	686
China	–	42,055	–
Colombia	1,605	17,893	1,015
Greece	3,016	17,060	466
Hong Kong	39,104	303,705	677
India	7,585	127,199	1,577
Indonesia	63	66,585	105,590
Jordan	1,605	4,670	191
Korea	3,829	181,955	4,652
Malaysia	12,395	222,729	1,697
Mexico	12,994	90,694	598
Pakistan	643	9,286	1,344
Peru	685	11,795	1,622
Philippines	3,478	58,859	1,592
Portugal	191	18,362	9,514
Singapore	24,418	148,004	506
Sri Lanka	365	1,998	447
Taiwan, China	6,082	187,206	2,978
Thailand	1,206	141,507	11,634
Turkey	477	20,772	4,255
Venezuela	2,657	3,655	38
Total	144,849	1,936,591	1,237
Developed Markets			
Japan	379,679	3,667,292	866
United Kingdom	205,200	1,407,737	586
United States	1,448,120	6,857,622	374
Total	2,032,999	11,932,651	487

Sources: International Finance Corporation (IFC); Swiss Bank Corporation (SBC); Federation Internationale des Bourses de Valeurs (FIBV); and author's estimates.

In December 1980, the 24 main investable emerging markets had a combined market capitalization of only US$144.9 billion, or 7 percent of the US, UK and Japan markets combined. By 1995, their market capitalization had increased to US$2 trillion or more than 16 percent of the market capitalization of those three developed markets. Growth of the market capitalization among emerging markets sky-rocketed to 1,237 percent by 1995, whereas growth in the three most mature stock markets registered 487 percent growth over the same period.

When reviewing the daily average trading volume between 1980 to 1995 of emerging and developed markets, the change in emerging markets jumped an astounding 1,930 percent. At the same time, developed markets increased only 995 percent. As a percentage of the daily trading volume, emerging markets still represent a fraction of the volume seen on developed markets. With a daily trading volume of US$4.3 billion, emerging markets represents only 14 percent of the US$30.2 billion in daily trading in the three largest developed markets (Table 1.3 overleaf).

Table 1.3 Average daily trading volume: major emerging and developed markets – estimated (US$ million)

	1980*	1995	% change
Emerging markets			
Argentina	4.95	45.31	815
Bangladesh	0.00	0.46	n/a
Brazil	24.15	322.34	1,235
Chile	2.49	45.83	1,741
China (Shanghai)	n/a	5.40	n/a
China (Shenzhen)	n/a	1.50	n/a
Colombia	0.85	8.50	900
Greece	0.39	23.24	5,859
Hong Kong	87.39	442.85	407
India	12.55	58.94	370
Indonesia	0.04	58.40	145,900
Jordan	0.63	1.98	214
Korea	8.50	633.17	7,349
Malaysia	11.69	319.64	2,634
Mexico	14.83	134.70	808
Pakistan	0.82	14.63	1,684
Peru	0.61	15.43	2,430
Philippines	2.81	58.55	1,984
Portugal	0.01	17.01	170,000
Singapore	16.60	278.00	1,575
Sri Lanka	0.01	0.80	7,900
Taiwan, China	20.47	1,365.44	6,570
Thailand	1.40	235.40	16,714
Turkey	0.05	204.58	409,060
Venezuela	0.27	1.96	626
Total	211.51	4,294.06	1,930
Developed markets			
Japan	731.50	2,720.00	272
United Kingdom	162.69	4,589.60	2,721
United States	1,862.80	22,874.00	1,128
Total	2,756.99	30,183.60	995

Sources: International Finance Corporation (IFC); Federation Internationale des Bourses de Valeurs; Smith New Court; Nomura Research Institute; and author's estimates.
*Note: Turkey – 1983, Bangladesh and Pakistan – 1984, Sri Lanka – 1985

The concentration of capital (the share of market capitalization held by the ten largest stocks) in the emerging markets varies considerably. The figures range from a high of 57 percent in the Philippines, to a low of 22 percent in Colombia. As the developed markets have no concentration higher than 18 percent, it is clear that there is a high absolute concentration of capital on emerging market stock exchanges. The average share of market capitalization accounted for by the ten largest stocks averaged 40 percent in emerging markets, while the corresponding figure in developed markets was a much lower 13 percent (Table 1.4).

Table 1.4 Capitalization concentration at September 1995: leading emerging and developed markets

	Share of market capitalization held by ten largest stocks
Emerging markets	
Argentina	46
Brazil	36
Chile	39
Colombia	22
Greece	44
India	29
Indonesia	35
Jordan	25
Korea	32
Malaysia	49
Mexico	47
Pakistan	42
Philippines	57
Portugal	35
Taiwan	34
Thailand	41
Turkey	56
Venezuela	48
Average	40
Developed markets	
Japan	14
United Kingdom	18
United States	7
Average	13

Sources: International Finance Corporation; *Euromoney*; and author's estimates.

The concentration of trading value is slightly more dense than the market capitalization concentration in emerging markets. This is because in many emerging markets, companies continue to be closely held by families or governments, limiting the size of the "free float," or those shares that are readily available for trading. Thus the average is 42 percent for emerging markets, with highs of 58 percent in Pakistan and 57 percent in Argentina, both countries with significant concentration of ownership. In developed markets, ownership is much more dispersed, leading to an average figure of 12 percent, including a low of 7 percent in the United States (Table 1.5).

Table 1.5 Trading value concentration: 1995 leading emerging and developed markets

	Share of trading value of ten largest stocks
Emerging markets	
Argentina	57
Brazil	54
Chile	43
Colombia	20
Greece	32
India	17
Indonesia	52
Jordan	26
Korea	36
Malaysia	51
Mexico	25
Pakistan	58
Philippines	53
Portugal	27
Taiwan	17
Thailand	26
Turkey	86
Venezuela	75
Average	42
Developed markets	
Japan	12
United Kingdom	17
United States	7
Average	12

Sources: International Finance Corporation; *Euromoney*; and author's estimates.

As with the developed markets, emerging markets often have more than one stock exchange. Brazil, China, India each have more than one stock exchange. In fact, in India there are more than ten active stock exchanges, many trading the same stocks in addition to shares unique to their region. In 1994/95, the total number of companies listed in emerging markets was 21,540, generating a market capitalization of approximately US$2.4 trillion. Obviously the average size of these listed companies was small as only 7,439 companies were listed in our sample of four developed markets but accounted for US$12.5 trillion in market capitalization (Table 1.6).

Table 1.6 Emerging markets: stock exchanges (1994/95)

Country	Exchange	Number of listed companies	Market capitalization (US$M)
Argentina	Buenos Aires	149	37,783
Bangladesh	Dhaka	183	1,323
Barbados	Barbados	18	497
Brazil	Sao Paulo	543	99,430
Brazil	Rio de Janeiro	576	185,350
Bulgaria	Bulgaria	26	62
Chile	Santiago	284	73,860
China	Shanghai	35*	10,695
China	Shenzhen	30*	4,078
Colombia	Bogota	190	17,893
Costa Rico	Costa Rico	118	434
Cote d'Ivoire	Abidjan	31	867
Croatia	Zagreb	61	581
Cyprus	Cyprus	41	2,525
Czech Rep	Prague	1,635	15,664
Ecuador	Quito	40	2,627
Egypt	Cairo	746	8,088
Ghana	Ghana	19	1,680
Greece	Athens	212	17,060
Honduras	Honduras	99	338
Hong Kong	Hong Kong	518	303,705
Hungary	Budapest	42	2,399
India	Bombay	7,985	127,199
India	Madras	700	1,600
Indonesia	Jakarta	238	66,585
Iran	Tehran	169	6,561
Israel	Tel-Aviv	654	36,399

Continued overleaf

Table 1.6 Continued

Country	Exchange	Number of listed companies	Market capitalization (US$M)
Jamaica	Jamaica	51	1,391
Jordan	Amman	97	4,670
Kenya	Nairobi	56	1,889
Korea	Korea	721	181,955
Lithuania	Lithuania	351	158
Malaysia	Kuala Lumpur	529	222,729
Malta	Malta	5	1,239
Mauritius	Mauritius	28	1,381
Mexico	Mexican	185	90,694
Morocco	Casablanca	44	5,951
Namibia	Namibia	10	189
Nepal	Nepal	83	244
Nigeria	Nigeria	181	2,033
Oman	Muscat	80	1,980
Pakistan	Karachi	764	9,286
Panama	Panama	16	831
Peru	Lima	246	11,795
Philippines	Makati/Manila	205	58,859
Poland	Warsaw	65	4,564
Portugal	Lisbon	169	18,362
Slovak Republic	Bratislava	18	1,235
Slovenia	Ljubljana	17	302
South Africa	Johannesburg	640	280,526
Sri Lanka	Colombia	226	1,998
Swaziland	Swaziland	4	339
Singapore	Singapore	212	148,004
Taiwan	Taiwan	347	187,206
Thailand	Thailand	416	141,507
Trinidad & Tobago	Trinidad & Tobago	27	1,138
Tunisia	Tunis	26	4,066
Turkey	Istanbul	205	20,772
Uruguay	Montevideo	20	183
Venezuela	Caracas	90	3,655
Zimbabwe	Zinbabwe	64	3,038
Total		**21,540**	**2,439,452**
Germany	Frankfurt	678	577,365
Japan	Tokyo	2,263	3,667,292
United Kingdom	London	2,078	1,407,737
United States	New York	7,671	6,857,622
Total		**12,690**	**12,510,016**

Sources: International Finance Corporation; Federation Internationale des Bourses de Valeurs; *Euromoney; Emerging Markets Factbook*; Risk Publications, author's estimates.
*Notes: "B" Shares

In Chapter Five, when discussing capital market development, we will go into greater detail about the composition and nature of emerging market stock exchanges. It is clear from the above, however, that emerging markets, while a minor global financial force at this time are expanding rapidly. An understanding of emerging market growth trends is critical to an appreciation of what financial markets will look like in the future.

There has been growing confidence in the emerging markets. Former creditors are now willing to place more money in those markets. The international market for developing country securities has continued to mature with better liquidity, a wider range of currency trading possibilities, longer maturities, narrowing spreads, and an expanding list of derivative products.

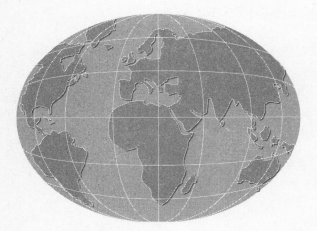

Chapter 2

Macroeconomic Trends in Emerging Markets

THREE FACTORS INFLUENCING MACROECONOMIC DEVELOPMENTS

A familiar construct employed in discussions of global events is the "First World" and "Third World." Today, emerging markets are rising out of what once was considered to be the "Third World." However, the reality is that low- and middle-income countries are not static – they grow, change and mature – moving through stages of relative development. In fact, over the past decade, we have witnessed previously unimagined rates of change in "Third World" countries, demonstrating clearly that there is, in fact, no "Third World;" rather a large number of countries passing through stages of evolution. What I'm interested in, as an emerging markets investor, are the factors which have combined at the domestic level to propel these countries forward, ever more quickly, towards wealth and security.

It is my belief that a confluence of demographic, technological and ideological shifts have broken the log-jam of development, and are functioning together to generate improvements in quality of life and expanded economic activity.

Demographic statistics illustrate clearly the trend towards lower infant mortality rates, reduced birth rates and lengthening life spans which is having a dramatic impact on the quality of life in developing countries. In turn, people who are healthier and live longer are better able to concentrate on improving themselves, primarily via education and expanded life experiences. And finally, more sophisticated life skills influence economic abilities and aspirations.

I have been impressed by the rapid rate of technology adoption around the world which is facilitating better communications and higher social productivity. Technological change is affecting everyone, regardless of economic development level, but in the emerging nations it has some unique features. In particular, technology has a telescoping effect, condensing the time-scale over which innovation and development progress. Nations don't need to reinvent the wheel and spend precious development funds on creating technologies which can enhance their productivity. Instead, economies are able to purchase or adapt existing technologies, zooming up the development ladder. Another variation is the capacity to leapfrog using technological inputs. While some societies were content with typewriters for decades before moving on to personal computers, many emerging economies find themselves able to entirely skip the typewriter stage, leapfrogging traditional developmental stages.

A growing awareness of the complexity of human economic endeavor, acknowledgment of the failure of central economic planning to raise the living standards of the world's people, and a belief that market economic systems are most successful in stimulating economic growth are evident changes in economic ideology. Tremendous political change has been spurred by ideological shifts, and can be seen in diverse events such as "people power" in the Philippines, the public disclosure of political corruption in Korea and of course the classic example, the fall of the Berlin Wall. Ideological change results in equally portentous economic change and is of particular interest to the emerging market investor.

Changes in economic thought throughout the world have led emerging markets to adopt broadly consistent policy programs, featuring liberal trade rules, open capital markets, free repatriation of funds and other policies consistent with free market economics. Many emerging markets are at various stages in implementing the specifics of such policies, but the commitment to move in the general direction seems assured. The volte-face from earlier policies of self-determination, which featured autarky, trade barriers, nationalizations and debt repudiation, has been remarkable. Market-oriented policy shifts have resulted in burgeoning world trade, the privatization of state-owned enterprises, substantially more active capital markets, more manageable external debt levels and tax reform.

All of these forces then – demographic, technological and ideological – are combining to generate increased economic activity in formerly poor and listless countries. Because emerging stock market investing is inextricably linked to broader socio-political and economic development, the emerging market investor must follow the development course in these countries much more closely than he might when studying higher-income countries.

DEMOGRAPHIC FACTORS

In 1993, low- and middle-income countries had a total population of 4.6 billion compared to only 795 million in the higher-income countries. Lower-income country populations therefore represent 85 percent of the world's population. In terms of space, 76 percent of the world's land area can also be found in lower-income countries. This is in contrast to the 31.5 million square kilometers, or remaining 24 percent of the Earth's land, that are occupied by higher-income countries. Of the total number of nations, 124 were in the emerging areas and only 19 in developed areas. It's not hard to see what potential exists in mobilizing 85 percent of the world's population to work towards economic expansion, utilizing 77 percent of the world's land.

Up until now, however, of the total world's estimated US$23 trillion gross domestic product, almost US$18 trillion of it was accounted for by developed countries, with only US$5 trillion emanating from lower-income countries, a minor 21 percent of the world output (Figure 2.1).

Owning such a large portion of the world's land mass, the emerging nations hold the key to vast natural resources awaiting utilization. The unlocking of these resources as a result of liberalized investment policies will have a dramatic impact on the economic growth of many emerging economies. One example of how large some of these investments can be was announced in

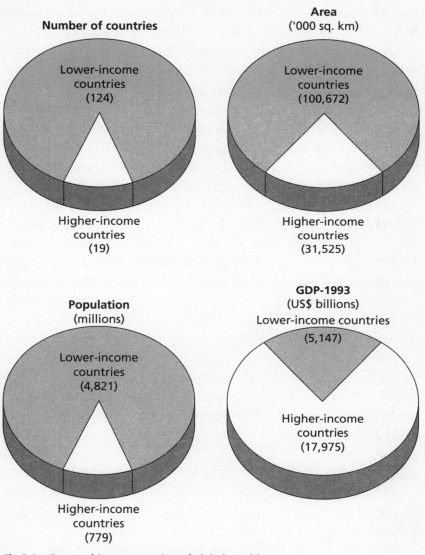

Number of countries

Lower-income countries (124)

Higher-income countries (19)

Area ('000 sq. km)

Lower-income countries (100,672)

Higher-income countries (31,525)

Population (millions)

Lower-income countries (4,821)

Higher-income countries (779)

GDP-1993 (US$ billions)

Lower-income countries (5,147)

Higher-income countries (17,975)

Fig 2.1 Geographic concentration of global wealth
Source: World Bank

December 1992, when the giant company Exxon reached an agreement with the Indonesian government to develop a gas field at a cost of US$17 billion. This development was reported to guarantee that Indonesia will be the world's leading exporter of liquefied natural gas into the next century. It will raise the country's natural gas reserves by an estimated 45 trillion cubic feet, to more than 100 trillion cubic feet and will include one of the largest offshore platforms ever built.

As is obvious, a fundamental gap between population, area and wealth exists in the world today. However, the following demographic, technological and philosophical factors give us reason to believe that this imbalance will not continue, and that the process of redistribution and enlarging of the pie for all will stimulate financial markets of the lower-income countries, making them the most dynamic industrial centers of the coming decades.

There are several forces at work, shaping the population structure of lower-income countries, that will impact on how development progresses. Table 2.1 and the text below give fundamental statistics, to clarify how demographic structural changes are happening and how they might contribute to economic and financial development.

Table 2.1 Demographic statistics

	1960	1993	% change 1960–93
Crude death rate (per 1,000 population)			
Lower-income countries	15	7	–52
Higher-income countries	11	10	–11
Infant mortality rate (deaths per 1,000 live births in that year)			
Lower-income countries	109	38	–65
Higher-income countries	28	7	–76
Life expectancy at birth (years)			
Lower-income countries	54	69	+28
Higher-income countries	70	77	+10
Total fertility rate			
Lower-income countries	5.6	3.0	–47
Higher-income countries	2.6	1.7	–36
Crude birth rate (per 1,000 population)			
Lower-income countries	41	24	–41
Higher-income countries	19	12	–35

Sources: World Bank, *World Development Report* 1981–1995

Infant mortality rates

The number of deaths per 1,000 live births is rapidly falling in low- and middle-income countries. Between 1960 and 1993, infant mortality rates in those countries fell by 65 percent, from 109 per 1,000 live births to 38 per 1,000. Happily, higher-income countries also achieved significant reductions in their infant mortality rate, dropping from 28 deaths per 1,000 live births to only seven deaths, an improvement of 76 percent over the same period.

Longer life

Life expectancy at birth has been moving up at a steady pace for the entire world, but at a faster pace in the emerging countries. Progress made between 1960 and 1993 has meant that life expectancy in lower-income countries rose 28 percent, compared with a 10 percent increase registered among higher-income countries. People are now expected to live well into retirement age these days, with average life expectancy in higher-income countries of up to 77 years. The lower-income countries are catching up fast, and are now at 69 years.

Longer life can also be demonstrated by using the crude death rate per 1,000 people in a given country. Once again, lower-income countries have scored significant gains, with deaths dropping between 1960 and 1993 from 15 to seven per 1,000 people, a 52 percent improvement. Higher-income countries are experiencing a stubborn consistency in their death rate, only moving from 11 to ten during the entire 33-year period.

Birth and fertility rates

Because life expectancies have been improved, birth and fertility rates are now declining. There is a faith among people in lower-income countries that their children will live a long and productive life, eliminating the need for many children. Additionally, as people are living longer, healthier lives, they can work longer and need fewer children upon which to rely in their old age. A United Nations' report has shown sharp drops in Third World fertility rates in the last 20 years due to significant increases in the use of contraceptives. The number of married women of reproductive age in the developing world who are using contraception has risen tenfold in the past 25 years to 380 million.

For all of these reasons, total fertility rates within the emerging nations during the period 1960–93 fell by an average of 47 percent, from 5.6 children on average to three children. Over the same period, fertility rates in higher-income countries fell by an average of 36 percent, from an average of 2.6 children to an average of 1.7 children. Another measure is the crude birth rate, which between 1960 and 1993, fell in lower-income countries from an average of 41 births per 1,000 people to 24 births, a 41 percent drop. At the same time, higher-income countries experienced a fall from 19 to 12 births per 1,000 people, a 35 percent decrease.

The dramatically changed figures relating to birth and death in lower-income countries have been achieved because of the impact of better health care. Lower cost medicines, wider availability of more effective medicines, better nutrition and better access to medical care have all contributed to better living standards. In Brazil, between 1950 and 1991, the number of physicians per 1,000 people rose from an average of 0.4 to 1.5, an increase of 275 percent. In Turkey during that same period, the average rose from 0.3 to 0.8, a 166 percent change. In Greece, the number rose from 1.4 physicians per 1,000 people to 3.1 per 1,000, which is a 121 percent change.

All of these demographic changes feed into one another. If the spiral is upwards, as is largely the case today among the majority of lower-income countries, the factors converge to speed development and social progress. The virtuous circle diagram (Figure 2.2) clearly demonstrates the inter-relationship between demographics and wealth generation. Once a cycle has been completed, it feeds into a repeated, but broader cycle. These demographic changes are the fundamental building blocks of economic development.

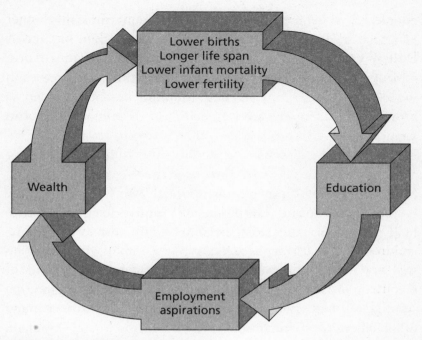

Fig 2.2 Virtuous circle of development

Effects of demographic change

Strides in the creation, production and distribution of new medicines and drugs, combined with the greater availability of food, has led to longer average life spans. People with a longer life span have more time to learn how to read, write and develop skills. Although more than 1 billion adults are still illiterate in the developing world, the advances made in literacy growth have been phenomenal. Better health care has resulted in improvements in the ability of people to learn, because better health is directly related to people's alertness, capacity for learning, and ability to cope with life. A prolonged life span makes investments, knowledge, and skills more worthwhile. For men, it often means better employment opportunities, or increased productivity resulting in bigger crop yields. In traditional societies, where women continue to be the principal child-care givers, the education of women leads to lower infant mortality rates. Healthier and better educated mothers strongly influence the early physical and mental development of their children. In fact, educating women often reduces the disparity between men and women in the society, leading to more co-operative home arrangements and increased participation of women in the paid labor force.

Education

Multilateral development institutions are increasing their emphasis on education in the developing world in an effort to help raise living standards. In almost all of the lower-income countries, adult literacy is steadily rising. Among the emerging markets in which we invest, Indonesia had only a 25 percent literacy rate in 1950. By 1995 the proportion of the population that was literate had risen to 80 percent. The same is true in many other emerging markets and is a key factor in development. Between 1940 and 1995, literacy in China grew from 8 percent of the population to 73 percent of the adult population (Figure 2.3). For 19 emerging nations, between 1960 and 1990, adult literacy rose by an average of 44 percent with countries such as Jordan, Pakistan and Turkey more than doubling their adult literacy levels. A number of countries have reached adult literacy levels of more than 90 percent, the same as the major industrialized countries.

These developments parallel the change that took place in Japan and other countries as they have emerged into developed markets. Between 1850 and 1920, for example, Japan's adult literacy rose from about 10 percent to over 80 percent. Now the new emerging markets are duplicating that development, but at a faster pace because of innovations in communications and education.

A better-educated person is able to absorb new information faster and apply unfamiliar data and new processes more effectively. Studies have found that a one-year increase in schooling can augment wages by more than 10 percent and raises GDP sig-

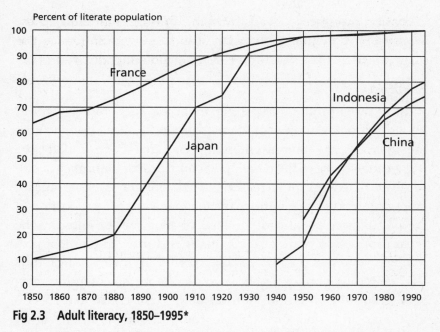

Fig 2.3 Adult literacy, 1850–1995*

* The literacy figures for France & Japan, after 1950 and 1970 respectively, are estimates. All 1996 figures are also estimates.
Sources: World Bank; author's estimates

nificantly. In Peru, it was found that if farmers had an additional year of schooling, it increased their probability of adopting modern farm technology by 45 percent. Similarly, Thai farmers with four years of schooling were three times more likely to use new fertilizers and other chemical inputs than farmers with one to three years of school.

Education promotes entrepreneurship. Entrepreneurs see new opportunities, are willing to take risks and change methods. They make the connection between innovation and actual output. These are the foundations of strong future growth which portfolio managers seek to harness for investors. These are the signals that tell us that an economy has the potential to emerge. Someone once said: "The road to success is paved with education."

Therefore, it is clear that countries with high rates of education have a measurable bias towards higher productivity, generating economic growth. It is important to know, however, that more than 1 billion adults are still illiterate in the emerging world. But given the improvement to date, such a figure only highlights the astounding potential growth latent in these populations as the virtuous circle of demographic change and education revolves.

Surplus

In turn, more productive people are able to generate a surplus, either of food or another tradable commodity. This leads to savings. Savings rates among emerging economies have tended to be higher than those of the developed countries for a number of cultural and demographic reasons. The younger average age of emerging market populations means that a greater proportion of the population has already entered or soon will be entering the most productive years of their life. It is during these most productive years that people are able to build up their savings, thus leading to a generally higher savings rate in the emerging markets. In addition, there are cultural factors which lead to high savings rates. In China, for example, the traditions of family unity and saving for future generations have led to high savings rates.

Asian savings rates have noticably outpaced those of the developed nations. Savings rates in G7 countries dwindled from 13 percent of GDP during the decade 1970 to 1980, to 8.1 percent in 1990 and 7.8 percent in 1992. It has been estimated by the IMF, however, that savings rates within Asia remain at 13 percent of GDP. This, of course, has led to higher rates of bank deposits and national reserves. Currently, an estimated 41 percent of global bank reserves are now maintained by the seven leading East Asian economies, compared with only 17 percent in 1980. Taiwan now has one of the world's largest foreign reserves.

Food

At one time, Malthusian pessimists feared that the continued expansion of populations in lower-income countries would create a global food shortage. On the contrary, as people living in emerging markets have been able to increase their education level and adopt new agricultural practices, technologies have been developed to solve food shortages, although the food distribution challenge remains.

For example, an estimated 2.7 billion people, primarily in Asia, rely on rice as their main source of calories. Improved rice culture, through research and new breeding, has resulted in an increase in

The impact of new technologies on the ability of the people of emerging countries to learn is great.

rice production in the past 25 years greater than the rapid population increase in Asia. During that time, the real price of rice has been halved and the predicted disastrous food shortage has not occurred.

Urbanization

Many lower-income countries have severe urban over-crowding and have difficulty providing municipal services to the steadily expanding population. These realities have created the impression that urbanization trends are a drag on economic development. Recent evidence, however, indicates that population density and the percentage of urban population appears to be favorably correlated with a nation's prospects for accelerated economic expansion. As nations become industrialized, there is a need for increased urbanization. There is a need for the agglomeration of more people required to sustain a service sector and to create a pool of readily available industrial workers. Economic growth does change land use and the locational structure of a country but it seems clear that the long-term rewards in quality of life standards make the changes worthwhile.

TECHNOLOGICAL FACTORS

The impact of new technologies on the ability of the people of emerging countries to learn is great. Some economists have stated that the four key elements for a country to generate a high standard of living include: (1) natural resources; (2) capital; (3) technology; and (4) a skilled workforce. In this section, we will review the contribution of technology to economic development.

The interplay between technology and people is evident. As the standard of education in emerging nations rises, the ability of people to absorb technology grows. For this reason, one economist said: "Talented people are a more important resource than any man-made device or corporate strategy."

Emerging nations can now take advantage of the technological developments which have been produced by the developed nations over the past century, and apply the very best of this technology to their own productive growth. With wealth to buy access to communications, and the education and leisure to use it effectively, technology is quickly being adopted by every household. The first purchase is invariably a television.

Television

The spread of mass communications, particularly television, has had a dramatic impact on how people view themselves in the world. This has resulted in further opportunities for the introduction of new technology. Television is bringing new ideas to millions of people in emerging markets, ideas which are having a revolutionary impact on their economic behavior. Observations all over the world indicate that the penetration of television is revolutionizing how people in even the most isolated regions think and behave. The impact of viewing a program such as "Lifestyles of the Rich and Famous" on slum-dwellers in Bombay or on farmers in China is not difficult to predict.

Between 1980 and 1995, the number of homes with televisions in emerging countries grew by 190 percent, compared to a 29 percent increase in developed countries. In some countries that started from a low base, the growth has been phenomenal. For example, between 1980 and 1995 in India, the number of homes with a television rose from 1.2 million to 20.2 million, an increase of 1,587 percent. In absolute numbers, there are now more television households in China than in the United States – 112.3 million homes with TV in China, versus 97.1 million homes in the US (Figure 2.4).

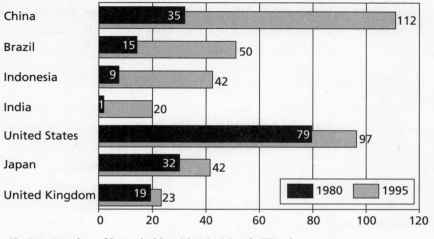

Fig 2.4   Number of households with television (millions)
Source: Screen Digest

Star TV, based in Hong Kong, is Asia's largest satellite network. It reaches an estimated 12 million households throughout
Asia in addition to hotels and restaurants in 38 countries from
India to Israel, and from China to the Philippines. In India, the
fastest growing market, the number of viewers increased almost
160 percent in nine months of 1993 alone, to 3.3 million households. Star TV's largest audience is in China with 4.8 million
households, followed by Taiwan with 1.9 million.

Television promotes business and itself is also a business.
Low-cost satellite dishes enable the establishment of small television networks in even the remotest and poorest areas. In central India, cable TV is provided by television shop owners, who
install a satellite dish for a few thousand dollars and then obtain
subscribers who pay about US$3 a month to receive the satellite
TV channels. Asia even has its own indigenous music station,
Channel V, which rivals MTV for the hearts and minds of youth
throughout the region. In all these ways – as a source of information, as a business and as an opinion-maker – television is
changing the way people in lower-income countries see themselves and see the rest of the world. It influences their expecta-

tions, their aspirations and their perception of what life has to offer them in the way of opportunity and living standards.

Telephones

Among lower-income countries, the number of telephones per thousand population increased on the average by 184 percent between 1975 and 1995. Growth in the installation of telephone lines per 1,000 people has increased over 200 percent in Indonesia, India, Brazil and China (Figure 2.5). At the same time, demand for telephone services has soared. Residents in cities often wait two years and pay exorbitant fees for telephones to be installed. In China, according to one estimate, each year the number of applicants rises by about 16 percent. The government is taking steps to increase capacity and is also improving communications in remote areas. A rural telephone services program is also being implemented in Indonesia, another far-flung country with 180 million people, but a very low telephone per person penetration ratio outside of the capital, Jakarta.

As a result of the introduction of mobile phones, emerging countries can now leapfrog past the obstacle of having a land phone line installed. The establishment of cellular operators is mushrooming right across the emerging world, creating modern, reliable telephone links almost overnight. It is almost impossible to overstate the growth potential in this area, both as a communication link and as an industry.

By the end of 1993, a joint venture between the state-owned Hungarian telecommunications company and US West Inc. was expected to complete a nationwide system of mobile phones in Hungary. Since starting in 1990, over 24,000 subscribers were obtained, with one-third using mobile phones as their only telephone because they were still waiting for one to be installed at home. Such a demand has encouraged companies such as US West Inc. to establish franchises in the Czech Republic and Slovak Republic, in Moscow, St Petersburg and 11 other Russian cities.

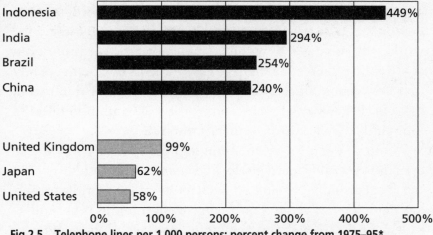

Fig 2.5   Telephone lines per 1,000 persons: percent change from 1975–95*

*Figures for 1995 are estimates
Source: ITU; World Bank; IMF; author's estimates

New telecoms technology

There have been a number of other strides in technology which will make wireless communication even more efficient and cost-effective. The movement from analog systems to new digital technologies will mean that both cellular and landline telephone systems will be able to expand capacity dramatically. Satellites are bringing cable television and possibly a satellite telephone system to emerging markets, enabling telecommunication links around the globe.

One firm in Colombia, a mountainous country with many unpassable roads and inaccessible areas, connects its cross-country operations via satellite. As the country's population is rather evenly distributed around the country, rather than being clustered in one or two urban centers, the firm opted to diffuse its corporate activities around the country, giving them a firm presence in every area of their market. Without advanced telecommunication capabilities, it would not be feasible to run the company this way. But new telecom technology is giving this firm a competitive edge and making it accessible in a modern way.

Facsimile machines, or faxes, are proliferating throughout the emerging world, so that information can be transmitted with even more efficiency. Previously, large volumes of written information that took days or even weeks to be delivered around the world can be available within minutes by fax. Faxes are even contributing to liberalization, as governments bow to the reality that they cannot effectively block information they don't want the world to know when it can be broadcast within minutes to thousands of news media outlets around the world.

Of course the great information highway, the Internet, is also opening emerging markets to information and investors. The Internet currently has limited availability in the world's emerging markets, but to say that it is growing rapidly is an understatement. It is penetrating emerging markets in the same way that it grew in the developed world, through universities and scientific research centers which are connecting to this global resource, so they can transmit ideas and information. When seeking information recently from Kazakhstan, I found that electronic mail sent via the Internet was quicker, cheaper and less prone to being garbled in transmission than sending a fax!

Effects of technological change

As must seem evident, the adoption of new technology is a big boost to economic development in emerging markets. Technological adoption is particularly crucial to capital market development. Much of finance revolves around accurate and swift information exchange, meaning that emerging markets cannot be serious participants in an international financial regime without ever-better telecommunications capabilities. Technology is also contributing to overall growth through productivity enhancements, technological upgrading of output and the capacity to produce higher value-added goods for trade.

Financial telecommunications

At all stages of the development process, international capital plays a crucial role in financing corporate expansion. Those markets which lack sophisticated telecommunications and computer technology to bring the latest prices and market changes to the international community are less likely to be considered for equity investment. As the need for substantial sums of money to develop huge infrastructure projects increases, the relevance of financial telecommunications can only become greater. Fortunately, planners in many emerging markets perceived this need early on, and made adequate resources available to the financial community, even in countries where the flow of information is otherwise strictly curtailed.

Productivity advances

The combination of better education and new technologies is having a dramatic and accelerating impact on productivity growth in the emerging nations. Countries considered to be on the "emerging" list often outrank their more developed counterparts in industrial and economic sophistication. *The World Competitiveness Report* (1993) found that Hong Kong, Taiwan and Singapore were all more time-effective at product innovation than were Sweden, the UK or Germany. Chile was faster than Norway or Canada. Figures concerning the number of engineers in a country, labor force equality, in-company training and computer literacy looked remarkably similar among the 15 emerging markets reviewed in the report compared to those for the 22 richer countries.

Studies also debunk the myth of less hardworking employees in lower-income countries. Recent research shows that not only does productivity in many of the emerging market nations equal or exceed that of the developed markets, but that when you include the informal sectors, the level of working hours in developing nations exceeds that of employees in higher-income nations. For example, one study showed that almost one-third of economically active Brazilians worked more than 48 hours a week, putting them second only to the Japanese, and ahead of the Germans, Americans, French, British and Canadians.

Access to advanced technology has allowed the industrial and financial sectors of emerging economies to come up the development scale much more quickly than was possible for the developed countries. Increased adoption of advanced technology generates greater economic returns, makes production and social organization more efficient and frees up labour resources to become involved in higher value-added work. The contribution of technology to increased GDP is inestimable and limited only by the availability of the educated workers needed to use it.

IDEOLOGICAL FACTORS

In the early 1960s, when I was studying economic development theory at MIT, many of the faculty members were spending a significant portion of their talents on understanding how and why countries grew and what could be done to stimulate economic expansion in the so-called "underdeveloped" countries. (Incidentally, the word underdeveloped was soon replaced, as the economists were reminded that, to some, it reflected ethnocentric thinking and was not very acceptable. Synonyms like "developing," "Third World," "the South" and "lower-income" were substituted.)

Trying to understand economic development in the 1960s was a humbling experience for the economists and officials in multinational assistance organizations. The US Agency for International Development spearheaded the global programs to produce economic growth in the less developed nations, but the results were disappointing.

Since the 1960s, economic thought has come a long way, and the importance of market-oriented policies and capital market development now absorbs a great deal of attention of the multilateral institutions. It is not surprising then, that the idea of emerging markets, as applied to portfolio investing, was originated by a World Bank subsidiary, the International Finance Corporation.

International aid

The case against international aid programs has been well articulated by many economists and observers. According to some estimates, subsidies in the form of grants or soft loans from the richer countries to the poorer ones since World War II mushroomed from a few hundred million dollars a year to about US$50 billion by the 1980s. The criticism is that the subsidies do not go to the poor people of these countries, but to their rulers, who are often directly responsible for the bad condition of their subjects. There is also the argument that such aid has the effect of keeping bad governments in place. Even Iraq, during the time when it was enjoying huge oil revenues in the 1980s, received millions of dollars of Western aid which allowed it to build up a huge military arsenal.

Aid has often been cited as being responsible for regional wars. One commentator has cited the cases of India and Pakistan, Iran and Iraq, Uganda and Tanzania, which were at war with each other but were receiving aid from the West.

One study has shown that since the early 1960s, African nations alone have collected more than US$300 billion in aid. In the 1980s, Africans were receiving about 22 percent of the West's total development assistance. In one case, US$9 billion was given to Tanzania between 1970 and 1988, more than four times that country's 1988 gross domestic product. Africa is littered with a number of "white elephants," including fancy airports, conference halls and new capital cities. These major projects have tended to enrich the country's leaders rather than help the population at large. One Lesotho chief has been quoted as saying: "We have two problems: rats and government."

As billions of dollars have been siphoned off into foreign bank accounts by despotic rulers, it is now becoming evident that aid has not stimulated economic growth, and may have even hindered it by inhibiting domestic, indigenous economic activity and putting off the need for necessary economic reform and changes in political structure.

Communism

The love affair between many emerging markets and Marxist economic ideology grew out the disaffection engendered by exploitative colonial relations preceding the Second World War. As these countries moved away from their colonial heritage, and attempted to build independent economies, they tried to adopt purposefully distinct economic policies that would accelerate their detachment from previous colonial rulers. However, such policies, including autarky, self-determination, nationalization, import-substitution and debt repudiation, also led to their decoupling from the international economic system as a whole and did not in the end lead to a better standard of living for their citizens.

These experiences were not lost on countries around the world. Even before the dissolution of the former Soviet Union, its influence on the economic policies of emerging markets had dwindled. Today, Russian officials talk about liberalization, privatization and cutting government spending in the name of economic stabilization. The failure of the economic policies of communism is pointing the way towards a change in economic philosophy in the developing nations of the world, away from centralist, socialist policies and towards market-oriented thinking.

Today, most lower-income countries are moving toward more liberal economic practices, gradually re-integrating with the world economy. Still wary of being exploited in a system they perceive to be designed for the benefit of wealthier nations, these countries are fast learning that free market practices can actually be made to work to their own advantage and often lead to surprisingly quick improvements in the domestic quality of life. It hasn't been easy, and political jockeying makes the adjustments come more slowly than objective economic analysis may deem preferable, yet it is possible to bring together the finance ministers of India, Indonesia, Argentina and Bulgaria and have them all speak the same economic language.

Probably one of the most articulate proponents of structural change is Richard Rahn, who flatly states that the capitalistic system is man's greatest invention and free markets are necessary for economic development. However, he mentions a number of key elements necessary for a successful economic system:

- the innovation of double-entry bookkeeping;
- fair taxation which does not expropriate or exploit;
- a social ethic which emphasizes hard work;
- the concept of private property rights which are forcefully protected;
- the idea of a free trading system globally;
- a fair and efficient legal system;
- low levels of government spending and therefore low taxation;
- low regulatory burdens.

The key concept is that free markets provide for free prices, which in turn supplies the market participants with valuable information needed for good decisions. This is tied in to the accounting system which provides for a measure of value, unlike the socialist accounting which muddies the information flow reaching the market participants. As regards taxation, he states that high marginal taxes tend *not* to produce higher government income. Professor Lafer's famous Lafer Curve illustrates this phenomenon best.

The convergence among the countries of the world in their economic views has begun to influence policy thinking in multilateral institutions, such as the World Bank. The trend is towards market policies, less government intervention, lower taxation and other innovations designed to stimulate private enterprise.

Effects of ideological change

During the post-colonial period for the lower-income countries, they attempted to distance themselves from colonial influence by developing and implementing their own economic and political strategies. To be sure, these were influenced by the *real politik* of the day, especially the Cold War. Ultimately, however, the indigenously derived development plans, which largely centered on restrictive trade policies, have been gradually abandoned and the public policies they led to slowly dismantled. In their place, largely Western conceptions of a free market are being instituted.

The "demonstration" effect of the success of free market policies in Asia should not be underestimated when evaluating the reform process among lower-income countries. While some Western economies flourished using free market economics, the widespread belief in much of the developing world was that Western economics could only work at the expense of other nations, such as themselves. But the experience of many Asian countries, starting with Japan and extending to Korea, Taiwan, Hong Kong and Singapore, had shown that free market economics can work for everyone.

Public policy has therefore taken a turn. While still reluctant to withdraw some protectionist measures, or still experiencing political lobbying against free market policies, many lower-income country governments have firmly placed their countries on that road to development. Though many bumps will impede progress, I expect the new-found belief in free market economics to carry these countries far.

At the same time, public aspirations have been fanned by Asia's economic growth and the general image of wealth that lower-income countries receive via the media of many countries around the world. These images influence social expectations and solidify the political commitment to reform and liberalization. This is an amazing process to witness and one in which I feel lucky to have participated.

MACROECONOMIC OUTCOME

Some observers have said that the 20th century could be seen as an age of failed experiments in socialism, including its fascist, communist and welfare-state variants. As the fixation with socialism lessens, they say, we are beginning to see some of the most backward regions of the world turning into the most dynamic. Probably the most important endorsement of market incentives has come from the World Bank, which did a detailed study of its own investment projects in developing countries and confirmed that: "… market incentives work."

Now the engines of development are not only centered in the developed countries such as the United States, Europe and Japan, but are being found in many of the emerging nations which are multiplying their resources by investing in other emerging countries.

One of the often overlooked ramifications of the global revolution in economic thinking, the move towards a market economy and a more liberal trading and investment environment is the multiplier effect of the growth in individual country markets on other markets. Now the engines of development are not only centered in the developed countries such as the United States, Europe and Japan, but are being found in many of the emerging nations which are multiplying their resources by investing in other emerging countries.

Stemming from the factors analyzed above, we can see several emerging markets economic trends as a result.

Economic growth

Current estimates indicate that the lower-income countries of the world, the emerging markets, will continue to grow at about double the rate of the developed world. That means that if we take the average real GDP growth of all the emerging markets in Africa, Latin America, Asia and some countries of southern Europe (Portugal, Greece, Turkey), the average growth rate in

1994 was about 5.5 percent, as compared to 2.8 percent for our sample developed markets. Stunning growth rates have been achieved consistently in countries that were once moribund – China, with 12 percent growth in 1994 while Peru experienced 12.9 percent in 1994. In dynamically expanding economies like Singapore and Malaysia, growth rates over 8 percent are the norm (Table 2.2). The convergence of demographic, technological and ideological changes will continue to propel all of these countries into the next century with better living standards and higher hopes.

Table 2.2 Real GDP percentage growth

	1990	1991	1992	1993	1994
Emerging markets					
Argentina	0.1	8.9	8.7	6.0	7.1
Bangladesh	5.1	4.1	4.8	4.9	5.0
Brazil	−4.4	1.1	−0.9	4.3	5.7
Chile	3.3	7.3	11.0	6.3	4.2
China	3.8	8.2	13.1	13.7	12.0
Colombia	4.3	2.0	3.8	5.3	5.3
Greece	−1.0	3.2	0.8	−0.5	1.5
Hong Kong	3.4	5.1	6.0	5.8	5.7
India	5.5	1.8	3.8	3.8	4.9
Indonesia	7.2	6.9	6.5	6.5	7.0
Jordan	1.0	1.8	11.2	5.8	5.7
Korea	9.5	9.1	5.1	5.5	8.3
Malaysia	9.7	8.7	7.8	8.3	8.7
Mexico	4.4	3.6	2.8	0.6	3.5
Pakistan	5.6	8.2	4.8	2.5	4.1
Peru	−4.2	2.8	−2.3	6.5	12.9
Philippines	2.7	−0.2	0.3	2.1	4.5
Portugal	4.2	2.2	1.5	−1.0	3.5
Singapore	8.8	6.7	6.0	9.9	10.1
Sri Lanka	6.2	4.8	4.3	6.9	5.4
Taiwan	4.9	7.2	6.5	6.1	6.2
Thailand	11.6	8.4	7.9	8.2	8.5
Turkey	9.3	0.8	6.1	7.5	−5.6
Venezuela	6.5	9.7	6.1	−0.4	−3.3
Average	4.5	5.1	5.2	5.2	5.5
Developed markets					
Japan	4.8	4.3	1.1	−0.2	0.6
United Kingdom	0.4	−2.0	−0.5	2.2	3.8
United States	1.2	−0.6	2.3	3.1	4.1
Average	2.1	0.6	1.0	1.7	2.8

Sources: *World Economic Outlook*, May 1995, International Monetary Fund; *Trend In Developing Economies* 1994, World Bank; and *Asia Pacific Consensus Forecasts*, Consensus Economics Inc.

Free trade

It is now widely accepted among economists that more open economies, i.e., those which have less distortions in their foreign trade regimes, grow faster. Analysis of various countries presents overwhelming evidence that open economies grow faster. Now it is realized that liberalization improves existing resource allocation across firms in various sectors, and within firms in a sector. Trade liberalization improves the efficiency of investments by allocating capital to activities that are most profitable. The result is higher GDP growth rates and higher growth rates in productivity.

The global liberalization of trade has had a profound impact on business and the operation of enterprises. Economic paralysis and stagnant economic growth in many areas were the result of closed-economy practices, such as high import tariffs. Such barriers to trade also kept out innovative technologies, and perpetuated incompetence and inefficiency. Only since the mid-1970s have the highly protective trade systems been gradually dismantled. Today, the trend is towards policies based on the free entry and exit of capital, a reduction in tariffs, the elimination of quantitative restrictions on imports, the elimination of price and exchange rate controls, and free determination of interest rates.

The best comparative analysis can be done by contrasting economic/industrial policy and outcomes between East Asia and Latin American countries during the same 1970–1980 period. East Asian countries almost unilaterally adopted export-oriented trade policies, while Latin American countries virtually unanimously relied on inward-looking import substitution programs. The results are well-known. Trade liberalization is now on the agenda throughout the Latin American region.

In fact, today we can find most participants in the international economic system joining one form of free trade association or another. Early examples were in Western Europe, which in 1957 established the European Economic Community (EEC), followed by the European Free Trade Area Association (EFTA) in

1960. In Latin America, the Latin America Free Trade Area (LAFTA) was formed, followed by the revitalized Andean Pact of Venezuela, Colombia, Ecuador, Peru and Bolivia, and the Mercosur Trade Pact linking Brazil with Uruguay, Paraguay and Argentina. In Asia, the East Asian Economic Group, the ASEAN Free Trade Area and the Asia Pacific Economic Cooperation groups were formed in 1988. In 1989, the Asia Pacific Economic Cooperation or APEC Agreement was reached, bringing together Korea, Japan, the ASEAN nations, Australia, New Zealand, the United States and Canada. Two years later, in 1991, China, Hong Kong and Taiwan joined APEC. NAFTA is the major North American free trade area (including Canada, the USA and Mexico), and an extension of its reach beyond Mexico and into the rest of South America is on the cards.

The Uruguay Round of GATT trade negotiations, in which over 100 countries representing more than 90 percent of world's commerce participated, was finally concluded in 1994, establishing cuts in tariff and non-tariff barriers. The liberalizations agreed upon were forecast to increase global output by some US$5 trillion over the next decade. The Uruguay Round was not only concerned with physical trade, but also with rules protecting international property rights, opportunities for investment, service industry market opening and generally greater predictability and access to global markets. A final accomplishment of the Uruguay round was the formation of the World Trade Organization, or WTO, to police the General Agreement of Tariffs and Trade (GATT).

The emerging nations of Asia have consistently shown the best growth-rate performance. This performance has, in many cases, come as a result of their successful export drive to the developed nations. While protecting their domestic economy from too much international competition, they have increased their share of world's exports and have become efficient and competitive producers. Utilizing large, eager and cheap labor pools and free enterprise-oriented policies, producers in those countries have used their labor cost advantage combined with technology to become major global exporters.

It is also important to note that they have been very effective in harnessing influence within developed country governments, particularly in the United States, to reduce import barriers to their exports. One example of their effectiveness was demonstrated when China in mid-1993 launched an aggressive campaign to win most-favored nation (MFN) treatment from the United States by dispatching well-publicized buying missions to major United States cities and offering large contracts to major United States corporations which could wield influence with the United States Congress and the Clinton administration. This was similar to the successful campaigns Taiwan launched for many years in the United States using the Communist threat to persuade United States political leaders of the need for liberal trade policies towards Taiwan, thus making Taiwan a major exporter to the United States to bolster the anti-Communist government.

Privatization

One of the most effective ways to reduce government spending, and thereby release financial resources for the private sector, is to privatize state-owned enterprises. Currently in many nations, such enterprises constitute a tremendous drain on the state's resources and budget, as the government is committed to allocating them resources to run their operations, regardless of their profitability or even viability. In fact, as liberalization has progressed, the newer private companies tend to be the most profitable, leaving the State to effectively subsidize State-owned enterprises, often on a massive scale.

An example of how privatization could be successfully launched and implemented was first demonstrated in the United Kingdom during the late 1970s and early 1980s. When the Conservative government, led by Margaret Thatcher, took office, the British economy was declining, and that decline was accelerating. The Conservatives were convinced that a major cause of the decline was extensive government control over industries. They concluded that state-owned industries would always perform poorly and that this poor performance would badly affect the entire economy. The previous Labor Government had nationalized the coal industry, the steel industry, gas supply, electricity generation, railways, docks, and a number of other industries. Practically all the telecommunications industry, aircraft and shipbuilding, much of car manufacturing, oil exploration and production, and even silicon chip manufacturing involved government ownership. The nationalized industries showed poor performance with, in some cases, negative return on capital, low productivity, high cost, high prices, inefficient use of resources, and poor service to customers.

John Moore, the man responsible for much of the privatization in the United Kingdom during that period, said that State enterprises inevitably performed poorly because the priorities of elected politicians were necessarily different from the priorities of business managers, and both sets of priorities could rarely be pursued simultaneously. Since nationalized industries did not need to succeed to survive, they naturally tended to perform poorly. He proposed that self-interest, as viewed by the socialists, was not some evil quality to be repressed, but was simply the urge for people to improve their life both for themselves and for their families. He said that this self-interest had been harnessed to drive progress since the beginning of time, and to pretend otherwise was to ignore one of the most powerful forces available for improving the quality of life for everyone. The British experience demonstrated beyond doubt, he said, that privatization improves the performance of former nationalized industries, and encourages more efficient use of resources throughout the entire economy. He went on to state that there are two equally important arguments for privatization: (1) the transformation in attitudes produced by individual ownership; and (2) the process which forces politicians to consider and focus on the State's more important role as regulator, and not owner, thus making it a more effective overseer of the public's interests.

In recent years, there has been a move towards privatization globally, most particularly in the emerging markets. South America has caught the privatization fever, and countries small and large, from Slovenia to Brazil have launched privatization programs. In some cases, the change in attitudes has been dramatic. Carlos Andre Perez was President of Venezuela when the oil industry was nationalized, but by 1993 he was at the forefront of inviting companies back and dismantling the nationalization.

However, privatization plans may be slowed if international investors cannot continue to be attracted to these markets. Over-reliance on international demand for stocks, instead of on the domestic market persists. In 1995, Indonesia was forced to scale back privatization plans because of the lack of demand for state-owned assets. Many countries do not have an established "equity culture" within their domestic investor base, and the potential for diversion of funds from privatization issues if returns are more favorable elsewhere is real. Governments, and the banks which advise them, become far too optimistic about the amount of stock which international investors are prepared to buy and the price they would pay. The sheer number of privatizations set to flood the international markets represents a daunting task for the bankers involved in arranging and under-writing the transactions. There is also the view that there is a great deal of risk in buying the stock of formerly State-owned enterprises (SOEs), as the newly privatized firms simply may not be able to compete. It is a simple risk/reward calculation that may be discouraging investors, international and domestic alike.

These countries differ from former Communist countries, because they moved towards nationalization of State firms out of a sense that this was the only way for small, newly independent countries with weak private sectors to develop strong basic industries, such as heavy manufacturing, energy and telecommunications. Today, the economies of these countries are thriving, and the State sees the wisdom of moving with the times and allowing their private sector to take over the operation of these SOEs before they turn into the moribund behemoths found in the former USSR.

In some cases of privatization, it is a means of releasing entrepreneurial activity. In almost all cases, private ownership is intended to help cement political and economic reforms being put into place, with the hope that once large changes have been made, it becomes impossible to return to the old system. Resistance to privatization can be great, particularly among those who benefited from State-ownership; the bureaucracy and those employees of the State enterprises whose jobs may be at stake. As one official said: "I never knew a turkey that has asked for Christmas to be brought forward."

It is important to note that privatization and industrial restructuring cannot effectively take place unless prices have been freed from control and subsidy distortions. A whole host of reforms must take place, such as foreign trade liberalization and the establishment of a realistic exchange rate. Also important is the need for a legal framework and an independent judicial system. The judicial system should regard competition as acceptable and to be encouraged. Also needed are competitive banking and financial markets to help mobilize and allocate financial resources on the basis of demand, rather than central planning. Privatization involves a change in thinking regarding private ownership and private copyright. This, in turn, is related to ideas regarding how a democratic civil society with personal rights and responsibilities should be established.

Manageable debt

The debt hang-over from the 1960s and 1970s has been gradually shrinking. The debt restructuring and bank financial packages that were started in 1984 had, in the main, been successfully completed by the end of 1992, although there were some packages still under negotiation. These debt restructuring initiatives have put debt-laden countries back on their feet and enhanced their reputations in the eyes of multilateral organizations and private capital sources. Improved economic performance has also enabled these countries to better service their debt from domestic revenue.

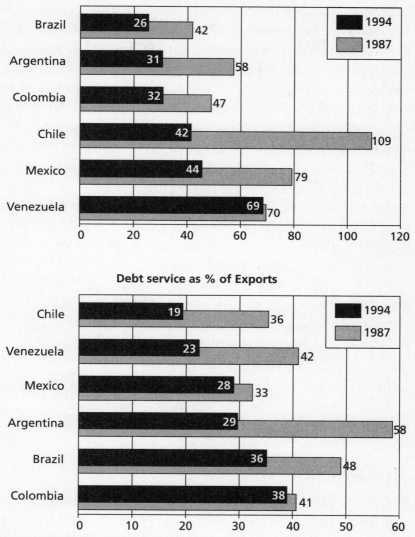

External debt as % of GDP

Debt service as % of Exports

Figure 2.6   Latin America: debt reduction

Source: Institute of International Finance

The Brady Plan debt restructuring in particular (where international banks are prepared to write off some debts in return for the restructuring of outstanding debt into US Treasury collateralized bonds with extended maturities and lower coupons), has had a dramatic impact on the ratio of debt service to export revenues. In Latin America this ratio declined from 57.8 percent in 1987 to 29 percent in 1994 for Argentina and from 36 percent in 1987 to a low of 19 percent in 1994 for Chile. Such declines in debt levels have boosted international capital market confidence in Latin America. Between 1987 and 1994 there was also a dramatic change in external debt as a percentage of GDP. Chile experienced highs of 109 percent debt to GDP in 1987, chopping that to 42 percent in 1994. Mexico too was able to reduce its debt GDP ratio from 79 percent in 1987 to 44.1 percent in 1994. By 1994, surprisingly, it was Brazil who had the lowest debt GDP ratio in Latin America, at 25.8 percent (Figure 2.6).

One important way in which the commercial bank debt of the various emerging markets was reduced was through debt conversions related to privatization. Between 1984 amd 1992, about US$40 billion of public-sector bank debt was converted to equity stakes in local companies through official debt conversion schemes.

There has been growing confidence in the emerging markets. Former creditors are now willing to place more money in those markets. The international market for developing country securities has continued to mature with better liquidity, a wider range of currency trading possibilities, longer maturities, narrowing spreads, and an expanding list of derivative products.

Tax reform

Will Rogers once said: "Income taxes have made more Americans into liars than golf." Albert Einstein said: "The most difficult thing in the world to understand is taxes." Probably one of the biggest depressants on the rate of capital formation is the risk of confiscation by governments via taxation. Economists are only slowly beginning to understand that the speed of economic growth is greatly influenced by the level of income taxes and that there is an inverse relationship between the amount of a country's total tax income and its economic growth rate. More specifically there is an inverse correlation between income tax revenues as a percentage of total taxes and industrial production.

While taxation in high-income countries persists at discouragingly high levels in order to support a cornucopia of social programs, in many of the emerging economies this is not the case. These countries have instead opted to encourage savings and stock market investment by not taxing capital gains. Such policies tend to encourage capital formation and transfer of money from traditional savings to equity investments. In addition, many emerging nations encourage owners of businesses to issue common stock through the stock market by giving tax benefits to listed companies. A number of governments are beginning to realize that by not having capital gains tax they promote growth and development. They realize that capital formation, if not taxed, will grow more rapidly and thus provide more employment.

Development directions

As is evident, the demographic, technological and ideological changes which have taken place in lower-income countries over the past decade or so are clearly influencing the direction and speed of overall macroeconomic development. Better health and learning, exposure to international media and world-class technology, and a willingness to embrace a more open economic philosophy are all promoting more effective social progress. The outcome can be seen in higher rates of economic growth, a willingness to engage in international trade, expanded ownership of the means of production through privatization of state-owned assets, and reduced overall levels of foreign debt. There can be no doubt about the vigor of the virtuous circle now turning in emerging market countries.

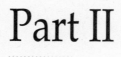

Part II

Country Reviews

What I have tried to provide in this section of the book is a quick historical picture of where financial and economic development has arisen in each region or country, followed by a more personal snapshot via "diary entries" that will illustrate for the reader some of the insights regular travel, visits and local discussion can give to the emerging markets investor

Chapter 3

Emerging Market Overview

The year 1993 was a great one for emerging market investors. Markets in every country soared, and gains in excess of 50 percent were registered as par for the course. But 1994 and 1995 came as a shock to such investors, who had developed the expectation that the potent combination of financial influences that drove the market up beyond its fundamentals could be indefinitely sustained. The important lessons learned were that long-term market growth is based on the natural capacity of a country to generate productivity enhancements and that pushing them up unnaturally fast only leads to indigestion later.

In 1993, the sharp upswing in emerging market stock prices attracted numerous merchant bankers and underwriters who saw good opportunities to expand their new issue and rights issue business. At the same time, many owners of companies saw an opportunity to sell their shares at high prices and raise new money for expansion. Perhaps more importantly, governments around

The interesting thing about markets, particularly stock markets, is that often behavior is exaggerated.

Asia and throughout the world saw excellent opportunities to accelerate the already-burgeoning popularity of privatizations by bringing their government-owned companies to the capital markets and selling shares at what they saw as high prices.

The convergence of rapidly rising prices, eager investors pouring their money into the markets, underwriters and merchant banks expanding their business, and companies rushing new issues to the market resulted in a very rapid rise in the number of shares available in all emerging markets. The interesting thing about markets, particularly stock markets, is that often behavior is exaggerated on the up and the down side. Sometimes everything is overdone: very high share prices, rapid increases in trading volume, sky-high earnings for the financial industry, too many new issues on the market at once, etc. It is exciting when it is happening but when everyone wakes up after the binge, hangovers are bound to be prevalent.

Aspects of emerging markets such as stock market performance or capitalization are constantly changing – by the time one reads such figures, they are already likely to have been supplanted by new developments.

After gigantic gains over the course of 1993, the reality of normal business operations struck local, regional and international investors in 1994. They realized that stock market prices most often lead, i.e., occur before, economic growth and company earnings growth, and often overshoot the growth in companies' earnings or the growth in economies. These realizations brought them to the conclusion that the very high growth in stock market prices experienced in 1993 were far in excess of what could be expected in subsequent company earnings growth or economic development, even in fast-growing Asia. This led directly to the correction in markets throughout the world and particularly in emerging markets in 1994 and 1995.

Because of the extreme volatility in emerging markets, I prefer to analyze countries in terms of (1) how practical investing is, i.e., ease of access and low transaction costs, and (2) the viability of the business community. Aspects of emerging markets such as stock market performance or capitalization are constantly changing – by the time one reads such figures, they are already likely to have been supplanted by new developments. What counts is the general direction of economic development and the general tone that prevails in a given country. What I have tried to provide in this section of the book is a quick historical picture of where financial and economic development has come from in each region or country, followed by a more personal snapshot via "diary entries" that will illustrate for the reader some of the insights regular travel, visits and local discussion can give to the emerging markets investor. These diary entries offer the reader a true picture of what an investor sees when visiting these countries and meeting daily with people who are involved in running a business, trying to make sense of the financial system, implementing policies, or just putting dinner on the table.

AFRICA

In 1995, which emerging market region of the world over a 12 month period gave investors a 40 percent return? Most would guess the dynamic economies of Asia, but in fact it was Africa. Sure, this figure was from an admittedly absurdly low base, but it highlights how quickly returns can be generated in emerging markets, and how quickly they can grow under the right combination of circumstances.

What I have tried to provide in this section of the book is a quick historical picture of where financial and economic development has come from in each region or country, followed by a more personal snapshot via 'diary entries' that will illustrate for the reader some of the insights regular travel, visits and local discussion can give to the emerging markets investor.

The countries of the African continent are slowly pulling themselves out of the mire, gradually converting to peaceful regimes and building their economies from the ground up. Yet the entire continent's total GDP, excluding that of South Africa, is still less than that of Belgium.

Most countries in the region are now adopting structural adjustment programs, while more and more of them have adopted realistic exchange rates, lifted exchange controls, cut subsidies and terminated price controls. Today, the continent has more than a dozen stock markets and as privatization gains ground, these markets should expand. Privatization has been slowed by ambivalent government support and by inflated valuations of African companies as a result of over-valued exchange rates. Banking, mining, and other commodity firms – tobacco, coffee, tea and sugar – are generally largest on the continent.

Equity market development is progressing in Africa. The Botswana stock exchange, which began trading in June 1989, had ten companies listed, for a market capitalization US$280 million. Nigeria's stock exchange has been widely influenced by the boom and bust cycle of its oil trade. In 1996 there were over 175 listed companies, giving Nigeria a market capitalization of US$1.3 billion. One of Africa's oldest stock exchanges can be found in Zimbabwe. In 1996, there were 65 companies listed on the ZSE, giving it a market capitalization of US$180 million. In 1996, Morocco's market was worth US$5 billion, Mauritius' was worth US$1.7 billion, Kenya's US$1.9 billion, Ghana's US$2 billion and Tunisia's US$2.5 billion.

The engine of growth on the African continent is indisputably South Africa. It is home to the largest conglomerate based in Africa, the giant Anglo-American Corporation, capitalized at US$13 billion. South Africa also possesses the world's 10th largest stock market, capitalized at US$250 billion at the end of 1995, with 640 companies listed. In light of recent reforms in South Africa, all local companies are laying plans to exploit the renewed international trade links and a more liberal trade regime. The pressure to abolish exchange controls exemplifies this new competitive spirit among South African businesses. There is also the potential for major South African privatizations, such as SA Telkom, Transnet, a freight transporter and South African Airways, which would give a big boost to the local stock market.

Ashanti Goldfields, based in Accra, Ghana, is the largest African company outside of South Africa, with a market capitalization of US$1.6 billion. It has metamorphosed from a struggling, undercapitalized, state-owned operation to one that today has interests in nearly a dozen African countries, and was floated in April 1994. Kenya Airways has undergone a similar transformation from its days as a badly run, loss-making state-owned airline. With a public issue in March 1996, Kenya Airways entered into a profitable alliance with KLM, and was on the road to sound business development.

Investors in emerging markets haven't missed this turn of events. At least 12 institutions have formed Africa funds, worth nearly $1 billion in investment targeted solely at the continent. Analysts advise investors to watch natural resource and tourism companies, industries with the most potential in Africa over the coming decade.

Investors feel more vulnerable in these markets however. They are truly "emerging." During the 1990s many African countries lifted exchange controls and at least partially freed up their exchange rates. This creates a level playing field and gives investors some comfort, knowing that the chances for market changes by government fiat are reduced. But with continuing political uncertainty and continued economic underperformance, the temptation to manipulate the markets still exists and not everyone believes that the government forces can resist.

ASIA

There is so much to be said about Asia. Its growth and its liberalization are setting examples for all economies, high-income and lower-income alike. Many studies have been done on the subject, most notably by the World Bank, to quantify their success. Fundamentally, most Asian economies embarked on determined, free-market-oriented financial and industrial reforms which gathered steam in the early 1980s, and which today are generating astounding economic returns. Gross per capita income is up, education/literacy rates are up, health figures are up, trade is up, consumption is up – the economic reforms have had a direct net beneficial effect on the people living in this area of the world. To do the reforms justice, I've selected a number of countries in the region and reviewed their economic structure in greater depth (Table 3.1).

Table 3.1 Asian Economic Indications (1994)

China		Hong Kong	
GDP growth (YoY %)	11.80	GDP growth (YoY %)	5.40
GDP per capita (YoY %)	424	GDP per capita (YoY %)	21,638
Unemployment rate (%)	2.90	Unemployment rate (%)	2.20
Savings rate (% GDP)	43.00	Savings rate (% GDP)	33.90
Forex reserves (US $bn)	51.6	Forex reserves (US $bn)	49.7
Inflation (%, national)	24.2	Inflation (%, national)	8.1
Market cap (US %bn)	1.6	Market cap (US $bn)	269
Co. listed	287	Co. listed	529
India		**Indonesia**	
GDP growth (YoY %)	4.30	GDP growth (YoY %)	7.30
GDP per capita (YoY %)	281	GDP per capita (YoY %)	884
Unemployment rate (%)	5.60	Unemployment rate (%)	2.40
Savings rate (% GDP)	20.40	Savings rate (% GDP)	34.60
Forex reserves (US $bn)	19.3	Forex reserves (US $bn)	13.2
Inflation (%, national)	8.4	Inflation (%, national)	9.3
Market cap (US %bn)	133.3	Market cap (US $bn)	53
Co. listed	4413	Co. listed	217
Korea		**Malaysia**	
GDP growth (YoY %)	8.40	GDP growth (YoY %)	8.70
GDP per capita (YoY %)	8,483	GDP per capita (YoY %)	3,699
Unemployment rate (%)	2.40	Unemployment rate (%)	2.90
Savings rate (% GDP)	35.20	Savings rate (% GDP)	32.30
Forex reserves (US $bn)	25.7	Forex reserves (US $bn)	26.2
Inflation (%, national)	5.6	Inflation (%, national)	3.7
Market cap (US %bn)	191	Market cap (US $bn)	195
Co. listed	699	Co. listed	478
Pakistan		**Philippines**	
GDP growth (YoY %)	3.80	GDP growth (YoY %)	5.20
GDP per capita (YoY %)	411	GDP per capita (YoY %)	966
Unemployment rate (%)	4.70	Unemployment rate (%)	8.80
Savings rate (% GDP)	14.60	Savings rate (% GDP)	19.70
Forex reserves (US $bn)	2.5	Forex reserves (US $bn)	7
Inflation (%, national)	11.2	Inflation (%, national)	9
Market cap (US %bn)	12.1	Market cap (US $bn)	56.8
Co. listed	724	Co. listed	189
Singapore		**Taiwan**	
GDP growth (YoY %)	10.10	GDP growth (YoY %)	6.50
GDP per capita (YoY %)	24,048	GDP per capita (YoY %)	12
Unemployment rate (%)	2.60	Unemployment rate (%)	1.60
Savings rate (% GDP)	49.70	Savings rate (% GDP)	29.00
Forex reserves (US $bn)	57.5	Forex reserves (US $bn)	93
Inflation (%, national)	3.6	Inflation (%, national)	4
Market cap (US %bn)	141.2	Market cap (US $bn)	246.4
Co. listed	229	Co. listed	313
Thailand			
GDP growth (YoY %)	8.50		
GDP per capita (YoY %)	2,416		
Unemployment rate (%)	2.60		
Savings rate (% GDP)	35.60		
Forex reserves (US $bn)	30.8		
Inflation (%, national)	5		
Market cap (US %bn)	132		
Co. listed	389		

Note: Asian numbers from *Reuters Asian Stock Sourcebook* 1996 and *Euromoney Guide to World Equity Markets* 1995

India

Indian economics and politics have been one long roller-coaster ride since independence in 1947. Severe disturbances, like the separation from Pakistan, acted temporarily to break the momentum of economic development in India. It is also true that as a large and diverse country, it has been difficult to arrive at a consensus over how economic development should proceed.

In the 1990s, however, India's direction seems clear. Over 200 million people in India form a relatively wealthy middle class, with advanced educational attainments, rewarding careers and a stable family life. There is no denying that a huge underclass remains, but this portion of the population is a potential bonanza to the country, as they are mobilized and brought into the industrialized activity of the country through economic expansion and job creation.

In 1995 inflation in India was a tolerable 8 percent, with US$17 billion in foreign reserves. GDP per capita is US$281 a year, but this is misleading, as a substantial middle class with an annual income over US$100,000 has appeared in recent years.

One of the most striking examples of the change in attitudes towards economic policies could be seen in India in late 1992 and early 1993. India was one the founders and prime mover in the 1970s to create centralist government-directed economic policies in opposition to free-markets, which at that time were believed to be hopelessly biased against the interests of developing nations.

From a reliance on state control and central planning, the Indian government is moving more and more towards a reliance on private enterprise. From the discrediting of private economic activity, the government has moved into a position of championing the business class as the way to prosperity and jobs for India's millions of poor. On the back of such policies, GDP growth was up to 4.8 percent in 1994.

To make his point clear, Prime Minister Narasimha Rao had a lawn party in 1993. He invited more than 400 Indian bureaucrats and ministers to his official residence, graciously welcomed them, served a generous spread, and then launched into a vituperative harangue on the damage to India originating in the socialism advocated by many of his guests.

Since then, India has proceeded to open its economy to international trade and to foreign investors. As a large and politically diverse country, India has experienced hiccups on the road to reform that have worried foreign investors. Incidents such as the politically inspired closure of an American fast-food franchise on the basis of spurious health reasons, or the reneging on a construction contract to build a power plant. In spite of these contrary notes, the country is broadly moving towards opening its 900 million strong consumer market to foreign companies.

Given its huge population and a savings rate of over 20 per cent of GDP, India's domestic stock market has grown rapidly. Market capitalization in 1994 was US$140 billion and over 4,000 companies were listed. In 1992, Indian companies raised US$5.8 billion in primary capital market issues, a 245 per cent increase over 1991 despite the fall of the market index. Growth of the market has been aided by the institution of unit trusts and investment trusts to mobilize domestic savings. The Unit Trust of India, which had a monopoly until 1987 on the unit trusts market in India, had a retail network of 76,000 agents and over 35 offices throughout the country. The government has now granted foreign fund management companies new licences to offer their products in the local market.

Progress on opening its stock exchanges is being hindered by delays primarily associated with the establishment of adequate share registration and settlement procedures. As things stand now, it is possible for foreign investors to buy Indian stocks, but this can mean having investment capital tied up for several months after the transaction, but before settlement.

Indonesia

Indonesia is another country in this region which has experienced the emergence of a substantial middle class and has the potential to really drive growth by bringing even more of its 180 million people into the industrialized sector. With GDP growth expected to continue around 8 percent annually, and per capita incomes of US$884 annually, Indonesia is rushing to upgrade its economic status.

Prior to the liberalization measures taken by the government, the stock market was a sleepy institution. I remember visiting the Jakarta Exchange trading hall, and just a few individuals could be seen holding a desultory bargaining session for a half hour each day. One gentleman was taking an afternoon nap on his table. Then, after the government liberalized foreign investments in the market, an explosion of activity occurred. The number of listed companies rose from 24 in 1989 to 217 just five years later, in 1994. Capital raised from new issues during that time was US$4.2 billion. In 1995 there were 21 new IPOs.

Malaysia

Malaysia is the economic success story of the decade. With a population of only 19 million people it has a stock market capitalization of US$195 billion (end of 1994) with over 475 companies listed. Per capita income has soared to US$3,700, with virtual full employment (the technical unemployment figure is 2.9 percent) and even a labor shortage in some fields. Inflation has hovered around 4 percent, while GDP growth sizzled at 8.7 percent, a rate of growth it has achieved almost annually for almost a decade.

The government announced in early 1993 the further privatization of 260 more government agencies following the successful public offering of several large companies. Dr Mahathir Mohamad, the Prime Minister, said that initially government employees resisted privatization, because they thought that it would mean loss of their job security. Today, employees in government agencies want privatization, as they now know it meant increased income and the potential for bonuses and other perks.

Further financial liberalization initiatives are being put in place, some of which would eventually permit foreign fund management companies to provide services to local investors. Malaysia has created an offshore financial centre on the picturesque island of Labuan, as part of its overall objective of enhancing its financial role in the Asia region.

Philippines

Following the resounding success of the privatization IPO for Philippine National Bank during 1995, now trading at a minimum 20 percent premium to its issue price, the Philippines crowned what was already a tremendously successful year in economic terms. Growth expanded by leaps and bounds. In 1992, GDP growth was a measly 0.9 percent, while in 1993 it was 2.0 percent. Beginning in 1994, the promised returns from political reforms were first evident, as GDP growth jumped to 5.2 percent and 1995 preliminary results indicated growth of 5.6 percent.

There are 189 companies listed in the Philippines, for a market capitalization of US$57 billion. Long excommunicated from international debt markets as a result of the debt default during the debt crisis of the mid-1980s (the only Asian country ever to have been rescheduled, and subject to an IMF restructuring program), Philippine borrowers are once again finding themselves welcome in the international capital markets. Their Brady bonds are trading at a premium while debt borrowing term maturities have stretched from one year to five years for bluechip companies. The national savings rate is rising, estimated at around 20 percent in 1995. Per capita GDP passed the US$1,000 mark in 1995.

Sri Lanka

With a change in government in 1977, economic policy was transformed from the socialist, centrally planned Chinese/ Soviet economic model to a market-oriented model. During its various terms in power, Sri Lanka's Freedom Party was instrumental in nationalizing almost all of the economy, including the major plantations and industries. This, of course, sounded the death knell for the market economy and economic growth in general.

The stock exchange fell into a deep slumber until the economic reform began in 1977. In 1990, the stock market was opened to foreign investment and political leaders called on the private sector to act as the engine of economic growth. Politically, the government saw the potential in economic development to diffuse radicalism, motivate disenchanted youth, and ensure that social benefits accrued to the population at large via market activity and job creation.

The Sri Lankan government has privatized a number of government companies involved in the importation and distribution of motor vehicles, textile manufacturing, ceramic-ware manufacture, leather tanning, packaging, hotels, and animal feed manufacturing. Borrowing a page from India's reform program, the government in Sri Lanka called their privatization scheme "peoplization," to assuage the fear of people who believed that the government might allow the country to slide back into foreign economic domination, as experienced during the British Colonial period.

By 1993, 18 of Sri Lanka's state enterprises had been 51 percent privatized, and another 31 enterprises were at various stages of privatization. In the Sri Lankan privatization program, 10 percent of the shares up for privatization were reserved for the company's employees, 30 percent were earmarked for Sri Lankan citizens in the initial offering, and the remaining 60 percent for successful bidders, either foreign or domestic. In some cases, companies with heavy debt loads, such as the bus system, were given away to employees without the State making any money. From time to time, progress in Sri Lanka has been blocked by bureaucrats charging that economic liberalization is destabilizing and uncontrollable. But the practical and enlightened former President Ranasinghe Premadasa stuck with his belief that "the engine of economic growth in this decade is the private sector." In order to defuse radicalism, he saw the stock market as a key instrument in achieving a redistribution of wealth. Unfortunately, Ranasinghe died at the hands of a radical Tamil separatist bomber.

Taiwan

Taiwan has for decades enjoyed a stable government conducive to economic growth with little unemployment, a well-developed infrastructure, large foreign reserves and minimal external debt. Inflation in Taiwan for 1995 was around 4.5 percent, while GDP growth was 6.4 percent in 1995. The country runs a consistent trade surplus and holds one of the world's largest foreign currency reserves, of around US$90 billion.

Reform in Taiwan has had the effect of stimulating economic activity and encouraging residents to become active in the local stock markets. Although Taiwan remains one of the more restrictive emerging markets, from 1983, foreign investors have been allowed to invest in the stock market indirectly through investment funds. In December 1990, regulations were passed allowing foreign institutional investors who met certain highly restrictive requirements to invest in the market directly. Change was also brought about by the installation of an efficient and cost-effective computerized trading system.

The results from the creation of the favorable investment climate are clear. During the ten-year period between 1977 and 1987, the index at the Taipei Stock Exchange did not move above 1,000 points. After reforms in 1987, however, it began to climb with a vengeance. During the three-year period from 1988 to

1990, the index rose from 2,000 to 12,000. While in 1987 the market capitalization of the Taiwan market was US$4 billion, in 1994 total market capitalization was US$246 billion. At the peak of the market, some Taiwan stocks were selling at more than 100 times earnings.

The number of brokers also rose with the market. In 1988, there were only 28 licensed brokers, but that grew to 372 broker- age houses. The number of active brokerage accounts rose from 700,000 to 5.3 million in a country with only 20 million people. It was estimated that one out of every three adults in Taiwan was active in the stock market. This was despite the fact that there was a relatively limited number of companies listed, with the number of companies rising from 123 in 1984 to 313 companies at the end of 1994.

To demonstrate the powerful effect of financial reforms on investment and capital market activity, it is worthwhile seeing what happens when reforms are rescinded. In 1995, the Tai- wanese parliament re-introduced a capital gains tax, which had been previously suspended in the late 1980s. After a one-day drop in the market of 6 percent, the President vetoed the bill and it is unlikely to be reintroduced.

Thailand

They say that Bangkok is a city of 12 million people by day and 5.8 million by night and a place where land prices have increased four times in the last ten years. Few countries have experienced the rate of change that Thailand has over the past decade. Such changes are particularly evident in Thailand's financial markets.

Today, Thailand is home to a thriving stock exchange, on which both foreign and domestic investors are players. In Thai- land, foreigners were restricted to participating in the local market, via a separate "alien board" established in the market to trade shares, but the lack of liquidity in many of the foreign "alien board" shares results in very volatile prices and also opens foreign investors to the risks of market manipulation. It also happened that foreign investors often reached their investment limit, and this affected foreign-registered shares, causing them to trade at a premium.

When in late 1992 the government floated a proposal (subsequently not carried out) allowing foreigners to invest legally in Thai stocks without being restricted by foreign ownership limits, the premium prices that investors had had to pay for the limited number of foreign-designated shares fell dramatically and caused significant book losses for some investors. For many years, foreign demand for bluechip Thai companies has outstripped supply. In addition to sometimes purchasing shares at a premium, other foreigners tried to circumvent the limits by purchasing local shares through Thai nominees. This was an illegal practice but the authorities did not take action to stop it for fear of driving away investors.

In its move towards modernization, the Stock Exchange of Thailand opened a securities depository center in September 1992 with computerized account balancing with the shares held at the center, in a bid to eliminate the need for physical delivery of scrip. This modernization had the added benefit of making it difficult for illegal practices, such as nominee share purchases, to continue.

Korea

I write this report from Kumi-City, Kyungbuk Province, Korea. This province is Park Chung Hee territory. The former President of South Korea, who was assassinated in the Blue House, was born in this mountainous territory near Gumi. It benefited from his munificence, with a technology university and industrial complex to provide jobs. The Kumi industrial Complex has more than 300 high-tech related manufacturers and more than 100 producers of electronic goods and components. This is a beautiful part of the country, with the deep green, mist-covered mountains and the shallow, fascinating Nakdong River passing through the area.

We are now on the Kyungbu Koso Toro – the Seoul to Pusan high speed road – which is the four-lane highway connecting the northern part of South Korea with the southern regions. Today, the drive takes about five hours but with a traffic jam like the one we are stuck in now, it could take much more. The traffic is at a standstill but I don't mind because I can work in the car with my portable computer. Also, the cellular telephone I picked up in Seoul works here, and I can call the Templeton offices anywhere in the world. I notice that in the truck sitting next to us in the traffic jam the driver is talking on his cellular phone too.

The main city in this area is Taegu, South Korea's third-largest city with a population of about 2.3 million. Since it is one of the country's five so-called "special cities," it enjoys a large degree of municipal independence from the Kyungbuk

Provincial government. Taegu lies in the center of the country, between Seoul (370 kilometers to the north) and Pusan (120 kilometers to the south), so it is strategically located. When Korea embarked on its export-oriented development strategy after the Korean War (1950–3), the area became the center of South Korea's textile industry. Kyungbuk Province, where the city is located, has a population of three million and is famous for the Ulsan shipyard, Korea's largest, and the Kumi and Pohang industrial complexes. The Pohang Industrial Complex is home to one of the world's largest steel mills, the Pohang Iron and Steel Company (POSCO). There are hundreds of iron and steel product manufacturers in the complex that rely on POSCO's output. The province is also famous in history, with the Kyongju city historical site. That city was the capital of the Shilla Dynasty, which ruled from 57 BC to 935 AD.

South Korea's economy is still growing fast, despite the fact that it is nearing a high state of industrial production and living standards. On the way to Pusan, we stopped at a department store and all nine floors of the enormous complex was jammed full with high quality goods. There was no shortage of shoppers either and we had to fight our way through the crowds to buy a shirt. I thought I'd get away with buying a low-priced, local-brand shirt. No way – Pierre Cardin, Countess Mara, Paco Rabanne, Yves St Laurent and other famous high-priced brands were all we could find. After a 30 percent discount because the store was having a sale, the price was still US$50 per shirt.

This area of the country still has a lower living standard than the big cities of Seoul and Pusan. Industry here is dependent on those major metropolitan areas. Most of South Korea's economic activity and infrastructure spending has been concentrated in those two main cities. To a great extent, Taegu's production facilities are manufacturing subsidiaries or vendors to large corporations based in Seoul that are seeking the benefits of the area's lower labor costs. What happens here, therefore, is dictated by what happens in the bigger cities, particularly Seoul. Sales and trading transactions happen in Seoul, while only production takes place here. Thus, there is a continuous outflow of funds, according to the Daegu Bank official we interviewed.

In 1994, the South Korean economy grew 7.9 percent, after increasing by more than 5.6 percent in 1993. Exports rose 17 percent in 1994, with heavy industry and chemical industries accounting for 68 percent of South Korean exports. Korea is no longer a source of cheap workers for labor-intensive light manufacturing industries. While exports of textiles, shoes and iron and steel products are showing a declining trend, exports of semiconductors, automobiles and general machinery are on the way up. However, in the restructuring of industry towards higher value added products and more sophisticated production, there is a need to import machinery and other capital goods. Thus imports rose 2 percent and caused a US$6 billion trade deficit. Inflation is well in hand, with a 6 percent increase – about the same as in 1993.

This year, the economy is expected to expand by 7 percent, driven by its strong exports. However, exports are meeting more and more competition from less-developed countries with lower costs, and as regional economic blocks such as the European Community and the North American Free Trade Area are formed.

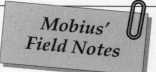

Mobius'
Field Notes

Vietnam

Since the mid-1980s, the government of Vietnam has taken a series of steps designed to convert the Vietnamese economy from a centrally planned system into a more mixed, market-oriented system. In the past five years, the Government's macroeconomic measures have reduced inflation, brought comparative stability to the local currency, improved export competitiveness and reduced public-sector borrowing.

It got a later start than others in Southeast Asia, of course, and must still do much more to build its economy up to its potential. But there have been many exciting signs of progress lately, and we see others ahead that should continue to improve the operating environment as we seek the best possible values for investors.

In July 1995 Vietnam became the newest member of the Association of Southeast Asian Nations (ASEAN), a well organized regional co-ordination body that includes some of the world's hottest economies. ASEAN should serve as an avenue for Vietnam's continued opening up to the world on both a political and economic level. Membership there may also help Vietnam gain admittance to the Asia Pacific Economic Co-operation (APEC) forum, an increasingly important body that for two years now has held summits each November drawing the leaders of the United States, Japan, China and most other Pacific Rim nations.

Such events can provide Hanoi officials with great exposure to the specific steps towards trade and investment liberalization that have worked so well elsewhere in the region. They could give Vietnam's reformists encouragement from outside to build a viable new foreign investment regime. This is something that is especially needed at a time when there is competition for capital among the world's emerging markets, especially among the Asian "tigers."

From a macroeconomic point of view, Vietnam's performance is excellent, with sustained, strong growth in real gross domestic product, a positive trend in its trade balance, and inflation largely under control. Many economic experts believe the country will achieve real gross domestic product (GDP) growth rates of about 10 percent for the rest of the decade, sustained by domestic demand, which, in turn, is being fueled by increasing private investment.

What we see overall here, then, is a fast-growing, if still poor nation for which there is great investor interest around the world. The big question, though, is whether the government will do all it can to establish a strong business climate. And to be quite frank, much still needs to be done on that front.

Many analysts see the lack of adequate reform as the single biggest obstacle currently keeping this country from developing even faster than it is. The fact that it has not experienced a Russian or Eastern European-style revolution overturning Communism should not necessarily be seen as an obstacle. Remember, neighboring Communist China has experienced a ten-fold increase in GDP since 1978 and has become the developing world's largest recipient of foreign investment.

Policy and law reforms have improved industrial output and labor productivity in state enterprises and, more importantly, increased the role of the private sector in the economy. The

Vietnamese government is encouraging foreign investors and in the past eight years it has granted almost 1,000 licenses for foreign investment projects, with total investment capital of about US$10 billion. During that time, both industrial and agricultural output have increased significantly.

The normalization of relations between the United States and Vietnam has created significant opportunities for US enterprises to participate in Vietnam's economic growth, and investment in Vietnam by US companies should provide even greater stimulation to the Vietnamese economy. Although many barriers to rapid economic growth still exist, the government has taken steps to address issues such as inadequate infrastructure, a primitive legal framework, a general lack of skilled and experienced managers, bureaucracy and corruption.

The "tiger" economies of Southeast Asia are the largest source of foreign investment capital in Vietnam. However, because Vietnam doesn't have an official stock exchange for trading company stocks, investing in Vietnam itself means making direct investments in individual projects, such as building a hotel or setting up a bottling plant. When portfolio investors such as Templeton want to invest in Vietnam, they must do so indirectly – by buying stocks in companies that are based elsewhere but that do business in Vietnam.

For a couple of years now there has been talk about creating a stock market in Vietnam. Unfortunately, there has not been much action. I still expect it all to happen, but little has been done so far. A local currency bond market is developing fast, *with the equivalent of about $345 million in Vietnamese treasury bonds targeted for sale this year, plus more in the form of newly allowed corporate issues. The Communist government of Vietnam realizes that foreign investment is important in helping the country develop its infrastructure and in helping enterprises compete successfully in Vietnam and in the world's markets. A fully functioning stock exchange, where company shares could be traded, would help achieve the government's aims. The Vietnamese government knows that a stock exchange will play a major role in attracting new foreign capital, and I look forward to the day that Templeton can buy shares on a Hanoi Stock Exchange.*

Philippines (28 July 1995)

*During July, the rainy season engulfs the Philippines, and the
traffic problems are exacerbated. Manila is now like
Bangkok. Flooded streets and a seat in traffic for one or two
hours for a trip that normally should have taken 15 minutes.
But such traffic problems are a sign of prosperity.
Automobile sales are booming on the back of lower interest
rates, higher incomes, and easier auto loan financing. The
banking sector is getting more competitive as the Ramos
administration's liberalization policies are beginning to take
hold. Banks and insurance companies are getting more
aggressive in their auto loan and housing mortgage policies
in an effort to grab a healthy share of the market before the
onslaught of foreign banks, who will be permitted to enter
retail banking in the Philippines soon.*

*Industrialists are having a problem with labor unions in some
industries. Sime Darby Tire, a subsidiary of the Malaysian
Sime Darby conglomerate, is facing hostile union pressure
and they are resisting because their competitors are able to
pay workers much lower wages. The Firestone plant which
was closed by majority owner Philex Mining and sold to Siam
Cement's subsidiary, Siam Tires, has hired all new workers at
one-third the pay now being demanded by the union at Sime
Darby Tire. The Firestone plant is now operating at a
production level of about 1,400 tires per day and by October
they will be up to 3,500 tires per day. Because of the lower
labor rates they pay, their costs are pesos 114 million lower
each year. While the minimum wage that they pay is pesos*

200 per day, plus a 57 percent benefits package of pesos 300 per day or a total cost to the company of pesos 500 per day, the cost for Sime Darby is pesos 450 per day, plus a 163 percent benefit package, or a total of pesos 1,170 per day.

The strike vote was held by the union on Sunday and the vote was overwhelmingly in favor of strike action. This time, the lawyer who organizes the unions and organized the strike at the Firestone plant has not taken any chances. While he overlooked some legal points when he organized the Firestone strike, thus causing the government to deem it an illegal strike and enabling the company to close down the plant, this time all the legal procedures have been followed, so that the union is able to strike at any time.

Goodyear, the third major tire manufacturer, is negotiating with the union and probably will not be as tough as Sime Darby. They take their orders from the Goodyear headquarters in Akron, Ohio, United States, and would be expected to be more lenient.

The strike came at the wrong time. Prices increased this year for tires because of increased demand but they have not been able to take advantage of this because of the strike action and because of the lack of inventory. While they normally would be able to make 2,900 tires per day, the output was down to 2,500 per day. That 500 tires per day makes a big difference. It is important that they hold the line against the unions because otherwise they will not be able to compete. Taiwan-based Chen Chung plans to arrive in October 1996 with a big plant with a capacity of 6,000 automobile tires per day and 14,000 motorcycle tires per day. All these tires will be for export as they can't compete with the small Philippine manufacturers. Chen Chung will pay the minimum wage of pesos 150 per day.

The small town of Puerto Princesa is the capital of Palawan province but it is difficult to tell that it is a capital. There is a small, well-paved airport, but there is a general lack of airport facilities. We were woken early in the morning at our room at the Asiaworld Hotel, five minutes drive from the airport, and told there was an emergency: we must leave right now because the airport road is to be closed down for go-kart races ... But we were too late, so we had to carry our luggage from the start of the airport road to the plane.

The town is pleasantly sleepy and provincial. A large group of adults with enthusiastic children in tow were there to see us off. This is an event. A take off and landing of a jet! But, wait a minute, isn't Palawan the place where all the offshore gas and oil is coming from in the Philippines? Doesn't the province benefit from this offtake? It does not seem like it. But this is the story of the Philippines. The center of the country is Manila and it gets the bulk of the riches. Mindinao, where the Muslim insurrection has continued for decades, has been likewise neglected. It has been the source of tremendous mineral and timber exploitation but has not retained much of those riches. But Governor Socrates is trying to protect his province from environmental disasters and has posted a sign in front of the small domed provincial capital building saying: "Our environment is not negotiable!"

We are here to visit a company called C&P Homes Inc, which is involved in the growth market for low-cost housing. The company's representatives tell me: "Real estate prices are up *but still our houses are cheaper than a car. A car depreciates but land does not. Car sales are up by 50 percent, so home sales should follow." The company's chairman started as a trucker of aggregate and then went in to contracting. He then discovered that the Filipino social security system helps finance housing and decided to go into low-cost housing. The housing units they build are expandable and come with a manual just like a car manual, telling the owner how to take care of the unit and how to expand it. In the Philippines, land is abundant, so they concentrate on low-rise buildings. They consider themselves home manufacturers. Everything is done on a mass production scale.*

 LATIN AMERICA

The main reason for the decline in share prices in Latin American companies in 1994 and 1995 was the financial crisis following Mexico's devaluation in December 1994. Lingering fears from the debt crisis of the mid-1980s caused investors to dump stocks when this new crisis arose much faster than might be the case in other areas of the world. In the year following the devaluation, the capitalization of the companies on the Mexican stock market shrank by 52 percent from US$176 billion to US$84.5 billion.

Soon though, foreign investors were returning to those markets, acknowledging that fundamental, underlying economic restructuring had taken place and that each market needed to be re-evaluated in the light of those changes. In particular there was been a swing away from the policies which contributed to the debt crisis in the 1980s. Latin American markets and firms need to be judged independently of one another and this is happening.

Argentina

In Argentina, Peronist President Carlos Menem was known as a nationalist and populist. Nevertheless he proceeded with privatization schemes, despite the fact that such privatization resulted in a weakening of union power (the base of the Peronista Party's support), and lay-offs for many workers. Argentina thus made privatization an essential part of its move to reduce government deficits. The President also tackled financial reform, made indispensable by the bank crisis which erupted in late 1994.

Due to the reforms, the Argentinian stock market has been expanding; in 1994 it was worth US$36.8 billion, with 156 companies listed. The solid macroeconomic conditions which currently prevail also contribute to confidence in equity investment. GDP growth in 1994 increased to 4.5 percent and the spectre of inflation appeared to have been vanquished, as inflation fell to 5 percent from its 1993 level of 7 percent.

Mexico

In Mexico, privatization has been very rapid. In the case of the government-owned banks, the government transferred ownership of almost the entire banking system to the private sector in a very short period of time. This was despite the fact that the US$7 million market capitalization of the government-controlled banks represented one-third of the entire Mexican stock market. In 1993, the Mexican government was finishing its privatization program by selling 37 more state companies. Up to that time the government had sold or closed 362 state-owned enterprises, with the sales yielding US$22 billion.

Further economic expansion resulted from the signing of the NAFTA agreement in January 1994, which attracted large streams of foreign direct investment and led to a net gain in employment. The market capitalization was around US$130 billion at the end of 1994, with 206 companies listed. Unfortunately this represented a 35 percent drop over the previous year, due to the devastating effect of the peso devaluation in December 1994. The devaluation of the peso led to a 40 percent loss against the dollar and sparked worldwide fears of other economic surprises in emerging markets.

Chile

Chile started one of Latin America's earliest privatization programs, and between 1973 and the late 1980s sold 470 state enterprises, accounting for almost a quarter of the country's output. Chile's GDP was less than a quarter that of Argentina, but it had the best-developed stock market in Latin America. The ratio of market capitalization to GDP in 1995 stood at 80 percent compared with 10 percent in Argentina and 20 percent in Brazil, thanks in part to the development of its own private pension funds. Telefonica del Peru was privatized in 1994. For a time, Chile was at the forefront of reforms, implementing programs such as private pensions, privatization and stock market development.

Uruguay

Uruguay's economy is heavily influenced by the much larger economies in countries surrounding it – Argentina and Brazil. Having caught the reform wind, in 1993 the government of Uruguay initiated a privatization scheme in which they planned to sell shares in the national airline, a telecommunications company and the electric power generating system. However, when the required national referendum was held, 70 percent of the voters rejected the privatization scheme proposed by the government. Although this defeat was largely interpreted as a rejection of the sitting government as opposed to privatization per se, it certainly cooled enthusiasm among politicians to pursue privatization of any kind. The nation's consumer prices index (CPI) rose 45 percent in 1994, while GDP growth hit 4 percent. There were 20 listed companies on the Montevideo Stock Exchange in 1994.

Brazil

With 75 percent public popularity ratings and control over two-thirds of the votes in the legislature, in 1996 Brazil's President Cardoso was in a position to really drive home his economic reform agenda. We saw that the Fiscal Stabilisation Fund was passed by Congress. The maximum tax bracket of 48.2 percent was reduced to 30.6 percent and the government was able to eliminate the practice of adjusting corporate financial statements for inflation, as a result of significant declines in inflation (down to 20.13 percent in 1995, with an even lower rate forecast for 1996).

To complete the government's first round of privatizations, Light Brazil, the national electricity provider, valued at US$1.8 billion was privatized in 1996. To kick off the following round, CVRD, the world's largest iron ore producer, was planning to sell off a 51 percent stake, worth an astonishing US$4–6 billion.

The interest rate drop in foreign markets, such as the US, and the improvement in macroeconomic stability in the region was bringing foreign capital back into Brazil's markets. As a demonstration of how strong interest in Brazil was, net foreign capital flows in January 1996 alone outstripped all such flows for the total of 1995! Of January's inflows, a net US$694.7 million went straight into the stock market.

Venezuela

Caracas is a spectacular city nestled in a valley surrounded by impressive mountains. The skyline bristles with high-rise office buildings, and from afar looks prosperous. But as you get closer to the city, you see that many of those high-rise buildings are just concrete shells and have not been completed. Many of these were started by banks, but after the financial crisis in 1994 when the banks failed, they became frozen in government hands.

This is the perfect metaphor for Venezuela's economy. A vibrant business sector hollowed out by repeated government intervention, nationalization, and grand development schemes which cost the taxpayers a bundle. Much of this activity occurred under President Carlos Andres Perez, during his first term in office in 1974. President Perez went on a nationalizing binge which covered the oil industry, the iron industry, a huge expansion of the steel industry, construction of government-owned hotels, shipbuilding, and culminated in the introduction of a vertically integrated aluminum industry, virtually from scratch.

Yet even Perez, during his second term in office, did a quick turnabout once the extent of the country's indebtedness was recognized. In order to secure IMF assistance, Perez began to unravel his state octopus. IMF terms required the removal of all the controls in the economy and privatization of the huge state enterprises. Many companies have been privatized or are in the process of being privatized.

Perez didn't last to see through his reforms. Rumor has it that fellow politicians conspired against him in revenge for losing perks that once stemmed from state-ownership. Ultimately, Perez was impeached for misusing 200 million bolivars (about US$2.5 million at that time) of secret funds.

Economic manipulation of such kind was largely disavowed by most Latin American governments in the mid-1980s, after which they struggled through drastic economic restructuring programs and moved towards market-oriented industrial and financial policies. They are now coming to reap the benefits of a newly competitive private economic sector and lower budget deficits/debt levels.

However, Venezuela delayed the day of reckoning, and was still grappling with high debt, IMF restructuring demands, and a confused sense of what the public will bear in terms of reform. President Caldera had the unenviable task of seeing through economic reform. Although once elected as president while a member of the country's reputedly most right-wing party, he crafted a coalition between himself and a combination of smaller parties, including the Communist Party, the Socialist Party, the Evangelist Party and a number of other strange bedfellows, in order to be re-elected in 1993. Together, the coalition members were nicknamed the "chiripas," and Caldera is labeled the "Big Chiripas." "Chiripa," by the way, means "cockroach."

According to some analysts, Venezuela currently has the most left-wing government in its democratic history, as a result of the strange assortment of allied parties commingled in the coalition. Caldera, who turned 80 years old while we were there on 24 January, however, finds himself faced with the task of turning myriad socialist policies into more business-

friendly, market-sensitive, fiscally conservative versions. During our visit, we were surprised to learn that Caldera was embroiled in an attempt to alter a labor law which provides for generous termination payments, a law which he himself sponsored in an earlier government!

Even though Caldera was elected on a platform of price controls to bring down inflation, he has had trouble implementing such policies. When price controls failed to do the job that they were intended to do, his popularity ratings plunged. Evidence of this came in the last gubernatorial election in December 1995, when Caldera's party was able to return only one governor out of 22 states. Moreover, during mayoralty races in 194 cities and towns, his party garnered less than 3 percent of the vote. What makes these figures even more expressive is that Caldera was at the height of his popularity when he imposed exchange controls in June of 1994. And the distortions wrought by price controls are amazing. For examples, it is now possible to purchase 24 liters of high octane gasoline for US$1. That's ten times cheaper than the price of bottled water! What the government should be doing is eliminating the massive subsidies within the economy, but the government is afraid to take this kind of measure. Caldera does not seem to have a clear picture of what he wants to do with the economy.

A businessman offered us his opinion: "The government does not have a clue. Caldera has never listened to people all his life. He makes all the decisions and overrides his own ministers so they cannot function. They must eliminate massive subsidies but populist governments think the people have no patience and thus are unwilling to accept things like the higher price of gasoline."

International credit rating analysts have expressed misgivings about the severe fiscal pressures facing the country and question whether the Caldera administration will implement the comprehensive economic and financial reforms requested by the IMF. At the end of 1995, the country was not servicing growing amounts of its internal and external debt and had entered into negotiations with the IMF on refinancing. The basis of the problem is government spending and the resulting fiscal deficit which is estimated to be as high as 10 percent of GDP. In an effort to stem the tide, the government has imposed new indirect taxes and is contemplating spending cuts to bring the deficit down to 3 percent of GDP, but many doubt the government's political will to make the required cuts in social programs and subsidies.

Currency devaluation is also touching the economy. In December 1995 the government devalued the currency by 41 percent from bolivar 169 per US dollar to bolivar 290. The government continues to be urged by the IMF to devalue further. The December 1995 devaluation was an IMF condition, in exchange for a US$3.6 billion stand-by loan. On the "parallel," or black market, the exchange rate went to bolivars 360 per US dollar. From positive growth of 9.7 percent in 1991 and 6.8 percent in 1992, Venezuela's economy sank into decline with the economy contracting in 1993, 1994, and 1995. High inflation, running officially at 57 percent in 1995 and perhaps unofficially as high as 70 percent, in January 1996 hit 5 percent a month.

The economic uncertainties touch the business sector directly. During our visit we interviewed the president of an appliance manufacturing firm. He explained the repercussions of some of the government's actions. "The government policies are forcing us to import to survive. When we import parts for our refrigerators and washing machines, we must use the Brady Bond exchange rate which is 350 bolivars to one US dollar. But finished products can be imported using the official rate of 290 bolivars to one US dollar. This means that importers of finished refrigerators and washing machines can import at a cheaper rate and put local producers at a disadvantage – even put them out of business, increasing unemployment."

Executives despair at the twists and turns of government policies which make their lives so difficult. They complain that the government is too "control-oriented," but is not familiar with the needs of business and thus continues to make policy errors which not only fail to achieve the government goals but also results in severe disadvantages for local business and the economy.

Despite its economic predicament, Venezuela is nevertheless a blessed country. It is rich in a variety of resources both human and natural. Venezuela can boast of spectacular beaches, diamonds, gold, bauxite, petroleum, natural gas, iron ore and seven former Miss Universes! In spite of political foot-dragging, a consensus seems to have coalesced around the necessity of economic reforms, leading to policy reforms.

An external vote of confidence has recently been received from the international oil community. On 23 January 1996 several international oil companies pledged millions of dollars in public tenders for contracts to enter into upstream operations in the country's state-owned petroleum industry. This comes 20 years after the petroleum industry was nationalized. It indicates that Venezuela truly has turned the page on a chapter of its history.

We continue our usual bargain-hunting expeditions, always seeking out the competitive, well-run firms able to make money under even the toughest economic conditions. There are many of them in Venezuela and we will continue to invest in such companies, believing that they are well-positioned to be the real winners as further national economic reforms are implemented.

Lima, Peru

The flight from Brasilia, in Brazil, to Lima, Peru, took about four hours. On the plane, I read an article in Hong Kong's South China Morning Post *about Peru's former first lady, Senora Susana Higuchi de Fujimori, and her efforts to oust her husband, President Alberto Fujimori, from power.*

She accused him of betraying the principles which got him elected and sponsoring bribery and corruption. In retort, he went on TV and said her allegations were the product of a deranged mind and stripped her of all the duties of First Lady. He also took their four children to live at the Ministry of Defence. She then started her own political party and found support among the poor people in Peru, who the reporter said, "Feel they are being made to pay the price of the Fujimori miracle and more particularly among the nation's women, who feel inspired by her example."

President Fujimori came to power in 1990 and started Peru on the path to a remarkable economic revival. The politics of Peru are strange and complex. Susana Higuchi's father was a Japanese immigrant entrepreneur who came to Lima with thousands of others in the 1930s. She was brought up in strict Japanese tradition but also as a Peruvian and a Catholic. She even considered becoming a nun. Alberto Fujimori's parents, on the other hand, had largely abandoned their Japanese heritage and were considered by Susana's parents as too liberal and lax, with no self-discipline.

When she discovered that her sister-in-law was selling clothes collected in Japan for the poor children of Peru and pocketing the money, she went public with it. In March 1992, President Fujimori led a coup against his own government and shut down the Congress to prevent the complaints being investigated. He then passed a law which allowed him to stand again for re-election as president but banned anyone else from his family from standing for election. It was commonly called the "Susana Law."

Inflation in Peru between 1990 and 1994 fell from 7,650 percent to 21 percent and real gross domestic product (GDP) growth rose from 2.6 percent to 10.4 percent – among the highest in South America. Tight fiscal control resulted in the budget deficit falling from 5.4 percent of GDP to 2.8 percent of GDP during the first three years of the Fujimori administration. President Fujimori rode a wave of popularity based on his success in beating the Shining Path guerrillas, reducing inflation and stabilizing the economy. But he dismantled the legislature and judiciary and has not properly rebuilt them according to some critics.

The April 1995 re-election of President Fujimori was based on a campaign against discredited political parties and traditional politicians in Peru. Four-fifths of Peruvian voters described themselves as independent, with no political party allegiance, so the election revolved around personalities, rather than parties. Fujimori's strongest point in his election campaign was his conquest of the Shining Path terrorist group, which was held responsible for 27,000 deaths and an estimated US$22 billion in property damage between 1982 and 1992.

The economic success in Peru can be tied to the impact of President Fujimori's economic liberalization program, increased government spending on infrastructure and new mortgage regulations to facilitate funding for house-building projects, which resulted in an expansion in the construction sector. According to some analysts, there is room for further growth as GDP contracted 25 percent between 1988 and 1992 and most Peruvian companies have excess capacity. Indosuez Capital has estimated that by the end of this year (1995), Peru's economy will have returned only to the levels it was at in 1987.

Peru is a major mining country, ranked seventh in the world in copper production, fourth in zinc and third in silver. There are 12 stock-market listed mining companies that produce copper, silver, lead, tin, and zinc. But the mining industry needs more money, estimated at up to US$7 billion over the next several years. Privatization in the mining sector during 1993 and 1994 included the sale of iron-ore mine Nierro Peru to Shougang Group of China for US$120 million. When I visited Shougang's steel plant in Beijing last year, the Shougang officials said they planned massive investments connected with the Peruvian mine, including a number of ships to carry iron ore from Peru to China. Some say that the Chinese paid too much for that mine.

Peru's privatization program has encompassed a wide range of government industries and new regulations ensure that Peru's external debt, estimated at about US$22 billion, is now eligible for use in privatization. At one point, all debt negotiations were stalled because of the repudiation of two debts by President Alan Garcia's 1985–90 government.

Peru shares borders with Ecuador in the north, Brazil and Bolivia in the east and Chile in the south. When my Peruvian friends talk about Peru they describe it in three parts: (1) the coast, (2) the desert, and (3) the jungle. Tensions on the border with Ecuador run high and the two countries fought a brief war on the border this year. The world's largest river, the Amazon, begins in north-eastern Peru, and Ecuador wants access to the river.

Visiting the spectacular private museum of Enrico Poli Bianchi, we were struck by the richness of the Peruvian cultural tradition. The search into Peru's long history by archaeologists has only just begun. One archaeologist told me that only 20 percent of the important sites had been explored. We often think of the Inca empire as embodying all that is Peruvian Indian history, but the Incas held sway for a relatively short time 500 to 600 years ago. Before that, there were Chimu, Chancay, Huari, Moche, Paracas, Chavin, Guanape, Kotosh, Huaca Prieta, Paijan and other tribes and cultures extending back thousands of years. Touring the Amano private museum, started by a Japanese Peruvian and faithfully kept by his widow, Rosa Watanabe de Amano, we saw fantastic statues and fine fabrics from the Chancay period (1000–1200 AD), Huari hats (800–1000 AD), finely decorated pottery from the Nasca period (1200 AD), and an exquisite vase in the form of a lobster from the Moche period (500 AD).

● MIDDLE EAST

In the Muslim countries of the world, the religious prohibition against charging interest creates a particularly fertile ground for the development of stock markets. In Pakistan, for example, in November of 1991, a religious group declared that bank interest and all other interest was prohibited by Islam in all its forms, regardless of whether a loan was taken for productive purposes or consumption. Stock markets are therefore encouraged, and recent liberalization moves by the government have resulted in a massive inflow of funds, not only from domestic investors but from overseas Pakistanis.

It is still difficult for foreign investors to buy shares in most Middle East countries except Israel and Turkey. In the case of Saudi Arabia, its stock market is closed to all non-Gulf Co-operation Council member countries as is that of Kuwait and the UAE. The most active and open of Arab stock markets are Jordan, Egypt and Morocco.

Egypt's stock exchange is capitalized at US$7 billion, while Morocco's is US$5 billion. Egypt has two exchanges, one based in Cairo and the other in Alexandria. They also have no capital gains tax. The sector best represented in the region's stock exchanges is banking and finance, with "hard" sector industries like petroleum and utilities coming next. Only Egypt's Cairo exchange has more than 100 company listings. At this time, Morocco is working through a very large privatization scheme, designed to boost market liquidity and give domestic investors an increased selection of investment options.

Another Middle Eastern country investors are discovering is Jordan, one of the most advanced and efficient of the Middle Eastern markets. With 117 companies listed at the end of 1994, the Amman Financial Market as the stock exchange is named, is capitalized at JD3.4 billion (US$2.4 billion). Foreign investment restrictions are gradually being dismantled, making it, together with Israel's stock exchange, one of the most accessible in the region. The neighboring exchange in Israel has 638 companies listed in 1994, valued at US$33 billion market capitalization.

Initiatives are afoot, though with no timetable, to further the growth of equity markets in the region by linking some exchanges, to create deeper, more liquid markets. Bahrain and Oman are already planning a stock exchange link-up, while talk of a pan-Arab exchange or Gulf-wide exchange make the rounds at Gulf Co-operation Council meetings.

Lebanon: the road to recovery

Beirut: Visitors can't help but be struck by the beautiful setting of this ancient Mediterranean city. During my time here, I've thought not so much about the horrors of the recent past as the bright prospects of the present and future.

Today the city is fast rebuilding from the damage of the bloody 15-year civil war that ended in 1990. It is clearly intent on taking back its historic place as the commercial and financial hub of the Middle East. As the regional peace process intensifies, we should see many investment opportunities develop here in the coming years.

It's easy to sense that the country and its capital are coming back to life through the world-famous energy of Lebanese businessmen and women. Construction is under way everywhere in the once-devastated downtown business district, so it's no surprise that the cement and glass industries were expected to be well represented when the Beirut Stock Exchange reopened in early 1996 for the first time since 1983. Those businesses are busy in an economy whose real gross domestic product (GDP) grew by 8.5 percent in 1994 and is due for 6 percent growth in 1995 and 1996. Many of them will need to raise capital through public listings to fuel their expansion plans.

The indications were that the Lebanese authorities would allow foreign participation from the outset on the revived exchange. They also are taking the important step of requiring tough disclosure standards from firms wanting to list, such as a minimum of three years of audited financial statements. Early French and British technical assistance is helping put the market and its regulators on solid footing, and there are, fortunately, no foreign exchange restrictions. We were also glad to see that a modern custody and settlement system called MIDCLEAR was created in advance of the market's re-opening. Given these positive steps and the traditional vibrancy of the private sector here, Lebanon's market capitalization may top $5 billion in a few years – perhaps becoming bigger than others in the Middle East such as Morocco, Egypt, and Jordan.

The bulk of the listings will, of course, be local, but there is also interesting talk of making Beirut a regional market with many cross-listings from other Middle Eastern countries. In time, this city may become an Arab version of Hong Kong, acting as both the regional financial nucleus and the window on to a much larger economy that has historically been under rigid state control and off limits to most foreign investors – I'm thinking not of China but Syria, which has four times the population of Lebanon (14 million, compared with 3.5 million) and could benefit substantially from the close interaction with Western financial markets. The Syrian government has been making initial moves towards privatization and other market-friendly reforms recently, and could see its ability to attract foreign investment brighten considerably if it follows the Palestinians and Jordan in signing a comprehensive peace treaty with Israel.

The re-opening of the Beirut market was only the latest in a string of impressive developments on the Lebanese investment scene. In early July 1995, for example, Prime Minister Rafik Hariri's government successfully placed its second Eurobond issue – an unrated US$300 million, five-year bond with spreads of 320 basis points more than equivalent US Treasuries. The first issue came last October, raising US$400 million with a three-year offering at 325 basis points more than US Treasuries. Mr. Hariri personally led the sales effort before the London international finance community at that time, bringing in more than twice as much as he originally expected. It all adds up to an impressive sign of investor confidence in this shrewd businessman – a self-made billionaire from the construction industry – and the stability he has brought since coming to power in October of 1992.

Perhaps an even better indicator is the estimated US$4 billion in returned flight capital that expatriate Lebanese have poured back into their country in the last two years. That means a lot in a country as small as this, and estimates are that there may be up to ten times that amount still being held abroad. We will be watching for signs that it is on its way home along with the estimated 200,000 expatriate Lebanese who have returned to their homeland from abroad in the past two years. No one knows the investment climate in an emerging market better than its own people, and I have yet to watch one of these countries take off before its own money returned from the safer haven it had sought overseas when times were tough at home.

Let's hope that is exactly what's starting to happen now in Lebanon, where services have always been the strength of its economy, currently accounting for about 70 percent of GDP. Tourism and financial services are certainly two of the growth areas in that sector both nationally and worldwide. A flourishing private banking industry has, fortunately, survived intact here despite the legacy of war and internal *strife. So have the beautiful beaches, mountains, ancient ruins, and other tourist sites. They should start drawing increasing revenues from domestic, regional and even some European visitors in the near future and be the source of considerable new development.*

There have also been signs of strength on the equity markets. Chief of these was the US$650 million public offering in late 1993 for shares in SOLIDERE, a US$1.8 billion public-private company created to manage one of the Middle East's biggest construction projects, the rebuilding of downtown Beirut. This heavily oversubscribed offering was restricted to Lebanese and other Arab investors. Eighteen months after the offering, the shares were trading on Beirut's new secondary market at about a 30 percent premium to their offering price. SOLIDERE's management is putting the US$650 million it raised into an ambitious 25-year infrastructure campaign to rehabilitate a 160 hectare-area in the city's central district. It is targeting 1.9 million square meters of new residential units and another 1.5 million square meters in office space.

Meanwhile, the government is also embarking on a second, more broadly defined program to rebuild the national infrastructure. Known as Horizon 2000, it envisions total expenditures of at least US$14.3 billion by the year 2002 from both public and private sources. The World Bank has already begun supporting the program with loans totaling more than US$100 million for irrigation rehabilitation and solid waste management, and has others in preparation worth a cumulative $170 million planned for power sector restructuring, road rehabilitation, and upgrading water supply systems. The European Investment Bank, Arab aid *institutions funded by the wealthy Gulf states, and other official sources are also channeling funds into the early stages of the program. It certainly should provide ample growth opportunities for all sides of the Lebanese construction industry in the coming years.*

Beirut's market could soon become one of the most active in the Middle East – a region that is fast catching the eye of foreign portfolio investors worldwide and thus seeing growing demand for quality listings. Performance in the Middle East markets has been good so far this year. According to IFC data, as of late July 1995 the Jordanian market, for example, was up 18 percent in US dollar terms, so far, this year. That made it the fourth best performing market in the developing world. The leader, by the way, lies a few hundred miles up the Mediterranean coast from Lebanon – Turkey, showing 32.1 percent gains, so far, this year. North Africa is also coming on strong, with the markets in Morocco and Egypt fast rising on the international investment scene, and Tunisia in the process of opening its bourse up to foreign investment for the first time.

Common ties of language, religion and culture may offer new opportunities for business co-operation among these countries and others in the Arab world as governments follow the global trend and become more private-sector oriented. Even more exciting as a growing theme are the new political openings for the thriving Israeli business community to partner Arab companies in making common use of the region's abundant financial, human, and natural resources.

Still, many uncertainties mark the future of Lebanon. Prime Minister Hariri has an odd habit of frequently throwing the country into brief political uncertainty by resigning and then quickly returning to office. There will probably continue to be political questions at least until the Lebanese presidential elections scheduled for this fall. A Syrian–Israeli peace treaty would also be a big help to the business climate in a country that still has 35,000 Syrian troops present and a volatile Israeli-occupied security zone in the south, near the biblical cities of Tyre and Sidon. And on the economic side, we also need to watch the recent trends towards falling central bank foreign exchange reserves and balance of payments deficits, which could put pressure on the local currency if the government spends as much as it intends to on infrastructure rehabilitation.

Risks such as these are inherent in emerging markets, and investors who cannot tolerate short-term fluctuations in search of potential long-term gains should not be involved in them. But we see Lebanon as an exciting country that should provide many opportunities for our funds' shareholders in the coming years, and we will be there with the same disciplined, value-oriented approach that we use in all the other countries we visit.

Mobius'
Field Notes

Oman

I wrote this article in Muscat, in the Sultanate of Oman, where I was attending a conference – Investment Horizon in Oman – regarding the development of Oman's stock exchange.

Omani men almost all wear the traditional long gown with an unusual bright and richly decorated turban and with a silver filigreed "khunjar" belt and a dagger with a richly carved silver case. The gown is normally white cotton or light blue or green and often covered with a thick overgarment of black or cream bordered with gold embroidery.

I arrived in the 24th year of the country's renaissance. In less than 25 years, the country has transformed itself, with a modern infrastructure of roads, houses, hospitals, power, communications and education. One of the speakers at the conference said that 25 years ago there were two schools, 80 students and one hospital. Now there are many schools and hospitals, and we have direct digital dialling from our hotel room telephones.

It was in Oman that frankincense, the aromatic resin taken from a tree, was once worth its weight in gold. It was exported throughout the old world. Southern Oman was the only place in the world where best-quality frankincense grew and for a long time it was the backbone of Oman's economy. Camel caravans carrying the precious sap moved westwards to Egypt, Greece and Rome while sailing ships carried it to India. Today, the frankincense-producing tree grows wild. The resin is harvested from April to June each year. About two thousand years ago, Roman historian Pliny described the Southern Arabian people as the most prosperous race as a result of their sales of frankincense. It was used in embalming, and some was found in the tomb of the Egyptian boy king Tutankhamen. Frankincense has been given a number of uses apart from being used as a fragrance, such as purifying drinking water, easing digestion and helping with heart and kidney complaints.

Oman has had a long tradition of seafaring. In 2,500 BC Oman was an important source of copper for the workshops of Mesopotamia. It was a stop-off point for trade between what are now Bahrain, Pakistan and Iraq. The rise of Islam resulted in Arab expansion and a golden age of Omani seafaring by the seventh century AD. The first Arab to reach Guangzhou, in China, was an Omani merchant, Abu Ubayada Abdulla, around 750 AD.

Oman was one of the first countries to adopt Islam when the reigning Julanda family gave their support to the Prophet Mohammed in about 630 AD. The area of Nizwa, where the Julanda princes Jeifar and Abd based themselves, was visited by Amir ibn al-As, emissary of the Prophet Mohammed, who persuaded them to embrace Islam. The Julanda dynasty seized control of the rest of the country from the Persians, who had been occupying Oman for more than a thousand years.

An independent Imamate was established in the eighth century AD. The Portuguese landed in Sohar and Muscat in 1507 AD on their way to India, and established themselves on the Omani coast to safeguard their lucrative trade routes. The forts that they built in Muscat still stand. In 1650 AD, Imam

Sultan bin Saif expelled them. Ahmed bin Said was elected Imam in 1741 and founded the Al Bu Said dynasty, which still rules Oman. The country became the only non-European country to hold colonies in Africa, mainly Zanzibar on the East African coast and South Persia and Baluchistan on the Indian subcontinent. This was in the period when Imam Said bin Sultan ruled, from 1804 to 1856. Upon his death, his two sons had a dispute which the British, who had good relations with the country since the early 18th century, mediated. One son got Zanzibar and the other got Oman. After that, Oman, deprived of its African territory and overtaken by Western commercial trade, declined as an economic power.

In the 1960s, the discovery of large quantities of petroleum started a renaissance in Oman. Sultan Said bin Taimur, accustomed to economic stringency, could not put the new wealth to good use. The succession of Sultan Qaboos bin Said in 1970 opened up a new era of expansion and infrastructure building. By 1975, a considerable infrastructure had been developed, with schools, hospitals, clinics, roads, and housing. Girls attended school for the first time, new ports were constructed at Mina Qaoos and Raysut, modern airports opened at Seeb and Salalah, postal and telecommunications services were established in 1974 and an earth satellite station linked Oman with the rest of the world. In 1975, a civil war in Dhofar was settled and in 1976 a comprehensive development program was launched on the basis of a series of five-year plans, which included diversifying the economy away from dependence on oil revenues and shifting investment from the public to private sector. The number of students rose from 900 (all boys) in 1970 to 250,000 (almost evenly divided between boys and girls) in 1993. Sultan Qaboos University was inaugurated in 1986.

Annual rainfall is low. Water is obtained from deep wells and 15 sea-water desalination plants powered by natural gas from Oman's oil fields. The newest technology combines desalination with generation of electricity. The country is planning a US$5 billion Liquefied Natural Gas (LNG) project. The project involves collecting gas from three main oilfields in central Oman and piping it 350 kilometers to the coast at Al Ghalilah, near Sur, where it will be liquefied before being loaded into insulated tankers and shipped to customers around the world. Potential customers for the gas include Guangdong Province in China, which is building a gas-fired power station due to start in the year 2000.

Emphasis is being put on industrial growth and industrial estates are being built around the country. Public assets are being offered for sale to the private sector in areas such as water, power supply and even road building. The government has instituted a number of incentives for industry such as interest-free loans and tax breaks. Oman co-operates with other Gulf states such as the United Arab Emirates in investing in sectors such as manufacturing, agriculture, trade and tourism.

Mining is growing in Oman. The country has two million tonnes of chromite reserves which have been mined by Oman Mining Company since 1992. In addition, there are an estimated 913 million tonnes of gypsum deposits, 100 million tonnes of silica ore (for glass manufacturing), and 116.4 million tonnes of coal reserves. Agricultural development is also being encouraged. Mushroom cultivation, poultry farms, and raising of livestock such as cows, goats, sheep, and camels are making the Sultanate the leading livestock producer in the Gulf region. Oman has one of the largest fishing industries among the Gulf Co-operation Council nations and Arab countries. In 1994, 12 fishing harbours were built.

Foreign investment has fallen short of the Government's expectations since most industrial establishments are, still, wholly Omani-owned. The mandatory 51 percent Omani stake in joint venture projects is seen as a barrier to securing overseas capital. In privatization, the Government is moving ahead selling shares in the Oman Cement Company and three major tourist hotels.

The Muscat Securities Market is housed in an imposing, new, four-storey building after having moved from the basement of the Ministry of Commerce and Industry. The market first opened to foreign investors in October 1993, with nationals from the Gulf Co-operation Council countries allowed to buy stakes of up to 49 percent in more than 30 Omani companies. The first public issue was made in 1971, of Oman Hotels Company. After the disastrous crash of the Kuwait stock exchange in the early 1980s, the government was careful to avoid such problems in Oman.

SOUTHERN EUROPE

I have been investing in the oft-neglected markets of Southern Europe for years now. This area was rife with socialist governments when I started, and while they may still be in power, they have generally changed their economic platform to be in tune with market-oriented reforms happening in other areas of the world.

In fact, as the European Economic Union has progressed, these countries have found themselves under pressure to conform to political and economic codes of behavior which they might not have selected if they had the independent option. Nonetheless, I feel that governments in Southern Europe are slowly steering a course towards more liberal markets and more laissez-faire business practices.

Such developments are evident in Turkey, where the government privatization program, as announced by the Public Participation Administration (PPA), intends to accomplish many things. The PPA's objective is to minimize state involvement in the economy, accelerate the further establishment of market mechanisms, enhance competition in the economy, decrease financial burdens of economic enterprises, deepen the existing capital market by providing wider share ownership, and provide an efficient allocation of resources. At the end of 1992, 80 companies had been privatized, raising over US$1.1 billion, of which US$285 million was raised via stock sales in the Istanbul Stock Exchange. This has contributed to a 1994 stock market capitalization of US$22 billion, with 176 companies listed.

Future privatization plans center on state-owned banks, which are costing the Treasury a lot to maintain, but only the steel producer Eregli Demir is close to moving into the private sector, and private groups already have large minority stakes. 1995 target earnings from privatization were targeted at US$5 billion, but only netted US$500 million, in light of political wrangling which mired the process. There are substantial, family-owned groups such as KOC – with holdings in listed companies producing automobiles, appliances and other products – and Sabanci – with ownership of banks and a wide range of manufacturing joint ventures. Nevertheless, they still have convoluted financial statements.

Similarly, Greece is trying to kick-start its stalled privatization plans. During 1996, the frequently-postponed partial privatization of OTE, the state telecom company, was expected to proceed. The new prime minister of Greece, Costas Simitis, was prepared to take a strong stand to prove Greece's intention of achieving economic convergence with the rest of the EU (not to mention solidify his own position within the government) and the OTE privatization was perceived as one crucial test of this.

Good news in Greece can be found in the progress being made on infrastructural investment. Several major projects, including the Athens airport, to upgrade roads and ports are in the works, and are currently at the government approval stage. One observer noted, "Should the reforms succeed, it will not only be a giant leap forward in the convergence process, but it will also reinforce political credibility, which will feed back again in the form of increased business confidence. If the government fails, this progress could soon be reversed. In this case, the dynamic implications for the country's political economy as a whole will be dramatic since it could lose even the slow train to the EMU."

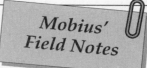

*Mobius'
Field Notes*

Athens

*Greece is an important emerging market, and, due to the
fundamental economic changes it is experiencing, along with
its growing integration in the European Community, I believe
it holds great promise as an area of investment for the Fund's
shareholders.*

*On a recent visit, I found Athens warm and welcoming after
a two-hour flight from cold, rainy Budapest. Upon arrival, I
was told that agreement had been reached concerning the
construction of a new Athens airport, one of many new
infrastructure projects expected to boost the Greek economy.
Certainly, the old airport has always been severely
overcrowded at the peak of the tourist season, but tourism
fell significantly in 1995, and some say it was due to the
congested airport. Others claim that European tour operators
conspired to boycott Greece because of rising prices.
However, inflation no longer presents the problem it did in
the past. In two years, it has fallen more than 14 percent to
below 9 percent, and the government expects it to drop to 5
percent. My economic consultants in Greece told me: "People
are getting so used to declining inflation, soon it will no
longer be news." Of course, even the government's goal of 5
percent inflation would be double the average for the
European Union (EU). As a member of the EU, however,
Greece will most likely move closer to many European norms,
including the rate of inflation.*

*While I was in Athens, one topic of great interest to many
people was Prime Minister Papandreou's health – some*

Greeks told me that the country would be in deep trouble if something happened to Papandreou, because it would result in a dangerous political-power vacuum. And yet, with the resignation of Mr. Papandreou on 16 January due to ill health and the subsequent election of K. Simitis as Prime Minister, we can see that Greek politics continues on a stable course with little substantial policy deviation. My assessment at the time was that the Greeks were being too sensitive to local political events, and that as their economy becomes more integrated with the European Union, it will be more difficult for local politicians to redirect the course of economic development. As the Greeks adhere increasingly to European Union rules and regulations, a number of decisions which previously would have been subject to populist pressures will be determined instead by Brussels.

Over the course of five days in Athens, I visited 14 companies, including Intracom, a telecommunications equipment manufacturer. Managers there told me Greece has a 52 percent penetration rate for telephones, which is high for an emerging market. However, you have to wait a year for a phone connection, telephone lines are of poor quality, and there is plenty of room for expansion of overall capacity and upgrading of existing technology. To me, this indicates the potential for growth in the Greek telecommunication industry.

We also visited Strintzis Lines, a shipping company, where we were told that the war in Bosnia had appreciably increased the demand for ferries to carry trucks and goods to Italy. Now, trucks and cars go by ferry to Italy and then north to the rest of Europe. Although this new trade route has attracted a great deal of competition, it is dominated by Greek firms.

As we left for the Athens airport, the driver told us we were lucky to be leaving because there was going to be a demonstration near the hotel later that day. During our visit, negotiations had been held in New York to end the long and bitter dispute between Greece and the Former Yugoslav Republic of Macedonia, which the Greeks insist on calling "Skopje" after its capital city. According to a United Nations plan, Greece would drop trade sanctions against its northern neighbor in return for guarantees that "Skopje" would change its flag and renounce any territorial ambitions. Apparently, the Greek and Macedonian foreign ministers had agreed to the plan, and the Greeks had decided to stop the embargo against Macedonia. However, die-hard opponents of the plan were arranging to hold a protest march at the peak of rush-hour traffic.

Of course, there is more political trouble in the region than just the "Skopje" dispute. But the day-to-day political situation in a country need not have a major long-term impact on investors, and market declines caused by political tensions are often a chance for us to increase our purchases of bargain companies. I believe that Greece's increasing alignment with the large European market will help drive long-term economic growth and that investing there now, offers the Fund's shareholders a potential benefit in the future.

*T*his chapter is dedicated to a study of how each of the countries covered in this section have had to alter Communist economic practices and replace them with more free market-oriented economic policies.

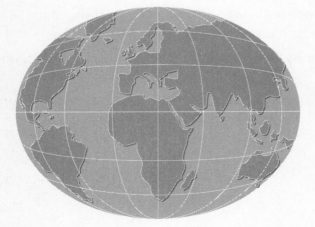

Chapter 4

Reform in the Former Communist Countries

The previous chapter reviewed the economic experiences of several emerging economic regions around the world. I wanted to set aside the discussion of the former Communist countries, however, for a separate chapter because their experiences are quite distinct from those of the other emerging markets and because they have many features in common. Many of these countries already have sophisticated industrial sectors and literate populations. But the effect of the Communist fiasco was to leave their economic systems in ruins. Today, we see these countries attempting to completely and fundamentally restructure their economic foundations over a very telescoped period of time. This has brought great privation in some cases, since newly privatized companies have often fired workers and as government subsidization of everything has been withdrawn. In other cases, the economic reforms have allowed totally new sources of wealth creation to appear, improving living conditions immeasurably.

Before continuing, I must acknowledge the correspondence I received from a viewer who objected to my use of the term "formerly Communist" in a widely televised commercial for Templeton funds. I appreciated his speaking up for those countries and those citizens who did not voluntarily adopt Communism as an economic model, but instead were forced to implement such a system by military conquest. I'm sympathetic to all those that are compelled to live within a social system to which they owe no allegiance, and admire the strenuous efforts of those working on the reform process, the daunting task that it is.

In this chapter, I am not making a political statement or assumption that all or any of the countries which adopted the Communist system did so willingly or fully. What this chapter is dedicated to is a study of how each of the countries covered in this section have had to alter Communist economic practices and endeavor to replace them with more free market-oriented economic policies.

CHINA

China is probably the most important, and most typical, of the emerging markets today. This is not only because it is the largest country in the world, but also because it is undergoing a fundamental change from being a closed, centralized Communist society to an open market economy. The characteristics that we see in China and the problems facing China are repeated in many emerging market countries around the world.

It is important to note that China is growing at a very rapid pace not only because of recent liberalization but also because of a combination of factors all converging to produce rapid growth. (Someone once said that it was like putting a dozen Atlas rockets on an ocean liner.) Between 1975 and 1984, average annual GDP growth was 7.2 percent, with growth accelerating to double digit levels by 1984. By 1985, real GDP growth had reached 13.4 percent and continued at high levels until 1989 and 1990, when there was a significant slow down, only to accelerate again, reaching 13.1 percent by 1992 (Table 4.1).

Table 4.1 China: real GDP growth

Year	% Change
1985	+13.4
1986	+9.7
1987	+10.9
1988	+11.3
1989	+4.3
1990	+3.8
1991	+8.2
1992	+13.1
1993	+13.7
1994	+11.5
1995	+10.2

Sources: IMF, *World Economic Outlook*, October 1995; *Consensus Forecasts*, Consensus Economics Inc.

China has many of the characteristics of other emerging markets including:

- expanding educational levels among the population;
- a high savings rate;
- low wage rates;
- high exports;
- a young population;
- a relatively primitive infrastructure and technology.

This combination of factors is providing the ingredients for higher economic growth rates. For example, the worldwide search for low-cost manufacturing helps the emerging markets, since the low-cost producers are able to gain a larger market share while high-cost producers are forced out of business. Those countries that have export advantages build up higher foreign exchange reserves.

In China, as in other parts of the world, particularly in the former socialist or Communist societies, there is a great deal of latent and expanding demand as a result of a "demonstration effect" generated by the availability of more information through the mass media, particularly television, about products in other parts of the world. This demand has not been fulfilled by the low-quality production of State-owned companies. This, combined with significant pentup savings, results in a potent brew.

It has been said that the socialist economic dynamics resemble a match thrown on a drought-plagued forest, where there has been a long period of economic depression or repression, and a great burst of economic progress is coming just as it has happened in other parts of the world and at other times. The potential demand for goods and services is difficult to calculate but it is clear that once the emerging markets economies are liberalized, there will be an explosive demand for a wide range of goods. In China as in other emerging markets the workforce tends to be among the youngest in the world with their peak earning years still ahead of them. In the case of Japan and Europe however, the aging workforce means that the upside potential for productivity increases is limited.

As with other emerging markets, China can now adopt the newest technologies and therefore leapfrog many of the existing levels of technology still being used in the developed countries. For example, in China and other emerging markets, cellular and optical fiber technologies now allow for a telecommunication system to be installed in six to nine months, instead of the 10 to 15 years required for landline systems, and at significantly less cost.

Another factor influencing development in China is the size of its workforce. Governments around the world are beginning to realize that unless they allow foreign investments, they will not be able to find jobs for all of the unemployed youths. In China, the rural workforce is estimated at 450 million while the urban work-force is almost 170 million. The urban workforce, between 1993 and 1994, absorbed 10 million new workers. Over 3 million people are expected to join the workforce every year through to the end of the century. The July 1990 census in China surprised officials when the total came to 1.13 billion rather than the expected 1.08 billion. The underestimation was approximately 50 million people or about the population of Korea.

> *As with other emerging markets, China can now adopt the newest technologies and therefore leapfrog many of the existing levels of technology still being used in the developed countries.*

Although the current government purports to be of the socialist/Communist mold, in fact a philosophical transformation has taken place in economic thinking. This is having an enormous impact on economic growth, as central control is being replaced by free market thinking. China has gradually made a number of important economic reforms. Since 1978, the People's Communes have been replaced by a "contract responsibility system" related to household output. Market forces have increasingly determined prices. Village enterprises in rural areas have been encouraged, so that a whole group of new entrepreneurial activity has emerged.

Beginning in 1984, the reform movement moved on to the urban areas. Here, more market-oriented systems have been allowed, with the establishment of special economic zones and the opening up of coastal cities to foreign investment and open trade. In 1991, reforms were initiated to rationalize the pricing system, reform the housing and social security system, and open up foreign trade even further. China has also been exposing its inland areas to the outside world, with an emphasis on rationalizing economic structures, improving technology and agriculture, trying to meet the ever-increasing demands for infrastructure such as power plants, roads and railways, and installing better financial systems for enterprises. Most important of all, the leadership in China has recognized that the fundamental resolution of the problems facing the country and further economic growth means accelerating the pace of reform and the opening of the economy.

Symptomatic of the changes outlined, in early 1993 it was reported that the People's University of China was abandoning courses in Marxism in favor of business studies. Fourteen new business subjects were made available at the University, which was originally established by the Communist Party to train young revolutionaries. The new subjects, such as real estate management and marketing, replaced the 17 courses related to Communist dogma that had died as a result of the lack of interest from the students. China's Communist Party school, the main center for training young party cadres, joined in by announcing that for the first time it would begin teaching China's leaders about stock market operations. These changes represented a radical change in thinking regarding economics in the former Communist nation and were just another sign of the demise of Communist thinking and the rise of free market reasoning.

China and other emerging markets are moving towards manufacturing and away from agriculture. As agricultural productivity increases, the number of workers needed in that sector declines. In 1995, the industrial output grew by 14 percent, while agricultural output grew by only 4.5 percent. Manufacturing, especially private sector production, is coming to constitute an ever larger proportion of the gross national product, in comparison to agriculture.

Chinese authorities, as with other emerging market leaders, are now realizing that they cannot continue to support money-losing State-owned enterprises (SOEs) which continue to drain the country's budgets. By 1995, more than half of the 72,000 SOEs were reporting losses, even when based on their own accounting systems. Premier Li Peng announced in early 1993 that he wanted to reduce the government's workforce by 25 percent and eliminate dozens of government commissions and administrative organizations. In order to avoid laying off staff, the plan was to spin off money-making enterprises from the various government organizations and departments.

The result was the explosion of business activities by government organizations, often taking advantage of their monopoly position or regulatory powers. In one case, the government-owned Foreign Enterprise Service Co-operation Organization (FESCO) used their government position to persuade foreign investors to hire local staff through its Organization. The company supplied staff and then took monthly fees from staff wages. FESCO has also diversified into several new areas of business: real estate, a joint-venture motorcycle helmet factory with a US company, a joint-venture printing plant with a Hong Kong firm, trading companies in Romania and Poland, real estate in Belgium and Holland, a tourist service, a car repair shop, an office equipment supply agency, and other investments.

The problem is that the Chinese are deadlocked over privatization, due to the question of ownership in State-owned enterprises according to some sources. When companies issue shares to the public, under current regulations, their worth cannot exceed 50 percent of the value of the enterprises' assets. As the shareholding changes, it becomes more difficult to define the nature of a company, which is then partly owned by the State and partly by the public. "Eventually, shares might be owned by State-owned companies, collectives, and individuals," a Chinese analyst said. "The possibility has given rise to great concern by central authorities who are afraid of losing control of enterprises and some state assets."

Moreover, the different agencies – the People's Bank of China (PBOC), the Ministry of Finance, the State-Owned Assets Bureau, State Economic Reform Commission, and the Stock Exchange Executive Council – are competing for regulatory control. The lack of a company law describing how to create, operate and dissolve a company, no unified accounting principles, no strong disclosure system, and no detailed requirements for evaluating a company's assets mean the privatization process will probably experience a series of crises during its progression.

Certainly establishing securities regulations has also presented the government with serious obstacles. The problems encountered in China are like a textbook case, where all the possible crises attendant to securities market development can be found. The government is just beginning to grasp the importance of proper securities regulation and enforcement. In the financial area, China has moved away from a central bureaucracy and allowed the establishment of specialized banks, trusts and investment corporations, universal banks, and various other financial organizations, including security firms.

In 1981 the central government started issuing treasury bonds. This was then followed by the issuance of bonds and shares by enterprises. Two stock exchanges were established in 1992, one in Shanghai and the other in Shenzhen, as well as a nationwide bond-trading system, centered in Beijing. Over the years, China has also opened commodities and futures exchanges. As more and more State enterprises were being turned into joint stock companies, many of them were listed on the two stock exchanges.

Today, Chinese companies are listed in a variety of ways. There are "A" and "B" shares listed on the two local exchanges, with the "A" shares sold to local investors and the "B" shares reserved for foreign investors. There are "H" shares of Chinese companies which are listed on the Hong Kong stock exchange and there are the "Red Chips," the shares of companies incorporate and/or listed in international markets but which conduct virtually 100 percent of their business in China. As at 1995, the number of listed stocks in Shanghai had grown to 169 "A" share companies of which 34 had "B" shares, with a market capitalization of around US$25 billion for "A" shares and US$1.4 billion for "B" shares. The Shenzhen exchange had 118 "A" share listings and 24 "B" share listings, for a market capitalization of around US$12 billion in "A" shares and US$813 million in "B" shares. About 15 companies were offering "H" shares in Hong Kong, for a market capitalization of around US$3 billion, while the seven "Red Chip" listings in New York had a market capitalization of about US$700 million.

Although there were only two stock exchanges officially recognized, Shenzhen and Shanghai, there were trading centers in other cities including Dalian, Shenyang, Chendu, Chongqing, Guangzhou, Fuzhou, Nanjing, and other major cities with most of them under the auspices of the PBOC. In the beginning, most of the securities companies were owned by the PBOC branches around the country from 1988 to 1991/92. A great example of the umpire taking part in the game as a player!

One of the problems facing China in 1982 was the lack of an independent regulatory agency for capital market operations. Initially, China's central bank, the PBOC, was responsible for regulating and developing Chinese capital markets. However, conflicts of interest were evident from the beginning. This is because, in addition to its role as a central bank, the PBOC also acted as a major universal bank with branches all over the country. Until recently, the PBOC had its own capital market operations, and this resulted in significant conflicts of interests. One observer said: "The People's Bank of China wanted to control and regulate the securities market but also wanted to profit by trading in it."

Having recognized the conflict of interest, the PBOC decided to cut its connection with its security firms and sold them to specialized commercial banks and investment trust companies during the second half of 1992 and into 1993.

Companies seeking a listing on the stock exchanges in China were required to gain approval from the PBOC. However, there were reports that employees of the PBOC in Shenzhen and Shanghai were demanding allocations of the highly desirable shares and holding up numerous underwritings. The PBOC also held direct interests in listed companies; Brilliance China Automotive Holdings, was 78 percent owned by the central bank's subsidiary, Chinese Financial Education Development Foundation and other affiliates. The Shenzhen branch of the PBOC had a stake in one of three investment funds and a national securities firm.

In addition to the PBOC, the Ministry of Finance, the State-Owned Assets Bureau, the State Economic Reform Commission and the Stock Exchange Executive Council among others were all involved in stock market regulation and operations in some way, which made the regulatory situation even more complicated. The China Securities Regulatory Commission (CRSC) was responsible for regulating stock exchanges and stockbrokers, new share issues, listing of bonds and other debt instruments, and commodity trading. But the PBOC was responsible for the approval of bond issues by financial institutions and the regulation of mutual funds. The Finance Ministry was responsible for treasury bonds and treasury bills. The Foreign Exchange Control Bureau was under the PBOC, but was quite independent, and was responsible for foreign bond issues and foreign exchange. The State Planning Commission decided the annual quotas for stock and bond issuance, both local and foreign. All of this regulatory oversight meant there was considerable constriction resulting in a backlog of demand and supply for stocks and bonds. If a company wanted to issue a foreign bond, approval had to be obtained from the provincial government, the CSRC, the State Planning Commission, and the Foreign Exchange Control Bureau. If it was a convertible bond, the stock exchange in Shanghai or Shenzhen had to also give approval.

Foreign investors in China continue to decry the lack of an adequate legal framework of clear business and economic laws, lax application of existing laws and regulations and inadequate court administration. Although the China International Economic and Trade Arbitration Commission has become one of the busiest arbitration centers in the world, foreigners who have won their arbitration awards have not been able to enforce them adequately since the central government courts in Beijing often are not able to make provincial courts enforce their orders or ensure that Chinese official organizations obey the court's judgment. In addition, it is not unusual for judges to favor state enterprises or the government in lawsuits. The Chinese judicial system is not independent from the Government; rather it is an instrument used to implement Government policy.

In 1992, one US lawyer involved in the securities business said that the stock exchanges in China would continue to expand and would be a great source of funds for Chinese enterprise but added: "The lack of a company law describing how to create, operate and dissolve a company, no unified accounting principles, no strong disclosure system, and no detailed requirements for evaluating a company's assets mean that the markets will have a series of crises during their development."

Examples of crises were already rife. In November 1991, when the Shenzhen Stock Exchange was about to distribute application forms for subscription to 11 company flotations planned for 1992. More than 100,000 Chinese investors from all over the country came to Shenzhen and camped outside the offices of financial institutions in an attempt to get applications. Again, in the summer of 1992, trouble emerged. Investors lined up in the city of Xiamen to buy application forms for shares and paid speculators up to two weeks' wages for the forms, without any guarantee of obtaining shares. Lines of people, some as long as one kilometer, formed at the 26 stations selling applications to enter a lottery to decide who could buy shares in four local companies; a car manufacturer, a fishery, and two trading companies. Speculators raised the price of application forms, originally costing five yuan, to 150 yuan in one day. Clearly it was a case of excessive pent up savings chasing too few stocks.

Obviously, China needs a sound regulatory framework. "The stock exchanges will continue to expand and be a tremendous source of funds for Chinese enterprises," said a US lawyer involved in the securities business. "But it's going to be fraught with potential complications unless the fundamental problems – structure of the system, the regulatory network, and disclosure – are dealt with."

Below is a series of "snapshots" of China, formed in mid-1995, as we toured several cities and businesses across the country. As China goes through the reform process, it is awe-inspiring to witness the trials and tribulations they encounter in the face of economic and structural reform.

"Snapshots" of China

Shanghai, 3 July 1995

We are now on the outer ring road in Shanghai. It is a four-lane, elevated highway surrounding the outer part of Shanghai, completed in December 1994. We came off the north–south section of the highway which appears to have been recently opened as it is festooned with celebratory banners. The progress in Shanghai is really amazing and the construction activity does not stop. As we drive through the city, cranes and structures under construction abound.

I just came from an interview with one of the Shanghai municipal officials. He said that their goal is to make Shanghai the financial and trade center for China and it seems that their planning and ambition is centered on that goal. The Pudong New Development area will result in an entirely new city at the mouth of the Yangtze River, complete with a major port, a new airport, office buildings, housing, a new stock exchange, etc. He said that although Hong Kong is now the largest port in China, eventually Shanghai will surpass Hong Kong. He added, however, that this will not mean Hong Kong will become smaller but that the entire financial activity and trade in China will be much larger and Hong Kong's share of the total activity will inevitably fall.

Shanghai is at the heart of an area which has been described as the largest market in Asia. Some analysts have said that the largest concentration of consumers in the Asia Pacific area is not Japan, not southern China, and not any single country but is in fact the Yangtze River Delta region. This includes Shanghai, and the provinces of Jiangsu, Anhui and Zhejiang. That market is estimated to constitute almost 200 million people, a population larger than Indonesia or Japan. Although foreign investors coming to China in the 1980s, concentrated on Guangdong, since 1990 the industrial focus has been on the Yangtze delta. It is from this region that one quarter of China's increased economic production came. The region has been growing faster than Taiwan or South Korea. In addition to the tremendous force that is Shanghai city, the autonomous townships and village enterprises make their own contribution to the growth spurt.

Shanghai is becoming central China's financial and services center. A number of industrial parks outside Shanghai are attracting investments. These areas are offering lower taxes and cheap credit to export-oriented enterprises and are not restricted by the same State quotas or targets to which the State enterprises are subjected. In a new industrial township outside Suzhou, US$1 billion is being invested, mainly by Singaporeans. There are 85 cities and towns in the delta, and 35 of them have a population of over one million people. The region is also attracting migrants – an estimated 9 million to date. This has created serious infrastructure, housing, security and other problems. While previously people in China could not move from one area to another, the situation has now completely changed and the country is on the move. To provide the necessary water, sewerage, rail, roads, power and housing services, a continued high level of foreign investment is essential.

Nanjing, Jiangsu, 6 July 1995

People here are concerned about the economic development of their province. The Governor of the province is from Jiangsu. The Jiangsu dialect is like Shanghainese. With 5.5 million people, Nanjing is the fourth largest city in the country, while the population of the entire Jiangsu province is 60 million. It is the largest in the country in terms of land area, with 100,000 square kilometers. According to our researchers in Jiangsu, this province is a leader in terms of economic development as they contribute a substantial amount in taxes to the central government. Shanghai is the first in paying taxes to the central government and Jiangsu is number two. Shanghai is a special city, like a province. Nanjing is the capital of Jiangsu Province.

The flight took about 30 minutes from Shanghai to Nanjing, taking off late at 19.30. This is the usual pattern when we travel. We leave after office hours for the next city arriving late at night in the next destination. We were the only ones at the deserted airport this late at night and thankfully it was not raining like in Shanghai, but there had been rains previously, and as in other parts of China, flooding is rampant. As we drove to the hotel it was clear that we had entered another construction site, like almost everywhere else in China we go these days. The building sites included many high-rise edifices. Our stay is at the luxurious Jinning Hotel (managed by the provincial government and the travel bureau of Jiangsu Province) which was built in 1982 to lavish proportions. It has a huge lobby encased in glass three stories high and a large fountain with a red marble ball free-floating under a strong gush of water.

The hotel has 822 rooms. Maintenance is good and the service is better than in Shanghai, in my view. I tried out my broken Mandarin but the replies came quickly in good English. (An indication of how good my Mandarin is.)

The manager said that the hotel wanted to issue "B" shares but the CSRC prevented that from happening. The reason given by the government for the restriction is that they want to list energy-related companies first. There is no stock exchange in Nanjing, but there are 50 or 60 places where people can buy and sell their shares. The people here are interested in the stock market and the percentage of investors to the entire population is second only to that of Shanghai. Most of the large brokers in China have sales offices here, all linked via networked computers with the Shanghai or Shenzhen Stock Exchange. People here, says one broker, like the Shanghai stocks because they are more volatile and there is a better chance to make money quickly. (Let's not talk about the chance to lose money quickly!) The exchange was established in 1992 and most of the people are short-term investors.

Unfortunately Nanjing is known for more than market speculators. This is the city where the notorious Nanking massacre took place during World War II. The Chinese claim that in December 1937 the Japanese killed 300,000 people in one week. And the reason? According to our driver, Nanjing was the base of the Kuomingtang army at that time and fiercely resisted the Japanese invasion. The Chinese soldiers cleverly removed their uniforms as the Japanese troops rolled in, but so hungry were the Japanese for retribution, they killed everyone in sight. In the memorial museum established to honor the dead, there are photographs of a whole floor of men's heads. Most of the people of Nanjing were killed by decapitation with samurai swords. Too terrible for words.

We are heading for Anhui Province to Maanshan (literal translation: Ma = horse, An = shadow, Shan = mountain). No highways here. The drive is ordinarily 60 kilometers, but due to flooding, today we have to take a detour and the distance will be 80 kilometers. Nanjing is on the Yangtze River. Both Nanjing and Maanshan are situated on the south bank of the Yangtze River. The Three Gorges dam project is loved in this province because it will benefit the entire province not only by preventing the flooding of the river but also by supplying power to the entire province. During June (according to the Chinese calendar, July by the Western calendar) it always rains. Along the Yangtze River there is lots of rain.

The project is in Hubei Province and will benefit Hubei the most. The Three Gorges is one of the most beautiful tourist spots in China, but the dam project is expected to ruin some of the tourist spots. The spot where the Chu Yuen Temple stands will be submerged, so local residents are trying to move it. Residents, too, are being moved away as the project gets underway. Even in this countryside everyone is building something. Bricks are strewn about as are lots of tiles used for exterior walls. What a contrast between the dull grey concrete of the old buildings and the new buildings with their shiny white tiles! As we move into the countryside, we find fields that are the deep green color of maturing rice plants. Two crops a year are harvested here; the early crop in September and the late crop around November.

They have the same type of big horned, grey water buffalos that one finds in Thailand. But unlike Thailand, it does snow *here and the temperature falls to about −5 degrees Celsius. People feel that it is the coldest place in China because they don't have heating in their houses. Further up north there is central heating and even their beds are heated so they don't feel the cold as much. We noticed at the Shangling factory that oil space heaters are becoming more popular. This is a function of the market. People with money use heat pump air conditioners to blow both cold and hot air. Others use electric space heaters coming from Italy and also the Philips brand from the Netherlands.*

The country roads are bad and once we hit a village it is chaotic with hawkers lining the roads and their customers blocking traffic. Sidewalks? Forget it. The way is blocked with hawker platforms piled with fruits, vegetables, sweaters, underwear, books, newspapers, someone cooking dumplings, etc. And where is the police officer who should be clearing the way? He's over there happily chatting with his friend. Over in the corner there is a crowd surrounding two women shouting at each other in some dispute.

We're now stuck in traffic in a small town somewhere between Nanjing and Maanshan. Let's try the mobile telephone we rented in Nanjing. Busy signal. Last night with the fax machine we carry with us and plugged into the hotel phone lines, we faxed the Singapore and Hong Kong offices. At the same time we gave them the portable phone number and asked them to call in but nothing's been received yet and it's 09.30. We use the callback service when making calls from our hotel room. Its more convenient and cheaper. The calls go through the US via satellite and then to the various destinations around the world. Last week we called our Moscow, Singapore and Hong Kong offices. One problem, like in many parts of Europe, is that in Nanjing they are still using the old electromechanical switchgear which uses pulse signals and not the digital tone dialling. So we must carry a pocket-sized tone generator to connect with our digital computerized dispatching unit in the US. Finally at 10.30 we arrived at Maanshan, the "steel city." What was supposed to be a one and a half hour trip took almost double that time.

As I travel around China the most prevalent descriptive word is for what I see "messy." People don't clean their bicycles, or polish their cars, the toilets are dirty. In a famous restaurant in Shanghai the red rug is black with embedded dirt, the streets are full of dust, windows are not cleaned. There seems no pride of ownership. Eddie Chow, one of our analysts, says that Chinese are not so concerned with details. Of course, it also has to do with economics as well, a desire for quick gains and to hell with the future. Also in a society where almost everything was owned by the "people," i.e., the State, why maintain it? But the loss in asset value by poor maintenance is inestimable and will have to be addressed by China eventually.

Chengdu Sichuan, 9 July 1995

Sichuan means four rivers. This is one of China's main agricultural areas and supports 10 percent of the country's population. There is a Chinese saying that whenever there is a revolution in China, it starts in Sichuan Province. In 1989 students protested here in sympathy with the far-away Beijing Tianamen protests and like those in Beijing were suppressed with police batons. Chengdu city's 3 million people are a small portion of the province's 100 million strong population. The characters in its name literally mean "becoming a city." Cheungdu was an urban center 3,000 years ago and a capital for the regional kingdom a number of times. As we drive toward the hotel, we see a 50-story skyscraper under construction looming above us. At the end of the main thoroughfare, Jin Min Nan Ro (People's South Road), dividing the city into West and East, is a huge statue of Chairman Mao with his hand raised in blessing.

From the airport a four-lane concrete highway is well-paved and as we enter the city the avenue is lined with large evergreen trees. One of the most noticeable new skyscrapers is the People's Bank of China. The city is full of tall buildings and grandiose new high-rises under construction. Traffic is bad now and will get worse. This is a bustling city with street hawkers, huge department stores, and a tremendous amount of activity. The Parkson company of Malaysia has five floors and two basements full of merchandise, beautifully presented, unlike many of the department stores we saw in other cities. While in hilly areas, we saw few bicycles, here the bicycles outnumber the cars, although the latter are also in abundance.

Inflation is high in Sichuan, having migrated from the coastal areas. It is now about 18 percent to 20 percent. We could see that when we tried to purchase some lychees from a street vendor, and the RMB 25 he demanded turned out to be more than the going rate in Hong Kong! Admittedly, though, they were perfect – big, round, deep red, juicy and delicious.

Sichuan was the first province to declare support for the family responsibility system. Other governors were afraid to declare their support for it for fear of being accused of being capitalist. Sichuan's family responsibility system decollectivized and returned the land to local farmers.

Responsibility for the farm production stimulated the farmers, and gave them an incentive to increase agricultural output in the early 1980s. Sichuan had been a leader in agricultural reform dating back to 1979. This province was also one of the first to adopt the joint stock company reform.

Sichuan has been the springboard for many famous events and personalities in Chinese history. The Nationalist forces established their base of operations here for a time during World War II. The notorious Empress Tsu Tsi started out here as the emperor's concubine. Of the famous ten marshals after liberation, seven were from Sichuan. The most famous poet in Chinese history, Li Bai, was born in Sichuan and lived during the Tang era.

In terms of total State-owned assets, Sichuan is placed second after Liaoning Province. In the 1960's relations with Russia were suspended, causing Mao to fear a Russian invasion of China. Factories were moved into the mountainous regions to avoid attack, so many wound up in Sichuan province. Surrounding Chengdu are wide, flat plains full of rice fields. More than 80 percent of the people are farmers, but education is held in high esteem. Book sales ranked first in China in absolute terms and third in per capita terms (first is Shanghai and second is Beijing).

China has seven military zones and one of those is in Chengdu. It is responsible for the entire southwest region of China. In 1979 the anti-Vietnam War was carried out by this military zone. Tibet is under the control of this zone also. In 1987 the Americans opened a consulate in the city, and the military command moved all meetings outside the city in order to avoid espionage by the Americans.

The next day, after bowls of dumplings for lunch, we were off to Mianyang in a Toyota van on a bone-jarring, vicious ride, driven by a daredevil who could qualify nicely for the Minneapolis 2000. The technique here is to make sure you cross the double line on the road. Driving is supposed to be on the right, but he must have been thinking of going to left-drive Hong Kong, because he decided to drive on the left so he could overtake everyone in front of him. On-coming trucks and cars also driving at high speed? No problem. Just drive straight at them in a little game of chicken and just when you both are going into a head-on collision, swerve sharply in front of the car you have just passed. The passengers? To hell with them. Let them bump back and forth against each other and the side of the van. The road between Chengdu and Mianyang is for the most part like a washboard. We didn't need a massage when we arrived, because we already had one in the van. However there were interludes of nicely paved highway, and it seemed that they were intending to build a better one. Unfortunately we arrived too early to benefit from that development!

After two hours of the drive through hell, we finally arrived and checked into the Linyuan Hotel. We had been warned to expect the worst in this remote part of China, but in fact we were ushered into lavishly furnished suites complete with American-made whirlpool baths. Of course, as in other parts of China, interior decoration and quality left much to be desired. They told us that Jiang Ze Min, the Communist Party General Secretary, President of the People's Republic of China and Chairman of the Central Military Commission had just visited and stayed in these suites. The walls were lined with silk damask and the windows covered with dark red velvet curtains shutting out all light and prying eyes. When I opened the curtains I could understand why they were needed. On the second floor of this three-storey hotel we were overlooked by a set of apartment-building windows.

The city, like other cities in China is under construction with a number of high-rise buildings underway. At the entrance to the city we passed an industrial zone where some factories were complete and more were under construction. This is reputed to be an electronics center. Since much of the high tech military work was done here, it is not surprising that it is being promoted as a high tech zone.

At the hotel, when it comes to facilities, the emphasis is on food, like most other hotels in China. In this case, there were 10 different types of restaurants offering Sichuan and Cantonese food. Health club? That's what they called it, but upon seeing it, I came to understand why Chinese executives are in bad shape. A flimsy rowing machine, broken down jogging machine, two unusable, stationary bicycles and a belt massager. In the same room were electronic games.

The reception area had eight clocks on the wall with times for New York, Moscow, Cairo, Singapore (with the wrong time), Geneva, London, Tokyo and Beijing. Only RMB-denominated Visa or Mastercharge cards were accepted. No American Express in sight. So we had to find some RMB cash fast. But we were hooked into the world by TV. In the room I flipped through the remote control buttons and found motorcycle racing from France with Chinese commentary, the "V" channel (Asia's answer to MTV) which was featuring a British punk rock group making sexy gyrations, Chinese music TV, a Chinese interview program, a program explaining TV games with kungfu fighters, a Chinese children's puppet show, and a Chinese news program featuring the trade row between Kodak and Fuji film.

At the Chengdu Communications Cable company the salary level for college graduate engineers starting at the company is RMB 200 (US$24) per month plus housing and food. Salary levels in this part of the country are lower than the national average because of the surplus of people eager to work. At the center of the city is the peasant worker market filled with young people in their 20s who have come from the countryside in search of employment. Some are in such difficult straits that they offer their services for free as long as they can get room and board. Lots of these young people are not needed on the farm to do the planting and harvesting, even in this rich land where they are able to grow three rice crops a year. Surplus family members thus go to the big city in search of a job so they can buy attractive things such as a bicycle, and color TV sets. They also dream of replacing their mud houses with a cement house. One worker returning from Beijing with a TV set to his home village was careful not to let other people in the village see his TV. He watches the TV quietly so no-one can overhear because he is afraid that when he leaves his home someone may steal it.

Dalian, 9 July 1995

We arrived at Dalian after a 40-minute flight but we wait on the tarmac for two hours, since there are some military air operations in Dalian which they don't want us to see.

Dalian's airport is rather new and neat-looking. The main hall has a glass roof three stories high with translucent blue *shades covering the entire area, giving a pleasant blue hue to the entire terminal. Like all the other places we visited in China, the city is another big construction site with buildings of 20, 30 or 40 stories going up. We stayed in a high-rise hotel over 20 stories high, the Furama Hotel Dalian. There are not many imported goods in Dalian, reflecting the relatively lower income levels compared to Shanghai.*

At one of the securities firms in Dalian, most of their business is not from brokerage activities but from financing activities. They borrow money from banks and other securities firms at 15 percent and undertake bond repurchase agreements with firms needing short term (three months, six months or one year) financing. These operations yield a margin of about 5 percent, the difference between their cost of funds and the 20 percent rate of the repurchase agreements.

These deals all flow through the Shanghai Stock Exchange with the Shanghai Stock Exchange acting as the counterparty for both sides, thus, in effect, guaranteeing the transaction. Although there is trading at the local Dalian trading center, all deals are settled in Shanghai or Shenzhen, depending on where the traded company is listed.

Chongqing, Sichuan, 11 July 1995

Chongqing is in the southeast part of Sichuan province and hangs on the deep gorges made by the Yangtze and Jialing rivers. It gets hot here in the summer and when we arrived we felt that heat. It is sometimes referred to as one of the "three furnaces" of China, the other two being Wuhan and Nanjing. It is from here that trips down the Yangtze River to the Yangtze Gorge start, taking three days to arrive at

Wuhan. The city is 8,000 years old and was the capital of the Kingdom of Ba in the 12th century BC. The name "Chongqing" in Chinese means "double celebration" or "double happiness." It was one of the treaty ports open to foreigners during the Qing Dynasty. In the late 1930s, during the Sino-Japanese War the Nationalist government had its temporary capital here, and Zhou Enlai lived in the city as he tried to work with the Nationalists against the Japanese. Various American missions under Stillwell, Hurley, Marshall and Wedmeyer tried to get the Nationalists and Communists to work together. The Communists ultimately took over the city in November 1949.

The airport at Chongqing is quite unusual and beautiful in a strange sort of way. It is done in white tile, but the architect must have admired Salvador Dali's paintings, because he gave an otherworldly feeling to the building. There are blue windows in the hallway. The control tower is like an onion stood on its stem. The entire building has few straight corners and curves around the site like a white caterpillar.

Driving into the city you see that the city has not escaped China's building boom. As we crossed the Jialing River bridge, one of three bridges between the two parts of the city (another bridge over the Jialing River and a bridge over the Yangtze River), we counted no fewer than 12 cranes on top of high-rise buildings going up. This city will be affected by the Three Gorges project, since the water level here is expected to rise, making it possible for larger ships to travel here from downstream. The roads here are better than in other cities we visited in China. The toll highway between this city and Chengdu, recently completed, is excellent. We heard that the city's mayor is trying to get Li Ka Shing, Hong

Kong's richest entrepreneur, to purchase the toll road so that those funds can be used for other projects. Although the toll road does not have heavy traffic, getting to it took some time and as we sat in traffic I discovered that I could call Hong Kong and Singapore from the Motorola cellular telephone, so no time was wasted.

Xiamen, Fujian

Here in Xiamen, situated directly across the Taiwan Straits from Taiwan, the pace of change has been dramatic. Fifteen years ago, this was a backwater and a bastion in the cold war between the mainland Communists and the Nationalists in Taiwan. During Chiang Kai-shek's reign in Taiwan, the Nationalists floated propaganda balloons from their forward positions on Quemoy and Matsu Islands to this city in Fujian Province.

The Fujian dialect is the same as that spoken by the "native" Taiwanese and was the main language in Taiwan before the arrival of the Mandarin-speaking Nationalist troops escaping from the victorious Communist forces. Taiwanese businessmen find it very comfortable to invest and work in Xiamen, and with relatives here, business goes more smoothly. The people here have sought progress by emulating Taiwan's industrialization. We visited two Taiwanese-invested factories here and were quite impressed. When we compared them with other Chinese factories we visited in Beijing and Shanghai, we found them to be more efficient and generally better managed.

All the people in Xiamen and, for that matter, most of the workers of China, are thin and wiry, lively and alert. With a *diet dominated by rice and vegetables, it's no wonder. Before the economic revival that China is currently experiencing, there was rationing of fats and oils and meat was in short supply. I remember noticing on previous visits to China that the people had often looked rather sickly. The situation is certainly far better now but people's lifestyles have not changed enough to alter what is essentially a healthy diet.*

Guangzhou, Guangdong

We are now ending a two-week trip to various areas of China to visit a number of companies, including the subsidiaries of various Hong Kong and Taiwanese companies as well as indigenous Chinese companies listed on the Shenzhen and Shanghai stock exchanges. Landing in Guangzhou Airport and arriving at the hotel I immediately feel the marked difference in general economic level of this city and province. Of course, all the passionate building activity is in evidence, just like so much of China. The difference is that Guangdong Province and its capital city Guangzhou have gone further. The influence from nearby Hong Kong is evident in the general training level in the service industry. The rugs in the hotels are clean, the floors are spotless, goods in the stores are nicely displayed, the front office staff speak English, the level of service is generally better and they are thus able to get a better price. The competition is also intense which, of course, benefits the consumers.

We have one of our meetings at the Dongfang Hotel. What a change! I had stayed here during my first visit to China in the 1970s, during the Guangdong Trade Fair, and at that time it was one of the few major hotels in the city. One day, I threw some old clothing into the waste basket but found the

*clothes cleaned and folded neatly on my bed that evening.
Back then, there was no need to lock doors or worry about
valuables because of the tight political control. But it was a
joyless and dull place. Today, the Dongfang Hotel is hemmed
in by high-rise buildings and its high room count has been
overshadowed by a number of newer hotels in the city,
including the hotel where I was staying. The Dongfang Hotel
has been spruced up to meet the competition with
spectacular Chinese decorations; a large, intricately carved,
wooden screen painted in gold, and three larger-than-life
size statues of the three sages.*

● EASTERN EUROPE

I personally find the most exciting aspect of emerging market development in the world today to be the creation of new equity markets in those countries transforming themselves from Communist/socialist economies to capitalistic free market economies. In eastern Europe, for example, the requirements of privatization have generated great interest in capital markets.

The urgency to privatize is nowhere felt more keenly than in the former Communist states of Russia, the CIS and Eastern Europe. After 70 years of State directed manufacturing, emphasizing output, not quality or profit, these economies have wrenching changes to make. The positive market forces that could be unleashed by privatization are stifled by fears of how these changes will be manifested in the workforce and homes of average citizens. Formerly guaranteed employment, housing and health care are no longer ensured for a large percentage of the population. Only the swift restructuring and expansion of economic activity can generate the wealth surpluses needed by these people to survive. Privatization is critical to that process.

To date privatization has been undertaken in the Czech Republic, Hungary, Slovakia, Poland, Bulgaria, Slovenia and Romania. They have progressed to varying degrees – Slovenia has 1,345 companies scheduled for mass privatization by the end of 1996, having already auctioned off 165 companies. Direct sales in Slovakia saw 550 companies privatized by July 1995. The programs in the Czech Republic and Poland have progressed on a larger scale. In the Czech Republic 1,900 companies were privatized in the first stage of a mass privatization in 1993, and a further 1,400 companies are to be sold via small-scale sales by the end of 1997. Poland's 1995 mass privatization saw 2,975 companies go public, with further sales and flotations scheduled throughout 1996 (Table 4.2).

Table 4.2 Privatization programs

Country	Phase of Program	Companies on List	Complete Date
Czech Rep.	MPP – I	1,900	6/93
	MPP – II	860	2/95
	Small-Scale Sales	1,400	12/97
	Strategic Dir. Sales	53	12/00
Hungary	Direct Scales	980	12/94
	Liquidation	537	12/94
Slovakia	Direct Sales/Auctions	25	12/96
	Direct Sales	550	7/95
	Direct Sales to Workers	N/A	12/96
Poland	Liquidation	314	12/94
	MPP	2,975	6/95
	Direct Sales	132	12/96
	Floatation	163	12/96
	MPP	413	12/95
Bulgaria	Direct Sales – I	796	10/94
	Direct Sales – II	243	12/95
	Direct Sales – III	517	12/96
	MPP	1,063	12/96
Slovenia	Auctions Sales – I	83	10/94
	Auction Sales – II	82	3/95
	Modified MPP	1,345	12/96
Romania	MPP	3,905	6/96

Source: Daiwa Europe Ltd.
Note: N/A = not available; MPP = mass privatization program.

The methods used vary greatly. They range from negotiated sales to foreign buyers, to mass public voucher distribution, to auctions to management and staff of the privatized entity. In this region, there are 27 countries, if we include the former East Germany, the Czech and Slovak Republics, the Yugoslav successor states, the Baltic states and the republics which once formed the Soviet Union. The scale of the work involved is enormous and unprecedented. Privatization is part of a process which is creating a market economy practically from scratch, with all of its legal, commercial, financial and institutional infrastructure. In the past, for example, most of the total value added in Poland was from the state sector, and for the Soviet Union, East Germany, the Czech and Slovak Republics, it was more than 90 percent.

Today, major leaps in private ownership have been made. By comparing the share of GDP accounted for by private sector firms, it is evident that privatization has massively restructured the nature of the national economy. The Czech Republic leads the region, with 70 percent of GDP coming from the private sector, rising from only 5 percent just a short time ago, in 1989-90. Hungary has gone from 25 percent private sector share of GDP to 60 percent by 1995. The deep significance of changes like this to a nation and to the labor force are difficult to over-emphasize, yet the process inexorably continues (Table 4.3).

Table 4.3 Private sector share of GDP (%)

Country	1989–90	1994	1995
Czech Rep.	5	65	70
Hungary	25	55	60
Slovakia	5	55	60
Poland	28	55	60
Bulgaria	N/A	40	45
Slovenia	N/A	30	45
Romania	N/A	35	40

Sources: EBRD, *Independent Strategy*, Daiwa Europe Ltd.
Note: N/A: not available

The general economic picture in Eastern Europe is still depressed, in spite of the inroads made on privatization. Considerable improvement is evident in the past couple of years, though, and there is evidence encouraging us to believe that this trend will continue. The weighted average growth rate for the region's countries (excluding the countries of the former Yugoslavia) has shown a fairly consistent upward drive. Back in 1991, these economies were actually shrinking at an annual rate of −11.4 percent, weakened further to −13.8 percent in 1992, then the decline began to slow to −6 percent in 1993 and −6.1 percent in 1994. In 1995 a dramatic slowdown in the decline to −1.1 percent was made, and forecasters in 1996 expected these countries to emerge on the positive side of the line with an average GDP growth of 1.8 percent. These are averages and include Russia which had negative changes in GDP through 1995. However, the averages also mask a number of countries who, like Poland, had a shrinking economy in 1990 but quickly emerged to a spectacular growth rate of 6 percent in 1995.

Actually, in 1993 we saw the beginnings of real growth in three countries – Poland, Romania and Slovenia. In recent years inflation has plagued Eastern Europe, peaking at a weighted average of 1,540 percent in 1992. This was followed by a dramatic decline in 1994 with further declines estimated for 1995 and projected into 1996, dropping to 41 percent. This high inflation scenario is a problem and has grave political consequences. The good news is that it is abating, but it is still at double-digit levels in too many countries of the region. Income levels in Eastern Europe vary widely, with extremes of US$7000 per capita in Slovenia and US$364 per capita in Albania.

Hungary

Hungary has significantly improved its economic circumstances by sticking with economic reform. At the end of 1995, Hungary had raised its foreign currency reserves to record levels, hitting US$11 billion, while at the same time making dramatic progress in reducing its current account and budget deficits. The Hungarian forint received recognition from the IMF and become a convertible currency. An IMF standby agreement was scheduled for signing in 1996, bringing Hungary more fully into the international financial community.

As for the privatization program, by the end of 1994, 980 companies in Hungary had been sold, including a refrigerator manufacturer, a car manufacturer, and a computer maker. There were still hundreds of companies, including a telephone company, pharmaceutical companies, hotels, a department store retail chain, breweries, and oil and gas companies waiting to be privatized. The government turned to mass privatization after learning that auctioning companies on a staged basis was too slow. As a result of looming government deficits, the urgency to sell State enterprises to raise cash was appealing. Taking the lead from the privatization program launched by the former Czechoslovakia, where vouchers were used, the Hungarians were proposing to offer low-interest, long-term loans to encourage small investors to purchase shares in the State companies.

Romania

Romania's 23 million people appear set to benefit from on-going economic reforms. GDP rose 6.9 percent in 1995, up from 3.9 percent in 1994, according to official estimates. Inflation gradually dropped but unemployment in 1994, however, remained high, at 11 percent, and the current account was perennially in deficit. Considerable in-fighting over reform speed and content exists, and the IMF has had to play referee on occasion.

In early 1993 Romania's privatization authorities published a list of the first 162 companies to be privatized as part of a broader scheme, designed to sell off 2,000 small companies during the following two years. Political stagnation in Romania hampered this process in the past, but a newly revised scheme, targeting mass privatization of 3,905 firms by mid-1996 was on track. In 1995, only 40 percent of GDP was earned by the private sector.

Poland

In Poland, the passage of a tight fiscal 1996 budget, demonstrates that the government was taking the budget deficit seriously. In fact, stringent fiscal and monetary policy survived several governments, despite populist rhetoric to the contrary. GDP growth in 1995 topped 6.5 percent, one of the few countries in the region to achieve such high growth. A sharply lower foreign debt burden was leaving more capital for domestic investment and further debt reduction. Interest payments as a percentage of exports dropped from 39.8 percent in 1989 to only 11 percent in 1993 and 1994.

At the same time, privatization continued, with more than 600,000 additional privatization certificates, of an existing 4 million units, being sold off to investors during the first week of January 1996 alone. In Poland, shares in Polish enterprises were being sold to the public as early as 1989, with the companies concerned providing a market in their own shares on a matched bargain basis. In early 1993 the first phase of privatization, involving the sale of medium-sized state enterprises, had been completed with 60 percent of their shares allocated to 15 to 20 national investment funds, 10 percent available for free distribution to employees and the remaining 30 percent retained by the state for sale later. The later sale would compensate owners of confiscated properties and provide allocations for a proposed national pension fund.

The second phase of the Polish program consisted of a public distribution of shares in the various funds, with all adults aged 18 and over and permanent residents in Poland eligible to apply for a participation certificate in each investment fund for a nominal fee. The certificates were then to be exchangeable for shares in the fund after a transition period.

Czech Republic

The sheer scale of privatization of state-owned enterprises in the Czech Republic has been monumental, and the speed with which companies have been privatized has been breathtaking. In 1990, only 2 percent of GDP was accounted for by the private sector. By mid-1994 this figure had risen to over 50 percent. The transformation of the economy from centralized command economy to market economy has hinged on the success of the radical privatization program. In the first stage of privatization small businesses were sold by public auction. So far 22,000 have been sold, the majority of which were sold before the end of 1992 when the Czech Republic was still part of Czechoslovakia.

The second stage was the introduction of a voucher privatization program, which was underway by the end of 1992, whereby books of vouchers were distributed to all Czech citizens over 18 years of age. The voucher books could be purchased for about an average week's wages. The vouchers were worth a nominal thousand investment points, which could be used to bid for shares in the enterprise being privatized, or alternatively could be exchanged for shares in mutural funds or investment privatization funds. In total, 6 million Czechs bid for shares of enterprises being privatized. It is estimated that 70 percent of the people who bought the vouchers handed them to mutual funds. The second wave of voucher privatization began in early 1994. The success of the initial stages of privatization has encouraged the government to press ahead with the privatization of key state-owned enterprises. The government has sought foreign strategic partners for its key industries to help with technology transfer and to raise much needed funds. For example, SPT Telecom a.s., the state-controlled telecommunications giant, has been partially privatized in two distinct stages. The first in 1994 saw 19 percent of SPT shares placed under the voucher scheme and in 1995, 27 percent of the shares were sold to an overseas strategic partner, TelSource. From this privatization, and others, the government raised nearly US$1.6 billion in 1995, sharply up on 1994 when proceeds from privatization stood at only US$7 million.

Slovak Republic

The first wave of voucher privatization in the Slovak Republic was accomplished by early 1993 soon after the establishment of the Slovak Republic as an independent state. Although a second wave of voucher privatization was planned for early 1994, as in the Czech Republic, it was first delayed and then canceled due to changes in government. When a coalition government led by the Movement for a Democratic Slovakia came to power they expressed concern that the scheme led to the concentration of shares in the hands of a few individuals and investment funds and that the owners did not have sufficient leverage over the management of companies to facilitate restructuring.

In June 1995, the government scrapped the voucher privatization scheme and replaced it with a bond scheme. Under the new scheme, citizens would be allocated a registered bond by the National Property Fund (NPF), with a face value of Sk10,000 (US$330) and a five year maturity. Investors could use the bonds to invest in privatized companies, purchase national insurance, contribute to pension funds, and invest in mutual funds, among other things. Under the scheme, privatization continued by direct sale to investor, with preference given to bids prepared by company employees. As a result, most privatizations have been accomplished through management buy-outs.

Due to the various delays in implementing the second stage of a mass privatization program, privatization in the Slovak Republic has been less swift than that of its neighbor, but is now progressing rapidly. Of 830 companies due to be privatized in the current round, 370 privatization projects had been approved by the end of 1995, with most due to be approved in 1996. The Slovak Republic has taken a different privatization course from its regional neighbors and although there has been some doubt over the transparency of the privatization process, it has also come in for some praise. This focuses on the belief that the new owner-managers are more likely to implement the necessary reforms than are the investment funds or dispersed individual shareholders who own companies privatized under the voucher privatization scheme.

Poland

*Poland is in the throes of a privatization transformation, as
are the other countries in this region. I'm optimistic about
the investment opportunities that it will yield in the years
ahead.*

*The Warsaw Stock Exchange (WSE) now has a five-year track
record. Its capitalization will increase, and as the
government's privatization proceeds, the market will become
more and more significant. The WSE was the world's best-
performing market in 1993 with an amazing 800 percentage
gain in dollar terms, then kept climbing to an all-time high in
March 1994 before crashing and losing half of its value. But it
has rebounded since. It operates in an institutional
framework that has been constructed in close co-operation
with top western experts financed by the World Bank, US, UK
and others. The Polish economy will keep growing with
increasing re-integration of trade flows into Western Europe,
and should pose many good buys as the decade moves on.*

*Thanks to the "shock therapy" liberalizations of Poland's first
post-Communist government and the continued reforms of
those that have followed, the overall economic situation is
looking very good today. Inflation has dropped from 684
percent in 1990 to close to 22 percent today. 1994's GDP
growth, 5.2 percent was the fastest in all of Europe. That's
remarkable when you consider that as recently as 1990 GDP
was shrinking by 12 percent a year, a time when former
Soviet markets were collapsing and new trade and
investment patterns with the West had not yet replaced*

them. Today, though, Poland has a new vitality fueled by an economic growth rate running about twice that of Hungary and the Czech Republic.

Poland has many things in common with Turkey, the Czech Republic, and other European emerging markets we track, such as:

- *a well-educated population anxious to increase purchases of Western consumer goods;*
- *skilled but inexpensive labor;*
- *an impressive young managerial class aggressively pursuing joint ventures with major Western firms interested in tapping into their country's agricultural, industrial and service sector strengths.*

Poland and the other strongest former East Bloc nations want to join the European Union by the end of the decade. This would reinforce positive recent trends, since by 1995 Poland already sent 63 percent of its total exports to EU member countries – up from 44 percent in 1990. Let's hope negotiations on EU entry can be completed in a reasonable time frame as part of the welcome trend we're seeing towards trade liberalization and integration in other parts of the world.

EU entry could help Polish companies, especially if it led to more access to markets in Germany, which by itself already accounts for 35 percent of all Polish exports. As long as local companies can defend their own domestic market position against new competitors, more trade with Germany should be good for Poland. And with Germany's economic strength and size the better it will be for Polish companies, whose dollar value of exports is up 19 percent this year compared to last year.

In the past few years major international firms like Daewoo, Heineken, Asea Brown Boveri, Pepsico, Fiat, International Paper, Sprint, the British glassmaker Pilkington, and ING Bank of the Netherlands have all made major direct investments in Polish companies. They're all betting on rising incomes in Eastern Europe's largest domestic market (population: 38.4 million) to provide them with long-term strategic opportunities through these partnerships, whose value is sure to be reflected in the local capital markets.

The international markets are also starting to notice Poland. In April the State-owned Polish Development Bank became the first institution from Poland in 15 years to tap the Euromarkets when it floated a three-year, $100 million deposit note issue. That was a good first sign of improved investor confidence. Investor confidence was also built by the 1995 landmark Brady deal, which reduced Poland's $14 billion commercial bank debt by about 42 percent, and the $791 million IMF standby agreement finalized in that same year. It would be very encouraging to see the markets welcoming Poland back into sovereign borrowing through the Brady debt reduction process, just as they earlier have done for Mexico, Argentina, the Philippines and other developing countries. That day may well be coming.

It also wouldn't be surprising to see a top private Polish firm do a GDR offering in the not too distant future, just as companies in other emerging markets like India, Chile, Mexico, Colombia and elsewhere have done. That would indicate investors see Poland's equities emerging into the big leagues, as well as its paper.

The progress in Poland has been truly impressive. The

Warsaw Stock Exchange reopened in 1991 after being closed for 52 years. From modest beginnings it has built a solid institutional foundation for itself, including:

- *a local broker network;*
- *computerized settlement on a delivery vs payment and trade date plus one day basis;*
- *private local and foreign custody institutions;*
- *a National Depository where local custodians may keep securities in the name of their customers.*

The Government's Securities Commission regulates the market, and to its credit requires considerable information disclosure by all listed companies, thus providing investor protection. Trading, clearance and settlement functions are automated, so you don't have to go through the irritating, paper-intensive back office struggles that some other emerging markets involve. These are all of fundamental importance for us, and while this is still a young market and has a long way to go, even at this point it doesn't involve anywhere near the kind of pioneering efforts required just next door in Russia, for example.

Despite all this, one of the first things you notice in looking at the WSE is its modest size compared to its potential. As at the end of 1995, market capitalization stood at about $6 billion. That made it only about one-third the size of Prague's stock exchange, even though Poland's population is almost four times the size of the Czech Republic's. The Polish market currently comprises only about 4 percent of national GDP – just one more sign that there's a whole lot out there in this highly promising economy that has yet to come on stream.

The big reason behind this, of course, is the slow pace of privatization in Poland compared to the Czech Republic or Russia. Why? Well, for comparison purposes, recall that the Czechs had continuous leadership under Vaclav Havel and the dynamic free market reformer Vaclav Klaus ever since the fall of Communism. They strongly supported what is considered one of the fastest, deepest, privatization programs the world has yet seen. Their stock market became surprisingly deep in the process.

Poland, on the other hand, had a string of coalition governments, and never built the political backing needed for a mass privatization program that had been discussed since mid-1990. Mass privatization began in 1995, but was unfortunately the subject of endless political squabbling. Setting it back considerably was the well-publicized scandal over February's privatization of Bank Slaski, in which local insiders made huge, quick profits when shares quickly started to trade at 13.5 times the Initial Public Offering (IPO) price. The Prime Minister then fired the Foreign Minister amid charges of incompetence in getting the shares to the public. In the subsequent wrangling three months passed before there was enough consensus in Parliament to install a new minister. With unemployment still a problem in the country that redefined labor politics for the world, no politician will want to support a program that appears to make a few people rich, but leads to large numbers losing their jobs.

The result is that there are so far only about 70 stocks listed in Warsaw. They are almost all companies that have made it through the slow case-by-case privatization process that has been used to date, such as major banks, trading companies, and some industrials and manufacturers. The Government initially restricted foreign purchases of certain "strategic" *equities. That, coupled with illiquidity problems and perceptions that Poland had higher political risk than Hungary or the Czech Republic, meant there was only minimal foreign participation on the WSE until this year. Yet about 500,000 domestic investors emerged in the process, which gave it a good base from which to grow.*

So it was mainly Poles who gained from 1993's huge gains, and mainly Poles who lost in 1994's steep decline. But now we can sense a greater foreign portfolio investor appetite. Outsiders are understandably attracted when the macroeconomic picture looks so good and the market's cumulative P/E ratio has come down to about nine – much more reasonable than the 32 of 1993. Liquidity is increasing now as domestic shareholders start to sell, and there still continues to be no capital gains tax.

The privatization outline called for the government to designate about 15 National Investment Funds (NIFs) to be managed in close partnership with world-class securities firms. Although much still needs to be resolved, the idea was that about 510 companies with total book value of $5.2 billion would be designated for privatization, with 60 percent of their shares going into these funds, 25 percent staying with the State and 15 percent going to the employees. Beginning in November 1996, up to 27 million adult Poles were to receive vouchers to be exchanged for shares in the investment funds, which were designed to speed up restructuring and improved corporate governance of the companies they hold. These NIFs would likely initially list under their own names on the Warsaw market, hopefully from spring 1996, and then eventually dispose of many of their assets through liquidations there as well.

In the meantime, the NIFs could serve as something akin to the "turnaround funds" that are well-known in New York. There was a lot of domestic criticism of the government's close involvement in NIF management teams and its decision to retain an important minority stake in the target companies – things the laissez faire Czech program never allowed – but the basic objectives seemed good, and there's no doubt the process would deepen the capital market. The World Bank and European Bank for Reconstruction and Development (EBRD) were closely involved in the process, both as financiers and advisers, which adds an important external checkpoint.

CIS

CIS stands for Commonwealth of Independent States and is comprised of Russia and former USSR regions which are now independent countries. Armenia, Azerbaijan, Georgia, Kazakhstan, Kyrgyzstan, Turkmenistan, Uzbekistan and Ukraine are just some of the exotic names which have now achieved sovereignty and are pursuing their own individual course of economic development. Some are further along in the process than others, and some have moved closer to free market policies than others. Political stability is also an issue in some areas. By and large, the transition to independence has been surprisingly straight, but further disruptions down the road cannot be ruled out.

While markets are still rudimentary, they are exciting for their frontier nature and the potential that exists when new countries gain the opportunity to control their own destinies. Production that was previously dictated by and in the interests of the central USSR Government can now be diverted, and reorganized to satisfy local objectives. These countries are particularly rich in resources, which are certain to serve as the backbone of their future economic growth.

It is my belief that the potential in the CIS is so large, and the need for Western assistance so great, that the CIS countries and Western investors will reach an accommodation in their negotiations on investment terms and conditions. Much of the value residing in the CIS is not adequately recognized today by the markets, because of the lack of information and, concerns about its reliability.

Kazakhstan

Five times larger than France and a third of the area of the United States, with a population of around 17 million, Kazakhstan is the largest former Soviet Republic, and has successfully made the transition to an independent State. In 1992, it was run by an old-guard Communist leader who had successfully evolved into a popular, elected President strongly in favor of economic liberalism. In 1993, Kazakhstan officials said they wanted their country to become a European Community member. They used

The formerly Communist countries face many problems in privatization, since the change represents a shift in thinking and a revolutionary transformation of thousands of companies.

Asia's fast-growing economies as their economic model, and consulted with leaders of those economies in an attempt to discover the reasons behind their success.

The beginnings of an ambitious mass privatization scheme came in 1993, and covered residential dwellings as well as State-owned enterprises. A combination of vouchers, auctions and tenders was used. To date virtually all residences have been privatized, while the Government retains approximately 39 percent, on average, of company shares it has expressed the willingness to further reduce these holdings.

Kazakhstan has significant natural resources still to be developed, and which will contribute significantly to its economic growth prospects. A major regional oil producer, Kazakhstan also has gold and base metals deposits. The tangled process of sorting out ownership and distribution of these resources is still being confronted by the local Government, but progress has been made. More importantly, the underlying commitment to reform and progress remains strong in this country.

Ukraine

The Ukraine is famous around the world for being Russia's breadbasket, and also for having suffered particularly harsh hardships under Soviet control. Today, the Ukraine is the second largest ex-Soviet Republic, with 52 million people. An ambitious privatization program was launched in 1993. It involved the free issue of vouchers, and the use of investment funds as intermediaries, as in the case of Poland and the Czech and Slovak Republics. It is estimated that about 40 percent of the shares in large enterprises would be privatized by that method, with the rest sold by more conventional methods to local and foreign buyers.

The formerly Communist countries face many problems in privatization, since the change represents a shift in thinking and a revolutionary transformation of thousands of companies. There are serious differences of opinion regarding what the objectives of privatization should be. In some cases it is a key to reducing Government debt, whereas in other cases it is seen as a way of luring foreign capital.

Ukraine can also rely on significant natural resources to further its development. Agriculture, aluminum, coal, and some gas production, are examples of sectors that will make an important contribution to national wealth generation. A broad, if outmoded, industrial sector also exists in the country. The Black Sea port of Odessa is a strategic asset set in the Ukraine, making it a center for shipping. A strong overseas connection with Ukrainian emigrants is also contributing to development, by providing the Ukraine with management and investment support.

Mobius'
Field Notes

Alma-Ata, Kazakhstan – October 1995

Alma-Ata, with a population of 1.2 million is very much like the cities one finds in Siberia. Large blocks of apartments and offices line the street in staid Soviet style architecture. There are wide tree-lined streets though everything was in a general state of disrepair.

At the Kazakhstan Hotel the "reservation charge" was US$120 and the daily room rate US$220 for what would pass for a "suite type" room which goes for US$85 in the US. The telephone in the room was not hooked to the hotel operator but is a direct line outside. If you want to call overseas you must make a reservation with the international operator who will connect you. Digital phones have not yet appeared in this hotel. Reservations in this enormous hotel, built in the mass Soviet style with plenty of granite and marble, are by appointment only with the female manager who appears at the hotel only occasionally. When we wanted to check in late at night, the lady at the desk demanded our passport and letter of introduction. From our point of view at that time, the number one investment priority was definitely a decent hotel with good service!

Kazakhstan is a large country with substantial resources. With a land area of 2.7 million square kilometers (1.1 million square miles), it is larger than Bolivia, Colombia, Egypt, Iran, Indonesia, Malaysia, Mongolia, or Mexico.

Flying out of Alma-Ata, we flew over China on our way to Hong Kong. We started out over the spectacular extensive snow-capped Tien Shan mountain range which serves as a rugged barrier between China and Kazakhstan. Looking at the geography with the high mountains separating China from Kazakhstan and the plains separating the country from Russia, it is easy to understand why the language most heard in Alma-Ata is Russian, and why the influence is so heavily Russian.

⬤ RUSSIA

The former Deputy Prime Minister of the USSR once said that improving the economic situation in Russia could be best summarized in three words: stabilization, liberalization and privatization. He said that there was a need to develop alternative uses for the savings of the people accumulated over many years, so that they were not only spent on consumer goods, but invested in things such as real estate developments, stocks, bonds and new private businesses. He summed up the need for privatization when he said that in the Communist Soviet system, there were no owners, but there were State bureaucrats dealing in such things as finance, land, raw materials, legal issues, and approval or disapproval of businesses. This was in contrast to a market economy where the private sector made those decisions.

Russia is one of the largest and resource-rich nations in the world. In addition, it has achieved some major advances in technology. As a result of the recent privatization program, over 100,000 companies were privatized and over 40 million Russians became shareholders in about 14,000 medium and large enterprises. This augurs well for the development of capital markets in Russia. Developments in Russia are moving fast and the early investors like Templeton gain exposure to the market, the better the possibilities of success.

The pains of Russia's transition are evident in its economic performance over the past several years. During this period, real GDP fell while inflation accelerated sharply. However, in the face of the overall decline in GDP the small private sector, especially in the services industries, has been booming. In fact, since much of the activity is not captured in the official output figures, the extent of the economic contraction may be overstated. Despite its economic problems, Russia maintains its status as a world superpower. This status affords Russia special treatment from both Western and Eastern governments, which have a strong interest in the country's economic success and political stability.

We tend to seek out countries that try to educate their populations. Russia holds interest for us because even under the Communist regime, they educated their people well technically, which augurs well for their future. It also helps, though, to have a minimum of Government interference, or at least a Government that facilitates economic growth, individual initiative and industriousness. Education is one thing, but there has to be a framework in which education can be put to use. Because at the end of the day, what is economic growth? It's productivity, nothing else. Only education and incentives can improve productivity. The incentives were missing in the Russian Communist equation, but that's all changing now.

As early as 1993, according to reports at that time, Russia's accelerating privatization program was approaching the point at which 20 medium and large firms were being auctioned almost every 14 days. By early 1993, the Russian Federation had already privatized 55,000 enterprises and, by the end of that year, its plan called for a total of as many as 50,000 small companies to be sold off, plus 10,000 to 15,000 medium-sized and large concerns. One London merchant banker said that, even if the Russian program reached 50 percent of its goal, it would easily qualify as the world's largest ever privatization program. The Russian privatization program, which began in October 1992, called for one voucher being issued to each of the country's 150 million citizens. Parts of the Czech, Slovak and Polish systems of distribution to the adult public, with investment funds acting as intermediaries, was chosen by Russia as one element for privatization of large enterprises.

The distribution of privatization vouchers free of charge through local savings banks to every man, woman and child (approximately 150 million people) was begun in late 1992. The vouchers could be used to buy shares directly or they could be pledged to investment funds to buy shares on their behalf. By the end of January 1993, 96 percent of Russians had received vouchers which they could exchange for shares in newly privatized firms at auctions. However, there was no regulatory system to control trading of vouchers and shares and in one case, 350,000 investors were swindled out of their vouchers. Two investment funds, Amaras and Revanche, advertised for people to invest their vouchers in their funds. They promised to pay 120 percent of the voucher face value after one month. But after the promoters collected the vouchers, they fled.

Russia, 30 November 1995

We arrived in Yekaterinburg at midnight local time and were met at the airport. Driving through the city, we passed the site where the last Czar, Nicholas II, was murdered. On the site is a very small circular log chapel and another log building which had been burnt by arsonists and was now being guarded by descendants of Cossacks, the military caste under the Czar. The Cossack black, yellow and white flag was flying there. On a drive outside the city at a police checkpoint we saw one of the Cossacks with a long moustache, in full uniform, on the opposite side of the street from where the regular policeman was standing. Our driver said that the Cossacks were not allowed to carry weapons but they did a good job in helping the police and kept good civil order. They beat people on the behind with a rotan if they misbehave. I told him that that's what they do in Singapore too and it is a good custom.

We also visited a new statue commemorating the Russian soldiers who died in Afghanistan. The large statue depicts an exhausted soldier sitting with his head bowed on his rifle. We also passed a new business center under construction which included a hotel, shops and other facilities being built under the supervision of an Austrian construction company – which would hopefully mean better quality construction since many of the buildings in Russia are not of good quality.

We were here to visit Sverdlovsk Energo. We were greeted by officials from the company at the hotel and driven around the city of Yekaterinburg, and then went to their plant on the outskirts of the city. The fuel they use produces a lot of ash, which can be used in making roads. They said they are thinking of exporting the ash to Asia. The plant was 13 years old. We were greeted by the general manager and a few officials. A US flag was hanging outside the plant and during the visit our guide told us that they had a number of visitors from America in their industry, which was good for international co-operation and understanding.

After trips to two plants in Yekaterinburg, we were comparing notes and talking about the Russian accounting system and what things were like before the recent changes. One Russian researcher said: "Twelve years ago, during Andropov, before perestroika, I was working in a plant producing rocket engines for the Russian shuttle and I figured out how to do a job in two days which normally would have taken five days, and the other people asked me, 'Why did you do that?,' since I was going to be paid the same anyway.

"In those days, all workers got the same pay. There were certain classes of workers according to qualifications but the differences were minimal. I received US$150 per month as a starting worker but an experienced worker would get US$180 per month. We would get free medicine but the quality was very poor. You could get the medicine free from the State doctor and it wouldn't cure you or you could pay extra and get the medicine which could cure you," he told me.

He also told me a joke about a woman who went to a Russian doctor and said that she had a headache and stomach ache, so the doctor took one tablet and broke it in two and said: "One half is for the stomach and one half for the headache – and don't get them mixed up!"

We went next to visit the Seversky Tube Works in Polevskoy. The drive from Yekaterinburg took about one hour through fields shielded by tall trees lining the road. At one point we passed the landmark and monument which marked the division of European and Asian Russia. The monument was covered in graffiti, and in a ditch at the foot of the monument was a pile of broken glass from beer, wine, vodka and champagne bottles. I was told that people come here to celebrate weddings and other special events.

We were about one hour late and we were told it was too late to arrange a visit to the factory. Our guide was Mr Alexia Degas, the Commercial Director. He had a businesslike demeanor and facial characteristics which were Chinese. He was very much at home in ruling the financial world at this company. His office was protected from noise by double doors. It was neat and his desk was almost clear of clutter and paper. He came right to the point. "What do you want? What is your business?" he asked.

I told him that we were interested in purchasing shares in the company, but before that we needed to learn more about the company. He said that we could have any information we wanted. I asked for audited financial statements, at which point he seemed exasperated, and then said that they did not want to spend US$500,000 on an audit by a Western audit firm. He finally produced a two-page balance sheet.

The flight from Yekaterinburg to Chelyabinsk was about 45 minutes. If we had driven it would have taken at least three hours over uncertain roads. The airport at Chelyabinsk is almost a carbon copy of the airport at Yekaterinburg, with exactly the same older-style building with a clock tower and a more modern building in the Soviet style attached to it. It was a rainy and cold mid-August day, but it cleared up later so when we took off again we could admire the yellow wheat fields scattered among the green forests.

We were here to visit the Chelyabinsk Integrated Iron and Steel Works. Our guide was Victor Kolchin, the Economic Director. He had light gray eyes, blond/brown hair, and a gray suit and tie, and his lined face was the essence of a hardened, long-suffering product of the Soviet planned economy. The difference between him and the other people I had met on this trip was that he was painfully honest. He said that he had been working in the plant since he had graduated from the university more than 20 years ago. He was facing a "difficult situation," he said, as he chain-smoked "Bond" cigarettes.

He told us that the plant was started in 1943 with a steel smelting operation. It was a combination of various plants moved from other parts of Russia in order to be safe from the German invasion. The design of the plant was based on a 1930s plan for a high-quality steel plant, but parts were added during the Khrushchev and Breshnev eras when there was a big push on to produce more iron and steel in an attempt to outdo the US When he gave us the output figures, we were shocked. He said that its capacity for stainless steel sheet production was 250,000 tons per year, but that in 1994 they had produced only 35,000 tons. Production capacity for stainless steel for pipes and other types of stainless steel was 300,000 tons per year but they actually produced only 40,000 tons in 1994.

That afternoon, we took off from Chelyabinsk at 12.50 and arrived in Magnitogorsk an hour later. The city is on a wide plain filled with wheat fields and dotted with small lakes and ponds. The earth looked rich and almost black. The Magnitogorsk Airport was almost deserted when we arrived and was the same again when we left. There were a number of planes parked on the tarmac but no real activity. We were now in the Republic of Bashkortostan, one of the republics of the Russian Federation.

We were met at the airport by a young man who was an assistant to the foreign relations bureau of the Magnitogorsk Iron and Steel Works. He was quite efficient but didn't say very much about the company. After a half-hour drive to the plant site, he took us to the highest point of a hill overlooking the complex. This hill is the site of the open-cast iron ore mine, which was the original source of iron ore for the plant. He said there is still some mining going on around the area and farther away. We then took a tour of the complex. It is a huge enterprise and from the hill we could see that the plant really comprised a small city, with numerous buildings and smokestacks. A few of the buildings were clearly quite new.

One of our hosts, Mr. Vladimir Ivanovich Shmakov, the Head of the Investment Department, was stylishly dressed, fast-talking and aggressive, with a very businesslike manner. He was obviously a deal-maker. He told us the plant was started in 1929 and began producing iron in 1932. Nowadays, they produce all sorts of iron and steel and they also produce consumer goods such as enameled kitchenware, wood furniture, meat products, baked goods, and dairy products. They also run a holiday resort, kindergarten, tramway, culture palace, etc. These operations are a legacy of the Communist days when the plant looked after the entire area's social needs.

In this section we consider in greater detail the unique conditions prevailing in emerging markets and how they lead to higher investment returns.

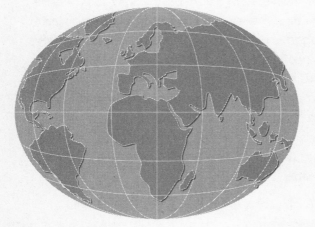

Chapter 5

Financial Growth in Emerging Markets

We have already considered the broad macroeconomic picture in emerging markets. In this section we consider in greater detail the unique conditions prevailing in emerging markets and how these conditions lead to higher investment returns.

● CAPITAL MARKET GROWTH

The term "capital markets" refers to the broad area of financial exchange of money, bonds, stocks and other financial instruments. The concept covers fixed income, debt, equity, foreign exchange and commodities (Figure 5.1). Such markets become necessary as financial transactions become more complicated. Simple bank loans and letters of credit are being elaborated by many kinds of derivatives in the course of sophisticated trade and economic transfers. This is especially true in a large economy, where a large volume of complicated deals are transacted every day.

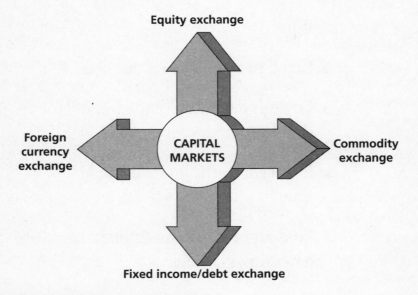

Fig 5.1   Representation of capital markets

Growth of capital markets is indicative of a deep and active market for the exchange of goods as well as money. Without reliable capital markets, the exchange of goods is hampered and private trade is slowed or made impossible. It is also an important mechanism for the transfer of capital surplus holders to capital deficit entities. For example, a pension fund may have funds available to invest, while a company may require funds for upgrading their production capacity. Capital markets enable an exchange of funds between these two market participants, via the sale of bonds by the company, the purchase of company stocks by the fund or more indirectly via the use of other financial instruments.

In Communist countries there is no theoretical need for capital markets, because the State believes it can efficiently allocate all resources, including money, where it is most needed and best utilized. Today, these ideas have been pretty effectively denigrated by the economic failure of Communist countries. As Communist systems are discarded, we find increasing numbers of countries reintroducing capital markets in order to achieve an efficient distribution of capital within their borders.

Open capital markets (as opposed to closed systems) serve as an excellent channel of foreign funds into a domestic economy. This is called "portfolio investment" and differs from direct foreign investment, in which foreign capital directly purchases equipment and land in order to manufacture in the domestic economy. We will explore the role of foreign capital in a domestic setting later on in this chapter.

For decades countries have employed many mechanisms for preventing the introduction of foreign capital into their economy. There has traditionally been a reluctance to allow foreign lenders to gain control over "national" entities via capital markets. Government officials of lower income countries have feared the potential for domination by higher income countries due to their ability to buy up all of the productive resources in the domestic economy.

In the context of this book, we will be examining primarily

equity markets. However, there are emerging market debt funds and there are advanced and sophisticated, debt markets in emerging markets.

EQUITY MARKETS

The expansion of emerging equity markets has been rapid. As local firms tap into investment pools through equity offerings they are able to invest in more new machinery, and to begin previously unaffordable research and development activities. And as such companies develop internationally recognized reputations, and are assigned internationally acceptable credit ratings, debt instruments become more widely utilized by firms interested in raising investment capital, but unwilling to dilute their existing corporate ownership stakes.

Emerging stock markets around the world constitute only around 10 percent of total global market capitalization (Figure 5.2). As of 1995, the total capitalization of the world's stock markets was about US$15 trillion, of which the United States accounted for US$8 trillion, Japan for US$5.7 trillion, and the United Kingdom US$1.3 trillion. The balance of global capitalization is that of the emerging markets, a paltry US$2 trillion. In 1995, Asia comprised 58 percent of emerging market capitalization. Latin America was next, with 20 percent, Sub-Saharan Africa comes in at 15 percent and the Middle East and Eastern Europe make up the final 7 percent (Figure 5.2).

It is worth noting, though, that emerging markets are expanding at a faster rate than the developed markets. Between 1980 and 1995, emerging markets grew by 1,283 percent, whereas developed markets grew at half that rate – 663 percent (Figure 5.3). The potential for growth of the emerging equity markets is also clear when one reviews the market capitalizations as a percentage of national GDP. The developed markets in the US, UK and Japan had a ratio of market capitalization to GDP which averaged 144 percent in 1994. The emerging economies, on the

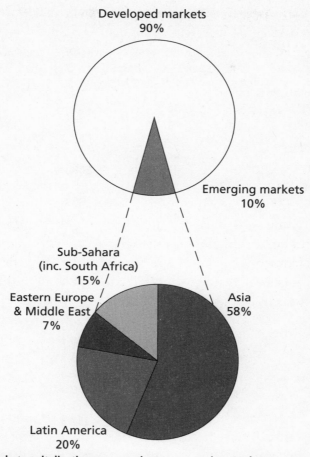

Developed markets
90%

Emerging markets
10%

Sub-Sahara
(inc. South Africa)
15%

Eastern Europe
& Middle East
7%

Asia
58%

Latin America
20%

**Fig 5.2   Market capitalization: perspectives on emerging markets
as at end-December 1995**

Source: Merrill Lynch

other hand, averaged only 64 percentage of market capitalization to GDP ratio. This in itself represents a significant catch-up. The corresponding figure in 1990 was only 33 percent. In the larger emerging markets such as Hong Kong, Malaysia, and Singapore, the percentage of market capitalization to GDP is quite high. The majority of emerging markets, however, have low ratios: 15 countries on our list come in with less than 50 percent market capitalization to GDP. These numbers indicate that the emerging markets have a long way to go before their full capacity for equity market growth is reached (Table 5.1).

Table 5.1 Market Capitalization as a percentage of GDP (as at 31 December 1994)

	Market capitalization (US$ billion)	GDP (US$ billion)	Market capitalization/ GDP %
Emerging markets			
Argentina	36.9	281.9	13.1
Bangladesh	1.0	25.8	3.9
Brazil	189.3	593.8	31.9
Chile	68.1	52.1	130.7
China	43.5	508.2	8.6
Colombia	14.0	65.0	21.5
Greece	14.9	95.6	15.6
Hong Kong	269.5	131.8	204.5
India	127.5	288.9	44.1
Indonesia	47.2	174.6	27.0
Jordan	4.6	5.3	86.8
Korea	191.8	379.6	50.5
Malaysia	199.3	70.6	282.2
Mexico	130.2	370.2	35.2
Pakistan	12.3	52.0	23.6
Peru	8.2	50.1	16.4
Philippines	55.6	63.2	88.0
Portugal	16.2	82.8	19.6
Singapore	134.5	69.0	195.1
Sri Lanka	2.9	11.7	24.8
Taiwan	247.3	237.8	104.0
Thailand	130.5	143.2	91.1
Turkey	21.6	132.5	16.3
Venezuela	4.1	55.6	7.4
Average			64.2
Developed markets			
Japan	3720	5108.0	72.8
United Kingdom	1210.2	423.1	286.0
United States	5081.8	6931.0	73.3
Average			144.0

Sources: International Finance Corporation; *Censensus Forecasts*; Consensus Economics Inc.; Institute of International Finance

In addition, current indications are that the number of companies listed on emerging stock markets is growing faster than in the developed markets. Between 1980 and 1995 the number of companies listed on emerging markets grew on average 137 percent, while the number in the three major developed markets grew by 53 percent. The growth figures in emerging markets was high, with 12 countries having well over 100 percent growth during the period (Table 5.2).

Table 5.2 Number of listed companies, 1980–95

	1980	1995	Change (%)
Emerging markets			
Argentina	278	149	−46
Bangladesh	22	170	673
Brazil	426	543	27
Chile	265	313	18
China	n/a	323	n/a
Colombia	193	117	−39
Greece	116	212	83
Hong Kong	137	532	288
India	2,265	7,500	231
Indonesia	6	238	3,867
Jordan	71	97	37
Korea	352	721	105
Malaysia	182	529	191
Mexico	259	185	−29
Pakistan	314	764	143
Peru	103	246	139
Philippines	195	205	5
Portugal	25	169	576
Singapore	103	247	140
Sri Lanka	171	226	32
Taiwan	102	347	240
Thailand	77	416	440
Turkey	314	205	−35
Venezuela	98	90	−8
Total	6,074	14,395	137
Developed markets			
Japan	1,402	3,005	114
United Kingdom	2,655	2,284	−14
United States	6,251	10,507	68
Total	3,436	5,265	53

Sources: International Finance Corporation; Swiss Bank Corporation; Euromoney; author's estimates

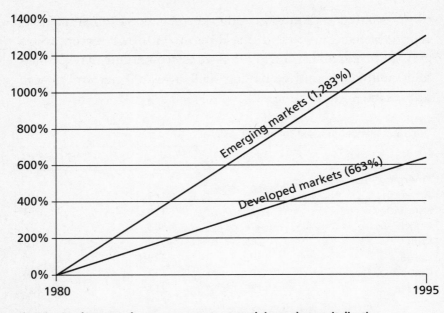

Fig 5.3   Market growth rate: percentage growth in market capitalization since 1980

Source: IFC; author's estimates

The reform of capital markets has gradually eliminated one of the greatest brakes on corporate expansion in emerging markets: the high cost of capital. Several changes in how capital is transferred mean that capital users can obtain investment funds at lower interest costs, with lower processing costs than ever before.

Increased availability of surplus capital

Stable economic conditions in the domestic market encourage citizens to keep their funds in the country and use them domestically, instead of squirreling them away at home or funneling them to other countries. Surplus capital was formerly transferred out of the domestic economy as quickly as possible, a process called capital flight, in order to take advantage of more secure financial systems elsewhere. Today, many lower income countries have a better grasp of their economic fundamentals, and that has led most domestic holders of surplus capital to keep that money in the country and invest it locally. In fact, the improved economic picture has led to foreign investment in emerging markets, on the scale of US$ billions every year (Figure 5.4). During the peak year of 1993 alone, over US$60 billion in equity capital moved into emerging markets.

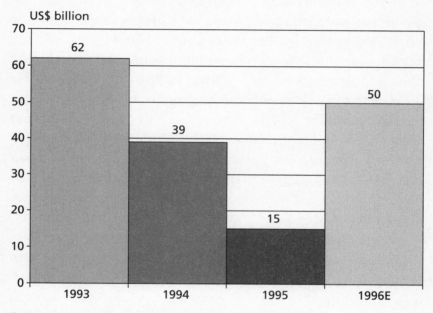

Fig 5.4   Emerging markets: equity capital in-flows 1992–6
Source: ING Baring

Reform of inefficient domestic financial markets

The actual process of making a financial transaction has been a great hindrance to wider market activity. The cost and time required to register certificates, ensure proper custodianship, transfer payments and lengthy approval processes have all conspired to drive many market participants away and into alternative forms of capital exchange. As governments have come to recognize the drag an inefficient market system places on the economy as a whole, wide-ranging reforms have been implemented and financial markets are gradually becoming efficient places in which to complete financial transactions.

Deregulating interest rates

Interest rates have long been a sensitive topic in lower-income countries, especially those with fixed exchange rates. Interest rate movements are the means by which an economy can be slowed or stimulated, as they act like a brake on an acceleration of spending. If interest rates rise to 25 percent but inflation stays below that rate, as a business person you are less likely to borrow money for the purchase of machinery, or as a consumer, to borrow money to purchase a refrigerator. It is also true that countries use the interest rates as a political tool, often to appease domestic interest groups. For this reason, interest rates in lower-income countries have often been fixed, changing only to satisfy domestic pressure groups. In this way, interest rates are highly politicized as an economic tool in emerging markets.

Many governments, however, are now coming to appreciate the benefits that accrue to the economic system if interest rates are depoliticized and left to act as independent market indicators, to float up or down with demand. This process of deregulating (and depoliticizing) interest rates has made open capital markets possible.

● CREATION OF NEW STOCK MARKETS

It is only in recent years that capital market development (especially equity markets) has been taken seriously by emerging market government planners and multilateral institutions. In the 1960s and 1970s, governments often looked at stock markets as merely gambling dens which drained financial resources away from the "real" economy. Gradually, however, meaningful literature on the subject of the role of capital markets in economic development began to appear, and it was gradually concluded that such markets played a vital role as allocators of capital and generators of capital for industrial growth.

Some observers have said that the growth of capital markets has a direct impact on the economic growth of the country. This is so because the development of equity markets focuses attention on the importance of the efficient allocation of capital. Efficient allocation of capital gives new entrants in the economic community access to capital, and assists income distribution. Experiences in the 1970s and 1980s do indicate that those countries which have had high economic growth also have successful equity markets. Brazil serves as an example, where growth rates fell after policies favoring the equity capital markets were reversed, while at the same time countries such as South Korea, which encouraged capital market development, experienced high economic growth. Of course, there are more factors to consider, since the establishment of an efficient equity market requires conditions similar to those required for a fast-growing economy. Such factors might be an efficient legal structure or rising educational attainments.

Emerging stock markets are expanding at a rate of at least twice that of the mature markets, as was earlier demonstrated in Figure 5.3. This growth can be seen via trading volumes and the number of stocks listed in those markets. Faster economic growth has resulted in higher savings available for stock market investments. Although from time to time, emerging markets are influenced by foreign investors, over time most emerging markets are dominated by domestic, not international, investors, and the dynamic of domestic savings is what is making those markets grow rapidly.

Although from time to time, emerging markets are influenced by foreign investors, over time most emerging markets are dominated by domestic, not international, investors, and the dynamic of domestic savings is what is making those markets grow rapidly.

Capital markets are absorbing an increasing proportion of the growth in savings which were previously almost exclusively deposited in banks. Market capitalization as a percentage of GNP is rising in the emerging markets and is proof of this trend. The expanding interest in emerging markets also provides an excellent opportunity for the emerging nations to replace debt with equity, and so ease the burden of interest payments. Unfortunately, this has not been recognized in a positive way by most developing nations because of the remaining fears of colonialism and foreign domination. However, attitudes are changing, and more governments are recognizing the value of portfolio investments as a means of attracting long-term risk capital. A number of countries, particularly in South America, have had successful debt for equity conversion programs. Chile has been a leader in this field and, as a result, has not only reduced its foreign debt burden, but has also attracted valuable foreign technology and managerial expertise.

More and more government officials of lower-income countries are coming to appreciate the importance of a stock exchange, first to channel investment capital into businesses and second, to act as a market for the exchange of financial securities. There is a growing realization that more has to be done. For example, in December 1992, President Fidel Ramos of the Philippines said:

"… with respect to the goal of developing our capital market, we are still short of the objective. The condition of our securities industry mirrors the economy as a whole, and is not quite developed and still short of what it could be. This is of special concern to our Government today because unless we are more dynamic and aggressive in the business of capital formation, we might as well forget our hope of reaching NIC status in 1998 … Let me emphasize this: the development of our capital market is the key priority and strategy of my administration. We realize that investments, both domestic and foreign, are key factors for sustained and sustainable economic development. These investments won't come unless investors are fully assured of a fair and efficient market-place."

Besides the obvious category of brokers and investors, securities markets contribute to systemic financial development in other ways. First, capital markets are useful to private companies, in prodding what is too often a moribund banking system to better satisfy their needs. By competing head on with banks to provide financing to the private sector, capital markets spur the banks to improve efficiency and service levels. Instead of going to the neighbourhood banker, and accepting usurious interest rates and fees to take out a loan, companies are able to issue debt via bonds or equity via company shares as alternative ways of raising necessary business capital. This direct competition for business drives banks to reformulate their policies and introduce competitive financial products, in order to retain traditional customers.

Securities markets also help banks in several ways. Secondary trading in securities held by the bank allows banks to secure their debt and to actively manage the risk profile of their balance sheet. Securities markets also contribute to the success of privatization programs. The potential for secondary trading, so that investors can liquidate their holdings, is what makes their initial investments in privatized companies attractive. Privatization adds significantly to the stock of equity available in an emerging economy, necessitating security market expansion. For all of these reasons, capital markets are a critical ingredient of reform in any growing economy.

EMERGING MARKET COMPANIES IN DEVELOPED MARKETS

As an alternative to their own thinly traded exchanges, some companies based in emerging markets are finding an eager welcome on the stock markets of mature economies. When we started the Templeton Emerging Markets Fund in 1987, the range of markets available to us was severely limited. We thus sought companies listed in New York and London which had most or a large proportion of their business and earnings from emerging markets. We found most such companies in London, where firms such as Antofagasta, a diversified Chilean company with major holdings in transportation and mining, and Ottoman Bank, a Turkish bank, were listed. Purchases of these stocks enabled us to obtain exposure to the economies of Turkey and Chile, whose markets were not yet open to us for more direct investment.

Today's enhanced reputation of emerging market companies has enabled firms to list directly on the major developed country markets. For example, in December of 1992, a Chinese firm, Brilliance China Automotive was listed on the New York Stock Exchange, by-passing the possibility of issuing "B" shares on the Shanghai or Shenzhen stock markets or an "H" share listing on the Hong Kong stock market. That issue was so well-received that the share price more than doubled and rose from the offer price of US$16 to US$33 at the end of 1992. The result of this resounding success was a rush on the part of mainland companies to list their firms outside their own markets in places such as Vancouver and Hong Kong.

Investors interested in Chinese shares were surprised that a mainland company could get a New York Stock Exchange listing and were rueful they had purchased "B" shares on the mainland exchanges, where due diligence and investor protection leaves a lot to be desired in comparison with the highly regulated US market.

● DOMESTIC PORTFOLIO INVESTMENT GROWTH

One big reason for domestic growth in equity investment relates to long-term savings. In a World Bank report on social security systems in Latin America, it was concluded that most systems in Spanish-speaking Latin America (Chile, Costa Rica, Ecuador,

Mexico and Peru) were decapitalized over a number of years. Social security institutions, even though they were autonomous under public charters, were required to invest exclusively in government bonds that paid negative real rates of interest during periods of high inflation. As the real value of their portfolios declined, the funds depended more each year on current revenues to finance current expenditures on healthcare services, disability and pension payments. By the end of the 1980s, none of the traditional systems held assets capable of supporting certain future obligations for pensions and survivor benefits.

This has led countries to move towards a private form of social security saving for individual retirement. In turn, this has generated a pool of patient, ready equity investment capital looking for a long-term home. Privatization of pension systems is also advisable because of their poor past investment performance. Chile was one of the first countries to move in this direction, whereas Mexico passed a law only in 1991 to create a compulsory pension fund system to be managed by the recently privatized banks. As such changes percolate throughout emerging markets, they are expected to increase domestic savings by US$1 billion per year. Once the pension funds start to invest in the debt and equity of private companies, they will have a significant impact on local bourses. As an example, new rules regulating Mexican fund managers require 50 percent of pension holdings to be allocated to equities, and the balance to other financial instruments.

Capital flight returns

Capital flight, as mentioned above, occurs when domestic money holders export their funds across borders, in the expectation that its store of value will be more stable in the other country than when kept at home. The phenomenon most often occurs in high inflation economic environments, in which the value of domestic currency undergoes repeated and drastic devaluations and loss of purchasing power. Such flight also occurs in countries with unstable political regimes, where the expectation of confiscation, extortion or other manipulation is high (Figure 5.5).

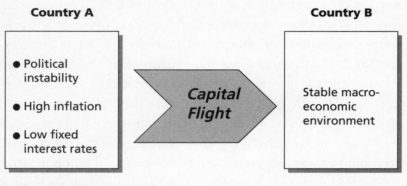

Fig 5.5   Capital flight process

Other reasons for flight can be low returns on bank deposit due to artificially low interest rates or an uncertain political situation, causing investors to store money offshore in case a quick exit is needed. A domestic capital market represents an alternative source of good returns and less currency risk than sending money overseas, in the absence of overwhelming pressure to send money out of the country. The existence of an independent, functioning, trustworthy market usually indicates that the circumstances requiring capital flight in the first place have changed.

Unfortunately, the process can become ingrained, especially where it is relatively easy to export the capital, say from Mexico to the United States. This loss of surplus capital has a strong negative effect on the local economy and is therefore an important problem for a number of emerging markets. The World Bank has estimated that between 1980 and 1984, capital flight from Argentina was about US$16 billion, US$40 billion from Mexico, and US$27 billion from Venezuela. In some years, capital flight from Argentina and Venezuela was equivalent to half the level of savings in those countries, in those years.

In addition to foreign institutional money, which may be harnessed by improved emerging equity markets, it is possible that considerable capital sent overseas from domestic sources may also be attracted back to the home markets. The dismantling of foreign exchange controls combined with the growth of capital markets in emerging nations has resulted in the return of that flight capital in many emerging nations.

In Pakistan in the late 1990s, liberalization moves by the Government resulted in a massive inflow of funds from overseas Pakistanis. One young Pakistani told me: "When the new measures were introduced, I sold my house and all other things I had in America and moved back here. One of my friends transferred US$5 million in a single transaction. We are all rejoicing that we can return to our home country and do the businesses we were prohibited from doing before these liberalization measures were introduced."

FOREIGN PORTFOLIO INVESTMENT IN EMERGING MARKETS

One of the challenges faced in emerging markets is gaining the support of government agencies associated with capital market regulation to permit foreign investment. There is a wide range of official attitudes to foreign capital. These attitudes can change over time, depending on the objectives of specific policies and officials. At times, government policies have even been known to work to the advantage of foreign investors. But the rules are more often designed to dissuade foreign investment, employing both discrete and explicit mechanisms to restrict international capital inflows.

Yet as was noted earlier in the book, governments are increasingly in agreement that foreign capital as a whole is not really dangerous to the domestic economy. It has long been my personal opinion that in fact foreign portfolio investment has a crit-

The introduction of foreign capital into a given economy allows the businesses in that economy to grow at a faster rate than would be possible if only domestic sources of capital were mobilized. In this way, foreign portfolio investment helps pull down barriers to economic expansion.

ical role to play in the world's capital markets. In the case of stock market growth in Taiwan and Indonesia, the introduction of foreign investors into the market definitely acted as a catalyst, stimulating local investment (Figure 5.6). Foreign investment also has demonstration effects, spotlighting companies that offer the most transparent financial information and best valuations. I have seen the same phenomenon in many other emerging markets – the introduction of foreign funds into emerging markets has a clear, beneficial influence on market growth and structure. Foreign capital is good for emerging markets. It stimulates the economy, boosts confidence and complements local capital invested in productive enterprises. When a foreign portfolio investor buys a new issue of stocks on the local stock exchange, the citizen or company who sold those stocks

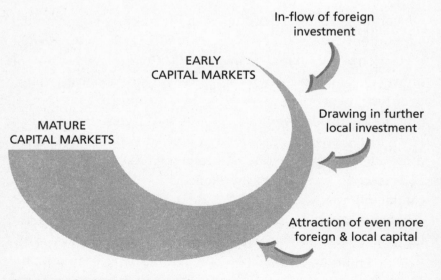

Fig 5.6   Foreign investment as catalyst

receives money that can be used to buy new, locally made, consumer goods, productive industrial equipment, or repay burdensome debt. The introduction of foreign capital into a given economy allows the businesses in that economy to grow at a faster rate than would be possible if only domestic sources of capital were mobilized. In this way, foreign portfolio investment helps pull down barriers to economic expansion.

Recognizing this, governments are now more likely to be selectively wary of foreign portfolio capital. Of particular concern to governments seems to be the notion of "hot" money. This kind of portfolio investment is perceived to be random, speculative and unreliable. Governments fear that such investment can effectively create instabilities in the domestic economy, by artificially moving currency values, or pushing up equity values beyond their fundamentals. Some countries have moved to restrict entry to short-term capital. The central bank of Malaysia, faced with a rapidly appreciating currency in 1993, laid the blame at the door of short-term portfolio capital, and required local banks to hold all foreign currency deposits for more than 120 days. This action did short-circuit the speculative capital flows, although it also had the negative side-effect of burning some investor's fingers and left a cloud over Malaysia's financial reputation for some time.

Yet even short-term capital doesn't necessarily deserve the approbrium heaped on it. A recent report from Lehman Brother's Global Economic Group has offered an alternative analysis of foreign portfolio investment, suggesting that there is little difference between short-term and long-term in terms of volatility and, by extension, impact on local economic conditions. Lehman's contends that it is not the time factor which matters to the economy, but rather the use to which the funds are put – whether it is productive or unproductive investment, to finance investment or consumption. Such distinctions should be heeded by emerging market regulators, as they help such agencies to implement more effective domestic policies without excluding foreign capital participation.

It is important for governments in emerging markets to acknowledge more openly the catalytic effect of foreign portfolio investments in the domestic market. The acceptance of foreign portfolio investors still has a long way to go in many countries. The reasons for this are not consistent. In some instances, it may simply be the case that the government is not comfortable with the concept of portfolio investment as practiced in the developed countries. This usually comes down to a fear of loss of control over key local businesses. Often local governments fail to distinguish between foreign portfolio and direct investments. Portfolio investors do not, as a rule, exert management control over the enterprises in which they invest. By their charters they are often forbidden to become involved in management and even are barred from sitting on the boards of directors of their investments. The reasons for this are obvious, since portfolio managers maintain holdings so extensive and varied that becoming involved with the running of all the companies in which they had invested would require untold time and manpower. Additionally, this oversight role would reduce the flexibility of the portfolio manager to move from one investment to another, a flexibility every manager values highly. An understanding of this should comfort those officials uneasy about foreign control over local enterprises.

Some governments are dismayed by the rush of foreign investors who temporarily push up local equity prices. It is true that many countries have experienced stock run-ups driven by foreign capital. Greece experienced this in 1984, Portugal in 1986, Turkey and Indonesia in 1989, Venezuela in 1990, and Peru in 1992. Such run-ups are disconcerting in the short run, but can just as easily be perceived as a boon to the local economy as a threat to it. Once markets have been open to foreign investment for some time, however, investors become increasingly familiar with specific companies, and are less likely to run-up the market as a whole. Instead, their investment decisions are more soundly based on the fundamentals.

Another anxiety felt among emerging market regulators is the potential for sudden drops in shareholdings, spurred by mass redemptions of foreign mutual funds without regard for local economic circumstances. It is true that most portfolio investors need to be able to liquefy their holdings on short notice, and quite frequently. The bulk of international portfolio investments are made on behalf of pension funds and open-ended mutual funds of unit trusts, where shareholder or pensioner redemptions are constantly received and where the fund manager is committed to honor such requests on demand. Part of the process of global financial development, though, is the education of investors towards long-term shareholding. In the case of the Templeton Emerging Markets Fund, for example, the annual portfolio turnover has averaged about 20 percent in recent years. Our average holding period has been five years. While we have the capacity to buy and sell investments in a given country in as short a time period as a week, it is more often the case that, as portfolio investors, we invest in all markets for the long term. This trend should alleviate regulator concerns about a mass exodus from their markets.

As a foreign portfolio manager, I'm entitled to my own grudge against regulators. One bugbear of mine regards capital gains taxes. Foreign portfolio investors put their investments at the service of local business, incuring risks along the way. They don't deserve to see their returns eroded by iniquitous taxes. While it may appear on the surface tax changes will raise extra revenue for government, in the end, such moves cost the country dearly in terms of the lost benefits that foreign capital brings. New export goods won't be manufactured, jobs won't be created, and valuable skills won't be acquired because adequate investment doesn't exist to finance these developments locally. When foreign investment is discouraged, domestic markets are deprived of a valuable source of financing. Capital gains taxes act as a deterrent to foreign capital investment, hurting the investor and the local economy. This should be obvious to market regulators and happily the incidence of capital gains taxes applicable to foreigners is diminishing.

Global institutional investment

Equity investments by individuals from higher-income countries into emerging markets are popularly done through mutual funds and unit trusts. These funds may target a given country, several countries or a region. In 1994, reports of the flow of funds in the US market indicated huge increases in mutual fund investment. It was also reported at that time that there was an increasing amount of new money going into foreign stock funds. Investments in shares is also increasing. As of mid-1990, when the New York Stock Exchange conducted its 12th ownership survey, about 51 million individuals in the United States owned shares in publicly traded companies or stocks in mutual funds, a 70 percent increase in ten years. The study showed that there were over 25 million mutual fund holders alone, nearly four times the total of 1952.

Additionally, institutional investors are increasingly accepting emerging market investments as a means of boosting their returns. It is estimated that by March 1995 US$119 billion were invested in emerging markets mutual funds. The number of such funds keeps rising, from 582 in 1993 to 960 by 1995. Gradually the investment boards of even the most defensive and conservative pensions funds in the United States, the United Kingdom and Japan have added "emerging markets" to the lexicon of institutional investors. According to a survey by Greenwich Associates, corporate pension fund managers were planning to increase the international equity portion of their assets to 7.5 percent by 1993, from the average 5.6 percent of 1990. As the total assets of institutional investors in the major industrialized countries are over $7 trillion and growing steadily, even a slight percentage increase in institutional investment in emerging markets will lead to substantial new capital flows destined for these countries.

On the back of this popularity, more than 50 money management firms now offer emerging markets products. The growth of emerging markets as a specific investment category has been driven by demand from clients, not investment managers, based on changing investment horizons. Individuals are far more comfortable with international investment exposure than they were a decade ago. Nonetheless, emerging markets have a long way to go – even now, the great bulk of money invested throughout the world continues to be invested in the investor's home market.

On top of institutional and retail investors in higher-income countries, we are now seeing investors from emerging markets themselves placing their savings in foreign mutual funds or unit trusts specializing in emerging markets. Thailand has something like 19 mutual funds currently on offer. Foreign fund management companies are salivating at the thought of selling mutual funds to the new global middle class. From Brazil to Singapore, sales offices are springing up and local ad agencies are taking aim at the new money crowd in targeted marketing campaigns. Foreign funds have already been permitted into India, with Morgan Stanley starting up in 1994, and Templeton just receiving its permit to market funds domestically as this book went to print. Further deregulation of domestic financial sectors is expected to open the doors wider for these new financial products and spur growth in the financial services industry in many countries that a few years ago experienced chiefly capital flight.

All of this investment demand must influence supply. It does – there has been a huge expansion in the number of companies tempted to list on emerging market stock exchanges. According to the International Monetary Fund, in the first half of 1992, international equity issues by emerging market companies amounted to US$5.9 billion, compared to only US$949 million in 1990. The cumulative total of new equity issues on emerging markets, between 1991 and 1995 was US$45.6 billion (Table 5.3).

Table 5.3 Emerging market equity issues (US$ million)

Emerging markets	1991 to first half 1995 Total
Africa	**1,211**
Ghana	398
Liberia	207
Morocco	8
South Africa	598
Asia	**23,667**
Bangladesh	26
China	5,713
Hong Kong	1,827
India	3,833
Indonesia	2,044
Korea	2,266
Malaysia	438
Pakistan	1,188
Philippines	1,886
Singapore	1,643
Sri Lanka	33
Taiwan	1.058
Thailand	1,712
Eastern Europe	**533**
Czech Republic	42
Estonia	4
Hungary	310
Poland	15
Romania	1
Russia	48
Slovak Republic	113
Middle East	**1,212**
Israel	1,212
Latin America	**18,957**
Argentina	4,142
Brazil	1,220
Chile	1,161
Colombia	305
Mexico	11,200
Panama	559
Peru	159
Uruguay	23
Venezuela	188
Total	45,580

Source: International Monetary Fund

CONCLUSION

The 1984–5 global recession, induced by the oil price shock, helped create the beginning of what is now described as the globalization of the world's security markets. The oil dollars that were generated by all oil-producing countries had to find a home somewhere, and the recycling of these dollars through the major financial centers of New York, London, and Tokyo created a boom in global finance and trade. At the same time, many emerging markets were just arriving at a developmental stage in which they welcomed foreign equity participation on local stock exchanges, utilizing the resources they attracted to build up their private industrial sector. The gush of resultant global capital flows has spawned a huge infrastructure of people, telecommunication equipment and systems to conduct international financial trades. Today the financial services industry which manages global equity flows is a multibillion dollar industry, redistributing the world's capital to those private entities in the best position to make productive use of it, and generating further capital and business expansion down the road.

Part III

Investment

There is a lot to think about in the course of selecting investments, especially emerging market investments. Once that's done, there is the on-going maintenance of performance valuation and comparison.

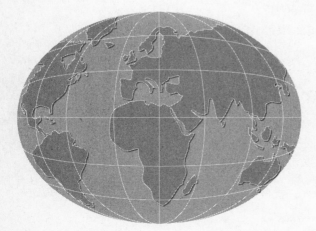

Chapter 6

Investment Strategies and Instruments

In general, stock market analysis tells us that bull markets run longer and gain more compared to bear markets which last a short period of time and move less in percentage terms. This is an important overall phenomenon of which to be aware, because it is a factor when deciding whether or not to invest. Market timing is difficult, but it is generally safe to assume that a bull market is coming and that the stock market will rise above its previous highs during that time.

> *My bias clearly rests with emerging markets, as I perceive them to possess a greater upside in the long term, given their inexorable climb towards full economic development.*

By way of example, let's look at the Hang Seng Index in Hong Kong. In August 1967, a bull market run began which ran for 65 months, and saw the index climb 2,754 percent from its starting point. The ensuing bear market lasted only 21 months, and saw a loss of 89.5 percent in the value of the index. The next bull began in December 1974 and over the course of 78 months the market put on 1,014 percent in value, to be followed by a 17 month bear run in which values declined by 59.4 percent. The point is clear, and can be demonstrated again in 1982, 1987 and it would appear to be starting over again as of January 1995 (Figure 6.1 and Table 6.1).

Table 6.1 Hang Seng Index: length of bull and bear markets

Start Date (month end)	Bull Market (% gain)	Length (in months)	Bear Market (% loss)	Length (in months)
August 1967	2,754%	65	89.5%	21
December 1974	1,014%	78	59.4%	17
November 1982	560%	58	45.8%	17
Nobember 1987	*556%*	*73*	*38.2%*	*13*
Average	*1,221%*	*67*	*58.2%*	*17*
January 1995 (to end-95)	50%	12	–	–

Source: James Capel Asia

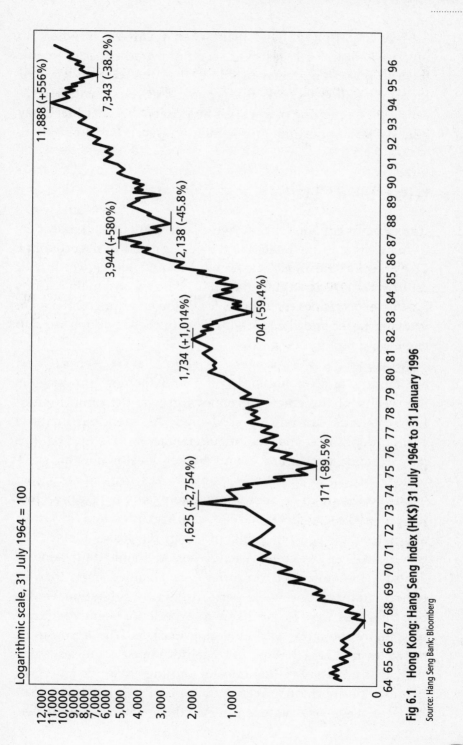

Logarithmic scale, 31 July 1964 = 100

11,888 (+556%)
7,343 (-38.2%)
3,944 (+580%)
2,138 (-45.8%)
1,734 (+1,014%)
704 (-59.4%)
1,625 (+2,754%)
171 (-89.5%)

Fig 6.1 Hong Kong: Hang Seng Index (HK$) 31 July 1964 to 31 January 1996

Source: Hang Seng Bank; Bloomberg

More importantly, then, than **when** to invest, is **where** to invest. My bias clearly rests with emerging markets, as I perceive them to possess a greater upside in the long term, given their inexorable climb towards full economic development. Specifically, I pick emerging markets for investment because I feel they offer the best opportunity for higher returns and diversification.

● HIGHER RETURNS

It is clear to any student of investment that stock market performance is strongly related to the performance of the economy. The question we must ask is: why should we expect higher returns from the emerging markets? There are two main reasons for this expectation: the economies of the emerging nations are growing faster and the stock markets of those nations are also expanding rapidly.

With inevitable shortages of almost every service and commodity, and an unfulfilled demand for new products as the wealth of the emerging nations grows, the opportunities for businesses can be unprecedented. As spending in those economies grows and the requirements for credit and finance expands, capital and equity market development are stimulated.

The performance of emerging markets can vary greatly. Over the period 1991 to 1995, markets like Argentina and Sri Lanka alternated between big gains and then big losses (Table 6.2). Others, like Peru, have consistently posted double-digit gains. In contrast, the developed countries, never gained more than 40 percent annually during the period under consideration. Developed markets were just as likely to experience negative returns as some of the more wild emerging markets. The lesson to be drawn from this is that investing in developed countries is neither safer nor a surer guarantee of earnings than are emerging markets. Furthermore, given the propensity of emerging markets to achieve very high earnings in the years that are positive, the investor has a better chance of attaining higher overall returns by investing in emerging markets.

Table 6.2 Market returns: emerging and developed stock markets: 1991–5 (percent increase in returns in US$)

	1991 (%)	1992 (%)	1993 (%)	1994 (%)	1995 (%)
Emerging markets					
Argentina	→ 396.6	−26.2	72.7	−23.1	12.7
Brazil	173.0	2.5	99.4	→ 69.2	−20.2
Chile	99.2	16.5	34.6	45.1	0.6
China (Shanghai)	–	−37.0	55.8	−39.1	−57.6
China (Shenzhen)	–	6.0	26.7	−38.8	−31.3
Colombia	191.5	38.9	34.7	28.9	−23.8
Greece	−18.7	−27.0	21.9	2.0	10.3
Hong Kong	49.5	28.3	116.7	−28.9	22.6
India	18.1	26.2	18.8	7.4	−34.2
Indonesia	−40.4	0.2	113.4	−19.3	12.0
Jordan	15.6	24.0	24.2	−9.8	12.7
Korea	−14.4	2.6	20.9	20.5	−6.9
Malaysia	12.3	32.3	102.9	−22.0	3.6
Mexico	107.3	19.9	49.1	−40.8	−26.0
Pakistan	172.3	−13.6	56.2	−8.5	−31.1
Peru	114.9	→124.2	37.2	53.5	11.0
Philippines	59.3	18.4	134.9	−0.6	−14.1
Portugal	2.3	−19.0	38.1	20.1	−1.1
Singapore	25.0	6.3	68.0	6.7	6.5
Sri Lanka	106.7	−33.9	65.4	−0.4	−38.0
Taiwan, China	−0.6	−26.6	89.0	22.5	−30.7
Thailand	36.1	42.9	103.0	−11.3	−1.4
Turkey	−26.9	−45.1	→234.3	−40.2	−10.6
Venezuela	48.4	−42.4	−6.9	−25.7	−29.5
Average (simple average)	**63.6**	**4.9**	**67.1**	**−1.4**	**−11.0**
Average (weighted average*)	**51.2**	**17.4**	**78.2**	**−0.3**	**−3.0**
Developed markets					
Japan	9.1	−21.3	25.7	21.6	0.9
United Kingdom	16.0	−3.7	24.4	−1.6	21.3
United States	31.3	7.4	10.1	2	→ 38.2
Average (simple average)	**18.8**	**−5.9**	**20.1**	**7.3**	**20.1**
Average (weighted average*)	**21.8**	**−4.2**	**17.1**	**9.0**	**22.9**

→ Best-performing market, * weighted by 1995

Sources: International Finance Corporation; Morgan Stanley Capital International; Swiss Bank Corporation; Smith New Court; Wardley James Capel

These rises reflect the faster earnings growth and the very low valuations on which individual shares can often be purchased and the rapidity with which changes can occur in the developing world. The opening of new markets, liberalization, privatization measures, and the high savings rates of those markets are all positive factors leading to higher returns. Where we have indicated that the various emerging markets indices throughout the world have shown very high returns, it is important to note that a comparison of what actual fund investments have achieved and the performance of the stock market indices is not wholly valid for two reasons. Fund managers, via their stock picks, may under- or over-perform the market indices, and two, foreign investment in many of the stocks incorporated into emerging market indices have only become possible recently, so that international fund managers may not even have had access to the best-performing stocks on any given counter.

DIVERSIFICATION

Diversification is a widely accepted principle of investing. Most often thought of in terms of diversification among a number of companies or industries, the value of diversifying among shares from different countries can easily be overlooked. But history in both the developed and emerging markets shows that markets do not move in unison; market leadership changes from year to year, and from one market to another (Table 6.3).

This is especially true of emerging markets. Out of our usual sample of 24 emerging markets, in no year between 1991 and 1995 did the same country out-perform all the others more than once. In fact, of the markets which led the pack in one year, few appeared in even the top five in subsequent years. Clearer evidence of the benefit of diversification, rather than putting all the investment eggs in one country basket, would be difficult to find.

For portfolio investors, the need for diversification of risk is great. Diversification of assets among many countries and many

Table 6.3 Annual best-performing markets: 1991–5 (percent change in total US$ returns)

	1991 (%)		1992 (%)		1993 (%)		1994 (%)		1995 (%)
Emerging markets									
Argentina	396.6	Peru	124.2	Turkey	234.3	Brazil	69.2	Hong Kong	22.6
Colombia	191.5	Thailand	42.9	Philippines	134.9	Peru	53.5	Argentina	12.7
Brazil	173.0	Colombia	38.9	Hong Kong	116.7	Chile	45.1	Jordan	12.7
Pakistan	172.3	Malaysia	32.3	Indonesia	113.4	Colombia	28.9	Indonesia	12.0
Peru	114.9	Hong Kong	28.3	Thailand	103.0	Taiwan, China	22.5	Peru	11.0
Mexico	107.3	India	26.2	Malaysia	102.9	Korea	20.5	Greece	10.3
Sri Lanka	106.7	Jordan	24.0	Brazil	99.4	Portugal	20.1	Singapore	6.5
Chile	99.2	Mexico	19.9	Taiwan, China	89.0	India	7.4	Malaysia	3.6
Philippines	59.3	Philippines	18.4	Argentina	72.7	Singapore	6.7	Chile	0.6
Hong Kong	49.5	Chile	16.5	Singapore	68.0	Greece	2.0	Portugal	–1.1
Developed markets									
United States	31.3	Switzerland	18.1	Finland	83.2	Finland	52.5	Switzerland	45.0
Netherlands	19.1	United States	7.4	Switzerland	46.7	Norway	24.1	United States	38.2
France	18.5	Netherlands	3.4	Norway	42.6	Japan	21.6	Sweden	34.1
Switzerland	16.8	France	3.4	Ireland	42.2	Sweden	18.8	Spain	31.2
United Kingdom	16	Belgium	–0.5	Sweden	37.6	Ireland	14.5	Netherlands	28.9

Sources: International Finance Corporation; Morgan Stanley Capital International

stocks leads to lower volatility, that is lower risk, without limiting the potential for gain. This is because a broader range of influencing economic and political variables impact your investments in different ways in different countries. A simple example is when oil prices are high, companies in oil-exporting countries like Indonesia or Venezuela will have more profitable returns, and generate a better a performance on the stock exchange, while companies in oil-importing countries, like Japan, may turn in weaker results and experience a drop in their share prices.

If US investors diversify from their US holdings by making investments only in, say, Canada, the diversification effect exists, but not as markedly as if the investor moved into emerging markets such as Turkey, Portugal, the Philippines, Malaysia, Brazil and Argentina. This is because the correlation coefficient, or ratio of times in which the markets move in tandem, of the Canadian stock market indices to the US indices have been found to be as high as 0.8, out of a total maximum of 1.0. This means that 8 times out of 10, when the US markets are weak, so are Canadian markets. In the end, a given portfolio has benefited from only a minor degree of diversification and risk reduction.

In the case of the emerging markets, the market correlation coefficient of the aggregated emerging markets against the US markets is as low as 0.077. Emerging market investments therefore serve to reduce the risk of volatility in a portfolio to a much greater extent than investments in other developed markets would (Table 6.4). The potential for gain also exists between two different emerging markets. Even individual emerging markets tend to move quite independently of each other, providing a great advantage to a diversified portfolio over single country investments. There is a correlation coefficient of only 0.20 between the Philippines and Poland, 0.19 between Thailand and Turkey. Korea and Brazil actually have a negative correlation, as do South Africa and the Czech Republic. Therefore, a portfolio with a selection of emerging market stocks, rather than a portfolio with one emerging market and one developed market is likely to gain greater diversification benefits (Table 6.5).

Table 6.4 Correlations between BEMI (Barings Emerging Market Index) and developed markets (Based upon weekly price returns 1 December 1994 to 30 November 1995)

Developed markets	BEMI	Asia	Latin America
FTA World	0.357	0.399	0.247
FTSE 100	0.376	0.423	0.278
MS EAFE	0.325	0.383	0.218
S&P 500	0.077	0.199	0.031

Source: ING Barings

Of course, the correlation coefficients cited are historical, and there is no guarantee that as the world gets smaller, with better and faster communications, and as global investors begin investing more in the emerging markets, that the correlation between the developed and emerging markets will not become greater in the short term. At least for the time being, the evidence points to wide discrepancies between market performances particularly over longer periods of time.

Perhaps just as important for higher returns is the range of variations and characteristics of equities found in emerging markets. For example, as of December 1995, the average price to earnings ratio, or P/E, in emerging markets was 17.1 but ranged from a high of 36 in Brazil to a low of 6 on China's Shenzen stock exchange. Price to book values in emerging markets during the same period averaged 2.1 in emerging markets ranging from 0.5 for Brazil to 7.8 for Greece (Table 6.6). Dividend yields ranged from a low of 0.6 for the Philippines to a high of 5.0 for China's Shenzhen market.

Table 6.5 Correlations matrix of IFCG total return indexes
(Based on monthly % change in total indexes over a five-year period ending December 1995;

	U.S.	MSCI	FT	IFCG Comp.	IFCG L. Am.	IFCG Asia	Arg	Brz	Chi	Chn	Col	Cze	Grc	Hun
U.S, S&P 500	1.00													
MSCI, EAFE	0.41	1.00												
FT, EuroPac	0.38	1.00	1.00											
IFCG Composite	0.24	0.34	0.31	1.00										
IFCG Latin Am.	0.38	0.23	0.20	0.65	1.00									
IFCG Asia	0.10	0.28	0.25	0.90	0.28	1.00								
Argentina	0.31	0.12	0.10	0.22	0.48	0.03	1.00							
Brazil	0.42	0.23	0.21	0.40	0.74	0.09	0.13	1.00						
Chile	0.26	0.08	0.05	0.44	0.53	0.28	0.26	0.29	1.00					
China	0.00	0.01	0.01	0.27	0.21	0.20	0.07	0.35	0.14	1.00				
Colombia	−0.02	0.01	0.00	0.12	0.10	0.09	0.00	0.16	−0.12	−0.35	1.00			
Czech Rep.	0.16	0.16	0.16	0.29	0.17	0.27	−0.06	0.38	−0.08	0.18	0.12	1.00		
Greece	0.21	0.34	0.33	0.33	0.05	0.34	0.02	0.14	0.20	0.20	0.23	0.48	1.00	
Hungary	0.29	0.38	0.36	0.43	0.62	0.18	0.36	0.52	0.45	−0.01	0.23	0.23	0.42	1.00
India	−0.08	−0.08	−0.10	0.40	0.31	0.33	0.12	0.27	0.40	0.16	0.09	0.44	0.29	0.57
Indonesia	0.28	0.12	0.09	0.57	0.25	0.55	−0.04	0.18	0.23	0.27	0.13	0.07	0.28	0.37
Jordan	0.09	0.10	0.10	0.22	0.10	0.22	0.09	0.04	0.14	−0.05	0.04	0.27	0.06	0.11
Korea	0.00	0.22	0.22	0.45	0.17	0.48	−0.05	−0.04	0.18	0.09	−0.07	0.09	0.11	0.30
Malaysia	0.20	0.24	0.21	0.62	0.18	0.71	0.00	0.03	0.11	0.27	0.04	0.36	0.14	−0.04
Mexico	0.19	0.14	0.12	0.56	0.82	0.29	0.41	0.31	0.32	0.07	−0.02	−0.01	−0.10	0.49
Nigeria	0.00	0.18	0.19	−0.01	0.09	−0.06	−0.04	0.06	0.11	−0.02	0.20	0.16	0.10	0.47
Pakistan	0.02	0.00	−0.02	0.24	0.16	0.23	0.06	0.03	0.07	−0.13	0.47	0.43	0.03	0.17
Peru	0.19	0.40	0.38	0.46	0.63	0.26	0.49	0.41	0.42	−0.09	0.13	0.17	0.16	0.48
Philippines	0.18	0.25	0.22	0.65	0.32	0.68	0.20	0.15	0.26	0.20	0.24	0.00	0.38	0.11
Poland	0.24	0.41	0.41	0.40	0.42	0.27	0.28	0.31	0.15	−0.09	0.32	0.41	0.20	0.47
Portugal	0.39	0.56	0.54	0.26	0.21	0.15	0.01	0.36	0.26	0.14	0.07	0.34	0.53	0.62
South Africa	0.03	0.35	0.33	0.53	0.11	0.65	0.26	−0.17	0.14	0.12	−0.27	−0.06	0.18	−0.04
Sri Lanka	−0.18	0.00	0.00	0.35	0.45	0.19	0.29	0.36	0.27	0.07	0.43	0.39	0.23	0.28
Taiwan	0.05	0.28	0.27	0.69	0.15	0.80	0.02	0.08	0.10	0.01	0.12	0.04	0.29	0.05
Thailand	0.19	0.05	0.02	0.61	0.20	0.69	0.11	0.03	0.33	0.20	0.06	0.11	0.18	0.11
Turkey	−0.11	0.07	0.05	0.20	−0.08	0.22	−0.13	0.06	−0.09	0.25	0.06	0.04	0.26	0.05
Venezuela	0.03	0.11	0.12	0.16	0.16	0.11	0.08	0.21	0.01	0.24	0.34	0.48	0.12	0.06
Zimbabwe	0.04	0.18	0.19	0.17	0.19	0.13	0.04	0.10	0.04	0.13	0.00	0.20	0.00	0.20

Source: IFC

Jor	Kor	Mal	Mex	Nig	Pak	Per	Phi	Pol	Por	SAF	Sri	Tai	Tha	Tur	Ven	Zim
1.00																
0.07	1.00															
0.12	0.14	1.00														
0.03	0.25	0.26	1.00													
0.13	0.16	−0.18	0.02	1.00												
0.20	0.05	0.21	0.17	0.06	1.00											
0.21	0.30	0.14	0.56	0.06	0.28	1.00										
0.13	0.04	0.64	0.28	−0.08	0.30	0.28	1.00									
0.32	0.21	0.28	0.38	0.16	0.24	0.21	0.20	1.00								
0.01	0.01	0.10	−0.04	0.05	0.10	0.25	0.13	0.49	1.00							
0.10	0.38	0.57	0.28	−0.33	0.31	0.10	0.60	0.12	0.06	1.00						
−0.07	0.30	0.09	0.35	0.07	0.41	0.27	0.08	0.26	0.13	−0.11	1.00					
0.12	0.21	0.41	0.13	−0.09	0.15	0.16	0.57	0.07	0.13	0.55	−0.02	1.00				
0.20	0.12	0.62	0.20	−0.11	0.28	0.21	0.67	0.15	0.05	0.49	0.05	0.40	1.00			
0.04	0.06	0.16	−0.13	−0.08	0.09	−0.06	0.19	0.09	0.13	0.11	0.02	0.17	0.19	1.00		
0.19	0.11	0.08	−0.05	0.12	0.15	0.18	0.20	0.22	0.13	0.01	0.33	0.01	0.13	0.11	1.00	
−0.05	0.02	0.23	0.15	0.12	0.00	0.40	0.23	0.35	0.15	−0.10	0.56	0.03	0.09	−0.12	0.25	1.00

Table 6.6 Emerging market valuations as at 29 December 1995

Country	Price/ earnings	Country	Price/ book	Country	Dividend yield
Emerging markets					
Argentina	15.0	Argentina	1.4	Argentina	3.5
Brazil	36.3	Brazil	0.5	Brazil	3.4
Chile	17.2	Chile	2.1	Chile	3.5
China (Shanghai)	10.4	China (Shanghai)	1.3	China (Shanghai)	4.6
China (Shenzhen)	6.6	China (Shenzhen)	1.4	China (Shenzhen)	5.0
Colombia	11.3	Colombia	1.0	Colombia	2.6
Greece	10.5	Greece	7.8	Greece	4.5
Hong Kong	14.3	Hong Kong	1.8	Hong Kong	3.4
India	14.2	India	2.3	India	1.8
Indonesia	19.8	Indonesia	2.3	Indonesia	1.9
Jordan	18.2	Jordan	1.9	Jordan	1.9
Korea	19.8	Korea	1.3	Korea	1.4
Malaysia	25.1	Malaysia	3.3	Malaysia	1.7
Mexico	28.4	Mexico	1.7	Mexico	1.1
Pakistan	25.1	Pakistan	2.2	Pakistan	2.4
Peru	14.5	Peru	2.8	Peru	1.3
Philippines	19.0	Philippines	3.2	Philippines	0.6
Portugal	14.8	Portugal	1.5	Portugal	3.3
Singapore	17.8	Singapore	1.7	Singapore	1.3
Sri Lanka	8.1	Sri Lanka	1.2	Sri Lanka	3.0
Taiwan, China	21.4	Taiwan, China	2.7	Taiwan, China	1.2
Thailand	21.7	Thailand	3.3	Thailand	2.2
Turkey	8.5	Turkey	2.7	Turkey	4.4
Venezuela	12.0	Venezuela	1.6	Venezuela	2.6
Average	17.1	Average	2.1	Average	2.5

Sources: International Finance Corporation; MSCI; Credit Lyonnaise Securities; author's estimates.

Higher returns and greater portfolio protection through diversification are the major reasons why virtually all investors should have some portion of their investment funds in emerging market equities. Nonetheless, there is real potential for volatility within each of these emerging markets, and no investor should be there for the short-term, unless they enjoy a gamble! Having decided that you will move into emerging markets, the next question to decide for yourself is how to invest. There are several ways that the sophisticated investor can gain exposure to emerging markets. This is the topic of next section.

EMERGING MARKET INVESTMENT INSTRUMENTS

The challenging world of emerging market investments holds great rewards, but also substantial risks for the investor. The criteria to be applied when evaluating the desirability of investments in those markets varies depending on your investment style and objectives. Obviously, as mutual fund/investment trust managers, we at Templeton believe in the efficacy of fund investment and will outline why below. However, some investors

Having decided that you will move into emerging markets, the next question to decide for yourself is how to invest.

have a preference for handling all the nitty gritty of purchasing stocks themselves, and to address these investors, we've included a review of domestic market stocks, depository receipts available on overseas counters and derivative instruments.

Investment instruments may be summarized as follows:

- open- or closed-end mutual funds or investment trusts;
- direct investment in stocks of emerging market companies;
- indirect investment in stock of emerging market companies listed in developed markets;
- derivatives, such as warrants and convertibles.

Investment in trusts and funds

We have already mentioned earlier in the book that mutual funds, as they are called in North America, and unit trusts, as they are labeled in the United Kingdom, have existed since the 19th century. However, they weren't called "emerging market" funds or trusts, as most financial markets around the world were pretty rudimentary at that time. Capital market development was not considered to be a critical component of economic development and little emphasis was placed on it. Emerging market trusts and funds as we know them today began in 1986, with the launch of an emerging markets fund for institutional investors by Capital International and the IFC. Individual investors were able to invest in emerging market funds in 1987, when Templeton launched its New York stock-exchange-listed Templeton Emerging Markets Fund Inc.

According to Lipper Analytical Services, Inc., of over 960 funds in existence at the beginning of 1995, there were 156 global funds, 155 regional Asia funds, 115 regional Latin America funds, 51 regional European funds, and over 480 single country funds. In some cases, the number of country funds for one country has exceeded even the size of the possible investments in that market. For example, as at early 1995, there were over 40 China funds offered with assets in excess of US$2.7 billion, but at that time the "B" shares available for foreign investor purchases in the Chinese markets of Shanghai and Shenzhen had a market capitalization of only US$2.1 billion.

> *There are solid reasons for selecting funds as your instrument of investment, gaining exposure to potential high returns and reduced portfolio risk while shielding yourself from the complications of direct equity market purchases.*

As with all types of financial instruments, emerging markets funds are not freely traded around the world. Each country has various restrictions and requirements regarding investors' purchases of certain funds. However, there is a trend towards global trading of funds as regulatory authorities try to co-operate. In Europe, for example, the USITS regulations allow funds registered in one country to be sold in other countries of the European Community. Not all barriers have been lifted, but Europe has taken a giant step in the right direction. It seems that in the not too distant future, funds, unit trusts or shares and other financial instruments will be freely traded across borders. I have come to recognize how international the funds have become, as I meet people during my travels from all over the world who have bought shares in Templeton funds (and who thankfully greet me with kind words!).

Investors around the world, in the US, UK, Germany, Hong Kong, India, Malaysia, Mexico, Poland, Thailand and Turkey, among others, are increasingly accepting the value of trust/fund investing instead of having individual stock trading accounts. Funds make the process of investing much more accessible, and require much less monitoring and research on a day to day basis. There are solid reasons for selecting funds as your instrument of investment, gaining exposure to potential high returns and reduced portfolio risk while shielding yourself from the complications of direct equity market purchases.

Closed-end funds

Some of the earliest investment companies were closed-end funds. In 1822, King William I of the Netherlands created what is today recognized as the first investment trust. It was formed in Brussels, Belgium, to make investments in foreign government loans. In the 1880s, similar investment trusts were formed in Scotland and England. One of the oldest closed-end funds is the Foreign and Colonial Investment Trust, which was formed in London in 1868 and is still in existence today. This and other such trusts were derived from trusts formed by wealthy families in the 19th century who appointed trustees to look after their assets. The trusts later became companies so that their shares could be traded widely and more investors could participate.

The Edinburgh Investment Trust was established in 1889 and was still in existence at the time of writing. In March 1889 it was reported that many of the holdings were in what then were probably considered developed markets, but which now would be considered emerging markets. For example, the Trust had many railway bonds of companies in Argentina, Brazil, Costa Rica, Cuba, Greece, Mexico, Philippines, Spain, and Uruguay. These railway bonds were giving about the same yield as the bonds of the US railroad companies, that is 5 percent to 6 percent at that time.

Closed-end funds have had a long history in the United States. They played a major role in the speculative era of the late 1920s. Many investors in this form of fund, which were highly leveraged during the roaring twenties, sustained major losses in the 1929 crash. As a result, the concept of closed-end funds faded into obscurity for many years. After World War II, open-end funds were more popular than closed-end funds. It was not until the 1980s that closed-end funds returned to popularity.

Notwithstanding the above, in 1951 the Israel Development Corporation, a closed-end fund, was listed in the US market. It was the first single country fund underwritten in the United States. In 1978 it was merged into AmpalAmerican Israel Corporation. Other closed-end funds formed were the Canadian Fund listed in 1952, and the Japan Fund which was listed in 1962 and was the first US closed-end single country fund of substantial size. In 1987, the Japan Fund became an open-end fund. The Mexico Fund was offered in 1981 and was the first of a long list of other listed country funds. The listing of the Korea Fund in 1984 created a great deal of excitement because of the high premiums that were immediately attached to that fund. In 1985, the First Australia Fund was underwritten and in 1986 a number of country funds investing in Europe appeared, including the Italy Fund, the France Fund and the Germany Fund. Also in 1986, the Taiwan Fund was offered and in the next year regional funds began to appear such as the Asia Pacific Fund and the Scudder New Asia Fund. The Templeton Emerging Markets Fund went public in 1987.

For closed-end funds in general, there was a bull market in the 1980s. This changed, and closed-end funds have been generally trading at a discount to their net asset value (NAV) until very recently. By 1995, emerging market closed-end funds raised

US$38.6 billion; and over 260 closed-end emerging market funds were in existence (Table 6.7).

Table 6.7 Emerging Market Closed-End Mutual Funds, as of 29 December 1995 (US$ millions)

Emerging markets	Number of Funds	Net Assets
Global	31	12,301
Africa	9	1,107
Asia	142	17,104
Regional	32	4,671
China	22	2,807
India	14	1,617
Indonesia	11	475
Korea	18	2,237
Malaysia & SIngapore	5	612
Sub-Continent	5	238
Philippines	6	489
Taiwan	10	1,311
Thailand	14	2,305
Vietnam	5	342
Europe	33	2,052
Regional	10	975
Hungary	3	203
Portugal	6	321
Russia	11	439
Turkey	3	114
Middle East	5	376
Latin America	40	5,639
Regional	21	1,929
Argentina	4	410
Brazil	6	601
Chile	6	1,741
Mexico	3	958
Total	260	38,579

Source: Lipper Analytical Services, Inc.

At the very early stages of emerging market development, closed-end country funds were a popular way of establishing emerging markets and putting them "on the map" among investors in America, Europe and Japan. By establishing a country fund, investors could gain access and exposure to an emerging market without facing all the problems encountered when entering the markets themselves. In addition, since these country funds were closed-end funds and traded on the major stock exchanges, they were liquid, and investors could enter and exit the market rather simply.

There can be significant differences between emerging markets funds' performance in view of the wide range of individual market behavior. One significant problem is that during certain periods of time, the emerging markets fund's share price performance does not correspond with the portfolio performance of the fund. There is an entire group of investors who concentrate their efforts on only purchasing closed-end emerging markets country funds, particularly those that are selling at large discounts to their net asset value. These investors believe it is only a matter of time until the share price catches up with or exceeds NAV. They have the added safety net of knowing that the NAV of a closed-end fund is also its ultimate "liquidation value."

Emerging markets closed-end funds have generally tended to trade at discounts to their net asset value, but the range of premiums or discounts has been wide. Generally speaking, those funds traded on US exchanges typically have had narrower discounts and higher premiums than funds listed outside the United States. A continuous discount indicates investor perception that the manager of the fund is not adding value to the fund, while a premium indicates that investors believe the fund manager's efforts enhance the value of the fund assets. In view of the recent trend for shareholders to force open closed-end funds in order to eliminate the discount to NAV, closed-end fund managers are having to justify their investment strategy more aggressively than ever before.

Thus one of the greatest advantage of closed-end funds is that they often sell at attractive discounts to their net asset values. In this way investors may purchase a basket of assets at a discount to their market value. In purchasing investment trusts or closed-end funds, purchase prices are listed in major publications. They are sold just like common shares, with the transactions going through stockbrokers, where normal commissions are paid. The key to the valuation of investment trusts or closed-end funds is the percentage difference between the share price and the net asset value per share. Other factors to be studied are the percentage of total assets held in cash, the geographical spread of the investments, and the historical total return measured in terms of the performance of shareholders' funds per share.

Open-ended funds

It is usually easiest to described open-ended funds as the opposite of closed-end funds. At the initial stages of emerging markets development, most fund managers were reluctant to establish open-ended emerging markets funds. They were fearful that in the face of large redemptions, always a concern with open-ended funds, the relative lack of liquidity in the many emerging markets would create problems. More recently, however, a number of global fund managers have started open-ended emerging markets funds, as they gain more experience in trading in the emerging markets, and as the emerging markets themselves grow in size and liquidity.

The differences between open and closed-end funds are numerous. However the most important difference is the relationship between price and net asset value (NAV). The NAV of a fund is based on the sum total of all the market values of the fund's securities positions in addition to cash and less any liabilities. The resultant net assets are then divided by the number of shares outstanding to arrive at the NAV per share.

Open-end funds or unit trusts, are continuously ready to offer shares to incoming investors at the current NAV plus any sales charges and expenses. They also stand ready to redeem investor shares at NAV less any charges or back-end loads. Closed-end funds must be sold in the market. The important element is that prices of open-end funds are directly related to NAV, whereas the share price of closed-end funds is determined by the market and may differ markedly from the NAV.

Both open and closed-end funds offer advantages, the most important of which are:

- diversification
- professional fund management
- lower costs
- convenience in record keeping.

In open-end funds there is a tendency for flows into the fund to increase at the peak of bull markets and outflows to increase in bear markets. This could make it difficult for the fund manager to perform at his best. However, if investors co-operate with the fund manager and invest more money when the markets are down, then, in fact, open-end funds could be more advantageous than closed-end funds.

Another advantage of closed-end funds or investment trusts is that investors may precisely control the price at which they purchase the shares. In open-end funds, the price at which the shares are purchased is not known until after the investor has made the commitment.

Investing in stocks of emerging market companies with domestic listings

The most rewarding but most difficult method of investing in emerging markets is by directly investing in stocks listed on emerging stock markets. Such direct investments, because of unique local conditions or local investor sentiments, can result in spectacular returns, or spectacular losses. More often than not the outcome is positive.

An investment of US$1 in Turkey's stock market in January 1989 would have been worth US$7.34 by July 1990, an annualized return of 634 percent. An investment of UK£1 during that same period would have been worth UK£7.21 by July 1990, an annualized return of 621 percent. An investment in Greece in March 1989 of US$1 or UK£1 would have been worth US$5.58 or UK£5.44 by June the following year, representing annualized returns of 458 percent in US dollars and 444 percent in pounds sterling. An investment in the Venezuelan market in January 1990 of US$1 or UK £1 two years later would have been worth US$11.34 or UK£10.80, annualized returns of 237 percent in US dollars or 229 percent in pounds sterling respectively (Table 6.8).

Table 6.8 Return on US$1 and UK£1 invested in emerging markets between January 1987 and May 1993

Emerging markets	Date invested	Date sold	Annualized return US$ (%)	Annualized return UK£ (%)
Argentina	Oct-87	May-92	71	69
Brazil	Dec-90	Apr-92	94	101
Chile	May-87	June-92	48	44
Colombia	Mar-87	Jul-92	50	44
Greece	Mar-89	Jun-90	458	444
Hong Kong	Nov-87	May-93	23	26
India	Mar-88	Mar-92	43	45
Indonesia	Oct-91	May-93	22	30
Jordan	May-89	May-93	16	15
Korea	Jan-87	Mar-89	60	53
Malaysia	Nov-87	May-93	18	21
Mexico	Dec-87	Mar-93	48	50
Pakistan	Jul-87	Dec-91	30	25
Philippines	Jan-87	Nov-89	82	80
Portugal	Dec-92	May-93	49	43
Singapore	Oct-87	May-93	17	18
Taiwan	Jan-87	Jan-90	117	110
Thailand	Feb-87	Jan-92	39	35
Turkey	Jan-89	Jul-90	634	621
Venezuela	Jan-90	Jan-92	237	229

Of course, these returns are calculated using the market indices and thus average all companies whether they rose or fell in price. However, shrewd individual stock selections could have realized even more spectacular results. Perez Companc, one of Argentina's largest companies, rose in price on the Buenos Aires Stock Exchange at an annualized rate of 340 percent in US dollars terms and 323 percent in sterling terms. In the one year between December 1990 and December 1991, the Eletrobras company listed on Brazil's stock exchanges rose in value by 2,900 percent in US dollars and 2,992 percent in pounds sterling (Table 6.9).

Table 6.9 Performance of Emerging Market Stock Indicies January 1987–May 1993

Emerging Markets	US$ Index			UK£ Index		
	Low	High	% Change	Low	High	% Change
Argentina	115	1,695	+1,374	67	931	+1,289
Brazil	42	158	+276	22	89	+304
Chile	286	2,052	+617	176	1,081	+514
Colombia	160	1,198	+649	100	624	+523
Greece	151	843	+458	89	484	+444
Hong Kong	1,086	3,742	+245	593	2,377	+301
India	134	560	+318	72	322	+347
Indonesia	50	74	+48	28	47	+68
Jordan	85	151	+78	54	96	+78
Korea	202	520	+157	132	308	+133
Malaysia	84	226	+169	46	144	+213
Mexico	175	1,855	+960	94	1,067	+1,035
Pakistan	113	309	+182	71	171	+141
Philippines	674	2,232	+231	441	1,424	+223
Portugal	330	491	+49	218	312	+43
Singapore	681	1,707	+151	397	1,084	+173
Taiwan	167	1,700	+918	109	1,010	+827
Thailand	128	674	+427	83	378	+355
Turkey	57	420	+637	32	233	+628
Venezuela	68	771	+1,034	40	432	+980

Investing in stock of emerging market companies via foreign listings

For those that prefer to take advantage of foreign stocks without going to a foreign market or foreign currency, ADRs (American Depository Receipts) and GDRs (Global Depository Receipts) are a relatively new innovation designed to give you just that chance.

Depository receipts are receipts for shares of a foreign company deposited in that foreign country but traded on a foreign exchange. For example, American Depository Receipts are traded in the United States. Normally American banks will have a custodial operation in the foreign country where the shares are traded. The shares are kept in the custodian's vault in that foreign country, and then depository receipts are issued against those shares. In the United States, Citibank, the Bank of New York and Morgan Bank are the largest issuers of depository receipts.

Global Depository Receipts are similar instruments but they are traded in international exchanges. They differ from American Depository Receipts since they provide issuers with a means of tapping global capital markets by simultaneously issuing one security in multiple markets. Global Depository Receipts can be registered, issued and traded in US public markets and listed on major US and non-US exchanges. If an issuer chooses to raise capital in the US private placement market, GDRs may be privately placed using the US Securities and Exchange Commission's Rule 144A, while at the same time being offered publicly in markets outside the United States.

Prior to the establishment of GDRs, companies were required to issue an ADR in the United States and then an International Depository Receipt (IDR) in Europe when accessing both markets. Global Depository Receipt issues often benefit from better co-ordinated global offerings, a broadened shareholder base and increased liquidity.

The placement of depository receipts in the United States was facilitated by the Securities and Exchange Commission's June

1990 Rule 144A (mentioned above), which permitted qualified institutional buyers to trade privately placed securities without waiting the previously stipulated two-year holding period that generally applied to privately placed securities in the United States. This increased the liquidity of privately placed securities for emerging markets depository receipts. Additionally, some ADRs have satisfied Securities and Exchange Commission accounting and disclosure rules for listing on the US stock exchanges. The result is that several American Depository Receipts have trading volumes which are now larger in their off-shore markets than on the local exchanges.

Depository receipts either in the form of ADRs, GDRs or IDRs are growing as a means of investing in emerging markets. In 1994, the total amount raised in depository receipts by companies from lower-income countries was US$18 billion, This is in contrast to a 1990 figure of only US$2.9 billion. Of the US$18 billion raised, Asian issuers accounted for US$12.1 billion, Latin American companies issued US$4.7 billion worth of ADRs/GDRs, and European and African issuers accounted for the balance.

The advantage of depository receipts is that they enable investors in America and Europe to invest in an emerging market company without leaving their home market. In many cases, the home market brokerage and other costs associated with purchasing and holding shares are lower than in the emerging market. By not going into the emerging markets directly, considerable administrative and other complications are avoided. In addition, dividend collection and distribution is completed much more efficiently since the sponsoring bank undertakes to collect all dividends, and then distributes them to the depository receipt holders after converting them into US dollars or the holder's home market currency.

The disadvantage of depository receipts is that they often sell at a higher price than the underlying stock in the home market, and they are sometimes less liquid than the underlying stocks.

Derivatives

The word "derivative" has nasty connotations attached to it after the collapse of Baring Bank and a number of other scandals centered on derivative transactions. The reputation of derivatives is only partially deserved; they have a place in the world of investment, as either protection or an opportunity to gamble. Some derivatives are relatively simple, but some are very complex and incredibly difficult to understand. At Templeton we have tended to avoid using these more complex investment instruments, because we have a rule that we won't invest in anything we don't fully understand, and which is not fully transparent.

Fundamentally, derivatives are created on the back of, or based on, underlying assets. These assets might be stocks, bonds, currency or commodities. They are two-way contracts in which one party promises to deliver and one party promises to accept the underlying asset at a future point in time at a predetermined price.

The job that they have been principally used to accomplish is two-fold. In the first instance, derivatives are used as hedging instruments, to offset a change in price in the underlying instrument, effectively buying a guarantee or promise that the asset will not change in price between now and the agreed upon future date.

However, it is easy see how tempting it would be to use derivatives to bet on the future price of an underlying asset. In this case, the investor is not buying the derivative to protect himself, but rather to expose himself, as he is gambling that the underlying asset price will move in the direction he predicts. This is where the danger of derivatives stems from.

Derivatives are available on virtually all instruments, in all markets. Emerging market derivatives may be found for fixed income instruments as well as equities. The equities area, our particular sphere of interest, is not currently extensively developed, but the range of derivative instruments in emerging markets is expanding.

In particular, in the emerging markets, there is often more demand than supply of stock scrip, so enterprising merchant bankers, underwriters and other institutions who derive commission income from this work have created derivative instruments priced off underlying equity assets. Because these instruments can be traded independently of the underlying stock, the supply of paper offering exposure to a given emerging market issuer is effectively multiplied. Effectively, such derivatives emulate the underlying emerging market securities and act as proxies for the real thing.

Table 6.10 Hong Kong derivatives markets by type

Type of derivatives	Average daily net turnover during April 1995	Net outstanding amount as at end March 1995 in terms of	
	(US$bn)	Notional Amount (US$bn)	Market value (US$bn)
Foreign exchange			
– Over-the-counter derivities	56.4	966.3	59.8
– Exchange traded derivatives	*	3.8	N.A
– Subtotal	56.4	970.1	N.A
Interest rate			
– Over-the-counter derivatives	3.5	476.9	6.4
– Exchange traded derivatives	14.3	189.2	N.A
– Subtotal	17.9	666.1	N.A
Equity and stock index			
– Over-the-counter derivatives	N.A	5.4	0.8
– Exchange traded derivatives	N.A	0.5	N.A
– Subtotal	N.A	5.9	N.A
Commodity			
– Over-the-counter derivatives	N.A	1.1	*
– Exchange traded derivatives	N.A	0.6	N.A
– Subtotal	N.A	1.7	N.A
Total			
– Over-the-counter derivatives	59.9	1,449.7	67.0
– Exchange traded derivatives	14.3	194.0	N.A
– Subtotal	74.3	1643.8	N.A

Notes: (1) The net figure is obtained after adjustment for double reporting between authorized institutions in Hong Kong. However, for equity, stock index, and commodity derivatives, figures are not adjusted for double-counting.
(2) Figures may not add up to total due to rounding.
(3) * Less than US$50m.
(4) N.A.: Not Applicable.

Source: Hong Kong Monetary Authority

The creation of such instruments is very tempting to all parties. It provides new sources of fee income for the people designing such instruments, it creates liquidity for the investor and it offers the company increased market exposure without diluting corporate ownership through equity offers.

For example, there are share warrants, options, futures, and share index futures contracts in markets such as Brazil, Hong Kong and Singapore. However, in many cases the depth of trading is limited. Below, we will review warrants and convertibles as these are the most likely derivatives to be found in the course of stock market investing in lower income countries (Table 6.10 and 6.11).

Table 6.11 Average daily turnover in notional amounts of foreign exchange and interest rate derivative contracts in April 1995

Country	Foreign Exchange US$bn	Rank	Interest Rates US$bn	Rank	Total US$bn	Rank
United Kingdom	301	1	296	2	597	1
Japan	112	3	477	1	589	2
United States	137	2	222	3	359	3
France	37	8	109	4	146	4
Singapore	**63**	**4**	**40**	**6**	**103**	**5**
Germany	45	6	47	5	92	6
Hong Kong	**56**	**5**	**18**	**8**	**74**	**7**
Australia	23	9	37	7	60	8
Swizerland	45	7	7	12	52	9
Canada	19	12	15	9	35	10
Belgium	22	11	10	10	33	11
Denmark	23	9	4	16	26	12
All countries	968		1,330		2,298	

Source: *South China Morning Post*

Convertibles

The most widely used derivative instruments in emerging markets are warrants and convertible bonds. Convertible issues have been particularly popular with Korean, Taiwanese and Indonesian companies in recent years. Convertible bonds have the characteristics of both debt securities and equities. A convertible bond allows an investor to buy a long-term option to convert his bond into the underlying common stock at a fixed price. The convertible bond pays interest, just like any other bond, and such interest is normally greater than the dividend income that would be received when owning the equity outright. The "strike price" or price at which the bond could be converted into equities is usually significantly higher than the price of the stocks at the time the bond is issued. During a decline of the equity markets, convertible bond prices may not decline at the same rate as the equity because of its interest paying characteristics.

Convertible issues have two means of generating returns: by their yield, and through capital gains. The complexity that convertibles introduce is in how to value each of these return-generating mechanisms. Investors may purchase convertibles in order to secure one or a choice of either within a given time frame. Even before making these comparisons, though, we seek to assure ourselves that there is a real yield, that is, that the interest rates offered are positive, after subtracting inflation. The possibility of a negative real yield is an important reason for not even considering investment in a convertible – unless the equity portion of the issue had some outstanding characteristics. When evaluating the attractiveness of a convertible, we must measure the relative merits of both returns.

In the yield category, our fixed-income people at Templeton have a number of criteria with which to evaluate a bond and these criteria would be applied. In the case of our equity specialists, we want to obtain a yield close to the current rate offered by corporate bonds in the domestic market as well as in the international market. As equity investors, the capital gains or equity characteristics of the convertible are the most important feature to us. In order to evaluate this, we return to the underlying equity issue's fundamentals. We complete the same evaluation process as we would for any equity issue. This involves comparative assessments which ask the basic question: "Is stock in this company a bargain?," a bargain being those issues which are:

- selling below their historical price after adjustments for capital issues;

- have a greater earnings potential than their own historical record;
- cheap compared to other issues in their own market, or other issues in markets around the world.

For example, if a stock had a convertible bond which had a yield of 5 percent while inflation was 3 percent, it would immediately be interesting for its bond value alone. In addition, we would consider the value of the conversion feature. It would be attractive if the share value was close to the current market price. So, if the current price was $10 and the strike price was $12 and if the company's earnings were growing at 20 percent a year, then there would be a good chance of the share price rising to the "strike price" or even beyond it. That would make it valuable to us, and we would consider purchasing it for its conversion features as well as its bond value.

But one must be careful. It pays to remember that the issuers' main purpose of issuing a convertible is to obtain better financing terms. The issuer tries to obtain financing at lower interest rates than issuing a straight bond by offering the conversion as a "sweetener." The buyer then obviously must expect the conversion price to be at some premium to the current market price. A convertible which is long-dated and stretches many years into the future, combined with a holder conversion option, is more attractive than one which is short-dated.

If the conversion premium brings the equity price to a level far above the current market price and above its all-time high, the convertible becomes unattractive. However, there are occasions in the secondary markets where we have been able to purchase convertibles with conversion prices close to the market price, even when the market price is at a low point. Expectations in this regard, therefore, are not totally unrealistic. Too often, convertibles are offered at the top of bull markets when the underlying equity issue is expensive both in terms of its own price history and in terms of the fundamental earnings power of the company. In such circumstances we stand aside.

Warrants

Warrants are options for a stated number of years which permit the holder to acquire shares at a fixed price (the "strike price" or "exercise price"), which are normally at a high premium over the share price at the time the warrant is issued. The warrant can be exercised by surrendering it to the company together with funds to cover the exercise price. Sometimes warrants are combined with bonds. This occurs when the warrants may be detached from the host bonds carrying them. Typically, warrants will trade at a fraction of the price of the common stock, but their price moves in the same direction. Therefore, investors buying warrants are able to maintain an interest in a particular equity with less outlay than if they owned the equity itself. And don't forget that you lose your entire investment if the stock price doesn't reach the warrant value. The investor can also lose because the relative movement in the value of the warrant is greater than that of the underlying stock, magnifying gains or losses alike.

PERFORMANCE MEASUREMENT

Performance evaluation is often relative – relative to your goals and investment objectives. It is also relative to the standards against which you wish to measure your performance, for example global indices, a specific market index, or alternative instruments like bonds or savings accounts. It would be pretty difficult to explain all of these relative measures, so in this section, I will stick to what I deal with most often – fund evaluation.

Measuring the performance of mutual funds and investment trusts or closed-end funds involves not only looking at the change in value of the fund's shares, but also the total return of the fund in terms of price appreciation and income. In the case of closed-end funds, it is important to examine not only the market price of the fund, but also the change in net asset value over time, since the two numbers do not necessarily coincide, in view of the premium or discount at which the funds may sell in the market. Some analysts prefer to compare the performance of funds against an index so as to determine whether a fund manager has under-performed or out-performed a particular benchmark.

There have been a number of stock market indices developed, designed to resemble various types of funds. In the emerging markets, the World Bank's International Finance Corporation (IFC), the Morgan Stanley Capital International (MSCI) Emerging Markets Free Index and Baring Securities' Baring Emerging Markets Index (BEMI) are the major indices against which individual emerging market fund performances are most often measured.

At the end of 1995, the IFC Index incorporated 26 countries, while BEMI covered 16, and 22 countries were used in the MSCI Emerging Markets Free Index. The Baring and MSCI Indices were formulated with the purpose of reflecting an index which would be closer to funds in which an actual investor could invest. To accomplish this, they exclude a number of countries where there were major foreign exchange or other restrictions inhibiting the in-flow and out-flow of foreign portfolio investor funds (Table 6.12).

There are some differences between each of these indices, that make their outcomes difficult to reconcile:

- updating frequency;
- exchange rates used;
- definition of emerging markets;
- which markets are included in the index;
- which indices are used in the overall combined index;
- country index weighting.

Of particular importance is that, in many cases dividend reinvestment is not included in the index. Adjustments are made in the indices for bonuses and rights issues.

I've always had a problem with analysts that principally measure fund performance by comparing them to index results. This trend of index following is particularly acute in the huge institu-

Table 6.12 Emerging market indices

	Baring	IFC	MSCI Emerging Free
Inception Date	07-Jan-92	Investable indices since Dec 88	01-Jan-88
Frequency of update	Daily	Monthly/Weekly	Daily
Published in	Baring Securities Emerging Markets Index monthly Updates, Reuters, Bloomberg and Bridge	IFC's Monthly & Quarterly Reviews, IFC's on-line database, Datastream, Bloomberg, FT and Reuters	MSCI Perspective – Monthly stand alone database updated with files sent via modem, Datastream and Bloomberg
Index denomination	US$	US$	Local & US$. Major currencies possible
Exchange rates used	Reuters quotes at 3 pm London Brazil: commercial rates, Philippines: weighted average, Thailand: BOT mid-rate	Most: IFS end-of-period rate Otherwise: WSJ or FT If Multiple: Free market rates	Reuters verified with Extel & Telekurs Brazil: commercial rate
Definition of emerging markets	GDP per capital min US$400, Manufacturing as percentage of GDP rising, Open Market	Low to middle-income country per World Bank's definition	Low to middle-income country per World Bank's definition considering investment barriers
Country indices used	Baring's own indices	IFC's own indices	MSCI's own indices
Country indices weightings	Foreign available cap. weighted sector balance and liquidity requirements	Stocks with combined market cap. of 60% of total market cap. per market cap. liquidity & industry classification requirements	Stocks with combined market cap. of 60% of total market cap. per market cap. & industry classification requirements with a top-down approach
Countries included and weighting (%)	As at 30 November 1995:	As at 29 December 1995:	At at 29 December 1995:
Argentina	5.9	3.7	3.8
Brazil	15.9	10.6	11.2
Chile	5.6	1.9	5.4
China	0.0	0.3	0.0
Colombia	0.0	1.4	0.8
Greece	1.5	1.6	1.3
Hungary	0.0	0.1	0.0
India	0.0	2.3	5.8
Indonesia	3.3	2.3	5.4
Israel	0.0	0.0	2.8
Jordan	0.0	0.2	0.2
Korea	5.8	2.9	3.3
Malaysia	13.1	19.8	16.7
Mexico	11.4	9.3	8.3
Pakistan	0.4	0.8	0.6
Peru	2.5	1.1	1.3
Philippines	3.7	2.8	3.0
Poland	0.0	0.3	0.3
Portugal	1.7	1.4	2.0
South Africa	13.8	27.0	16.4
Sri Lanka	0.0	0.1	0.1
Taiwan	6.8	2.8	0.0
Thailand	7.5	4.7	9.9
Turkey	1.1	2.3	1.3
Venezuela	0.0	0.4	0.4
Zimbabwe	0.0	0.03	0.0
Adjustments for bonus and rights issues	Yes, using the chained paache mehtod	Yes, using the chained paache method	Yes, using the chained paache method
Dividend reinvestment	Not included in the index	Available in the Total Return index series for all indices	With Gross Dividend within 2 months

tional investment markets. Lopsided trend-following behavior by investment managers is inspired by the tendency for such managers to be evaluated on the basis of various market indices or benchmarks. Investment consultants who advise large pension funds and other institutional investors regarding which manager to select will ask the fund managers: "What's your benchmark? Which emerging market index do you use to gauge your performance?" It is then not unusual for the fund manager to find that his answer to that question becomes the benchmark against which his performance is measured in the future!

A variation on this theme is to have the consultants combine the performance of a number of managers and make that the benchmark objective. The institutional investors manager's performance is thus measured relative to an index or their own peer group of other managers rather than by an absolute total return yardstick. The result: the managers become index or benchmark followers, seeking to emulate the index or their colleagues in the industry as closely as possible.

By far the best evaluation of mutual funds performance should include annualized rather than cumulative numbers. Total return is defined as what the investor realizes from owning a fund, or the change in his investment's value over the time period, assuming dividends and capital gains are reinvested in additional shares of the fund. It is important to see those annualized returns over a period of years in order to understand the performance of a fund. It is impossible to multiply a fund's 15 percent annualized return by five and conclude that its cumulative return was 75 percent, since such calculations miss the compounding effect. If, for example, a fund earned 15 percent in one year, US$100 would become US$115. In the second year, if it earned 15 percent the base would be US$115, so the result would not be US$130 but US$132.25. An annualized return of 10 percent therefore would have a cumulative return in five years of 61.1 percent, and an annualized return of 20 percent would have a cumulative return of 248.8 percent over five years.

Lipper Analytical Services publishes the Lipper Emerging

Markets Funds Service which covers those emerging markets funds that are more easily traded by international investors. This, together with Morningstar and Micropal are the principal sources of objective reviews and statistics on mutual funds and investment trusts around the world.

There is a lot to think about in the course of selecting investments, especially emerging market investments. Once that's done, there is the on-going maintenance of performance evaluation and comparison.

The above information serves as a good primer on the subject, in terms of introducing the products available to investors and how to keep an eye on them. In the subsequent chapters, further information which should help emerging market investors to monitor and evaluate more fully their investments is provided.

Good portfolio management requires an integration of all relevant information in order to achieve the best results.

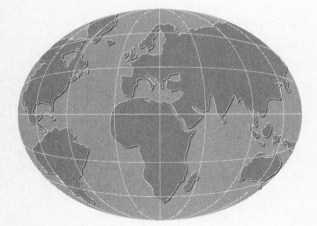

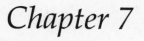

Chapter 7

Evaluating Stock Picks

A lot of magazine space has been used up over the years, as well as analysts' time, deducing how a fund manager becomes successful. All kinds of terminology have sprung up to describe the strategies employed – "technical," "style analysis," "bottom-up investing" – not all of which are especially useful to the average investor. Instead of rehashing the debate, I've chosen to outline my personal investment approach and explain why I think it makes sense for the investor.

● VALUE ORIENTATION

The emphasis on value in investing is not universally accepted and, when accepted, is often not applied. Sir John Templeton has said that there is a tendency for too many investors to focus on "outlook" or "trend." It is my belief that more opportunities may be uncovered by focusing on value. Studies have shown that over the long term, stock market prices tend to be influenced by the asset value and earnings capabilities of listed shares. Also, share prices tend to fluctuate much more widely than real share values. Therefore it is unlikely that index funds will ever produce the best total return performance.

The value approach to investing was first and best defined by Benjamin Graham and David Dodd in their 1934 book *Security Analysis*. In the book, they articulated the system of buying value shares whose price is cheap relative to factors such as earnings, dividends or book assets. But studies have also revealed conflicting conclusions regarding its application. For example, one study showed that investing in shares with a low ratio of share price to cashflow was a better strategy than buying shares with a low price-to-book ratio. Others indicate that price earnings ratios are the best determinant of future price.

Many investors now speak of "value investing," but few actually diligently apply the value-investing principles and the hard work necessary to find real value. Those investors who do work hard at it are inevitably rewarded. The investor who purchases a stock because of basic value can enjoy a certain peace of mind. If, after purchasing a stock at a low price in relation to value, the price continues to decline, then it is simply a better bargain than it was before. On the other hand, the speculator who purchases in the hope of a quick profit places himself at the mercy of market fluctuations because he can succeed only be selling his shares to other speculators at higher prices.

We at Templeton take value-oriented investing very seriously, and it is our main determinant in making an investment decision. However, we and global investors in general are constantly challenged by the need to make reasoned comparisons between companies in different markets. In such conditions different accounting systems can play havoc. There is thus a need to carefully evaluate the company accounts to determine how different numbers were calculated so that there is a full understanding of their meaning and so they may be compared to the accounts of another country. Value is of course relative, and it is the analyst's job to make comparisons which are valid, based on a consistent mechanism for making accounting adjustments.

> *Many investors now speak of "value investing," but few actually diligently apply the value-investing principles and the hard work necessary to find real value.*

SHORT AND LONG TERM

Another issue on which I am particularly concerned is that of evaluation or measurement of returns. Over the years we at Templeton have consistently emphasized that our investment approach is long term. I have had to write many letters to individual investors in our funds who criticized us for not taking opportunistic positions, when it is repeatedly stressed in our fund reports that this is not at all our approach to investing. Another way in which observers forget or ignore our long-term approach is obvious when they ask questions like, "Why have your funds experienced a poor performance over the last six months?" I must continually remind investors and commentators that this is the wrong question, and that we don't measure ourselves in this manner, and that therefore in our eyes there is no "poor" six-month performance.

One problem facing the world today is the tendency for people to think in shorter and shorter timeframes. A recent study indicated that stocks in US companies were held for an average of two years, whereas in the 1960s they used to be held for seven years. Some shareholders look for a quick return on their investments, and thus business executives are increasingly driven by the same mentality. This short-term philosophy is detrimental to the health of the company and the investor. Unless companies and investors take a longer-term view, growth prospects are limited and planning becomes stunted. Taking a long view of emerging markets will yield excellent results for the investor prepared to be patient and willing to apply sound and tested principles in a diligent and consistent manner.

The approach we take in our reports is not to focus on the short term since we are investing the funds entrusted to us not for a three-month, six-month or even one-year period, but for at least a five-year period. Over the many years that Templeton funds have been investing, we have found that striving for short-term performance increases the risks to shareholders and actually results in poorer returns. Only by taking the long view will we be able to do the best job for investors.

'Long term" can, on the other hand, be a frustratingly vague term, especially when your retirement savings are at stake. We have therefore adopted five years as our principal time frame of reference. A ten-year time frame may be better than a five-year time frame insofar as it forces us to look further into the future which is what successful investing is all about. Unfortunately, taking a ten year view is extremely difficult and there is a tendency to lose bearings and make unrealistic forecasts. The five-year focus seems to be the most practical and realistic.

Of course this requires support from shareholders, because if they become unhappy about a temporary decline in the value of their portfolio, and send us a letter complaining about this short-term performance, then it becomes difficult for us. I personally believe that such declines in our net asset value could be viewed as good opportunities to purchase more of our shares. If investors are committed to taking a short-term view, then they should not be buying our funds.

Related to the issue of market cycle is the percentage of fund assets held in cash at any one time. I have been in turn vilified and glorified for my willingness to hold large cash positions if I don't see any "bargain" stocks available at a given time. By our standards, cash positions of 30 percent or even 40 percent are not alarming. It is important for investors to remember that "cash" is always working earning interest while we gradually find good bargains. We simply do not focus on the percentage of cash held in the portfolios but on how many bargains are in those portfolios. While some investors may have been concerned at certain stages about our cash positions, they subsequently applaud us for having cash readily available to purchase stocks when prices are low.

BOTTOM-UP VERSUS TOP-DOWN INVESTING STRATEGIES

There is continuing controversy over the optimal strategy to apply to emerging markets portfolio management, or for that matter any equity portfolio. On one side of the fence is the "bottom-up" investment school of thought, and on the other are the "top-down" investors. Let me make clear from the outset that I think the arcane debate over the merits of narrowly defined investment strategies is a waste of time. Any good fund manager applies all the investment information they can obtain to make a decision, and is unlikely to satisfy pure patterns that are merely convenient definitions.

I have tended to favor a "bottom-up" approach. It means that I place the most emphasis in my research on finding the best companies globally in all emerging markets, and try to review the prevailing macroeconomic conditions from the point of view of the local company. That is, I'm concerned with macro-economic conditions, to the extent that they may hinder or help a bargain company achieve its objectives. Bottom-up investors allow country allocation to follow stock selection.

The direct alternative to this approach has been labeled "top-down" investing. According to this notion, a top-down manager will first select the countries in which he/she would like to invest, through the analysis of the economic and political environment in those countries. Secondarily, the portfolio manager selects individual stocks within those markets, looking chiefly at consid-erations such as liquidity and market capitalization, factors which would influence the manager's ability to enter and exit the market easily. Top-down investors start with the assumption that markets are inefficient, particularly new or emerging markets, and they hope to catch these inefficiencies before market devel-opment eliminates them, or before other international investors move into a new market, bidding up stock prices in the process.

A recent review of these approaches in *Emerging Markets Investors* magazine statistically compared the performance of funds, differentiating them by their strategy, "top-down" or "bottom-up." While such studies are not conclusive, as the strat-egy definitions are broad and loose at best, it was gratifying to find that only two of the top ten funds professed to emphasize a "top-down" approach to investing. In fact, the magazine study reported that "bottom-up managers who invest in all emerging equity markets have outperformed their top-down counterparts by 50 percent over the last three and a half years."

Micropal's Emerging Market Fund Monitor magazine also identified bottom-up strategies as winners over the long term.

They found that bottom-up funds outperformed top-down funds in the six distinct time periods under evaluation, between March 1992 and June 1995. The bottom-up strategy showed particularly good results during bull runs, suggesting that in good times, a well-run company is better positioned to benefit from market trends than mediocre firms. On a risk-adjusted basis, the bottom-up funds scored 57 percent better than the top-down funds on an average monthly basis over the period under review.

To my mind, though, these categorizations of "bottom-up" and "top-down" are gross over-simplifications, and it is difficult to find managers who neatly fit those descriptions. The subject is fraught with dangers, simply because definitions of investment styles tend to pigeon-hole a particular manager and leave them with fewer options. More often than not, some managers would tend to emphasize stock selection whereas others would tend to emphasize country allocation, but both would at all times be considering macroeconomic and macropolitical as well as individual stock differences. It is difficult for any manager to ignore matters regarding earnings, growth and momentum of companies, the evaluation of companies, interest rates and their impact on alternatives facing investors in a particular market, liquidity of the market, market capitalization of companies (particularly as emerging markets funds grow and require larger single investments to make a significant impact on portfolios), economic policies of the country, the political environment and market-related factors such as investors' sentiment and market rumors.

RESEARCHING EMERGING MARKETS

Information sources

"A verbal promise isn't worth the paper it's written on." Samuel Goldwyn

In emerging markets, we are continually reminded of the need for independent research and careful checking of what company officials and underwriters tell us. An investor must constantly be aware of the influences and biases affecting him. These influences and biases are strongest in the places where one spends the most time and from where one obtains the most information. For this reason, the emerging markets analyst must try to visit all the countries in the emerging markets areas as often as possible, and read news and research reports originating from all over the world. Investors must try their best to exercise a great deal of objectivity in their analysis of all the relevant data, so that local or foreign, company-specific or industry-specific data may be given appropriate weighting.

There must be an ability and willingness for the emerging markets researcher to obtain information from all relevant sources, whether it be local or international. In other words, total reliance cannot be placed on just local information or on only foreign information. The best sources of information for emerging markets investors are (1) the staff of a company in which you are considering an investment, (2) the staff of competitors, and (3) the audited financial statements. If you read about it in the newspaper or a magazine then it is probably too late (except maybe to do exactly the opposite of what the article suggests!).

With brokers becoming ever more involved in merchant banking and taking positions on their own behalf, they have become a poor source of information. In fact, it is now downright dangerous to act solely on information from brokers or merchant bankers, since there is a growing tendency for them to put forward information designed to promote a particular stock. Furthermore, if the broker is distributing a glossy publication to hundreds of investors, then the chances are low of the company still being a bargain by the time you read about it. Therefore brokerage house research reports can only be used as leads and background information.

For the same reason, it is not wise to unquestioningly accept ratios such as debt-to-equity ratios or price/earning ratios (P/E) from brokers. Be sure to check the definition and methodology they are using. For example, brokers in Australia add cash back in when calculating the debt-to-equity ratio, which makes the situation look brighter, and their P/E ratios often include extraordinary gains which should be noted when they appear. Brokers in Malaysia often use pre-tax profits to calculate P/E ratios.

Devote less time to reading periodicals and talking with brokers, and instead use that time to try to get to know the company's staff and its competitors. Always use the company's audited financial statements as the primary information source. If you find a particularly good independent and reliable information source, use it but make sure it really is reliable.

One debate, which is taking on greater importance as global and emerging markets investing expands, regards the benefit of obtaining data from advisers and analysts based in the country in which the investments are being made. The question is being asked with particular urgency as the number of investors moving into emerging markets escalates and as more capital is finding its way to emerging market stocks, with which most fund managers are less familiar. As the competition heats up, funds will be able to distinguish themselves only on the basis of superior stock selection, rather than whole market movements.

Can wholly local information sources boost portfolio returns? Experience has shown us that total reliance on a locally based analyst or adviser is not sufficient and will eventually lead toward returns inferior to those produced from a more comprehensive approach. For wise portfolio decisions, two important perspectives are necessary. First, the global outlook and experience which comes from having invested in many countries, and second a more detailed and intimate knowledge that comes from a local presence, especially about individual companies.

It is important to incorporate both perspectives by having local and country-specific information collated, digested and then contrasted to global data. This analytic process yields much more powerful results than research which leans heavily on one or the other source of information. Locally gathered information, for example, provides insights into the real success of a business, as measured against similar companies in the same country experiencing the same economic conditions. Global information helps the investor to see what international economic or political forces are gathering steam and may alter the local business environment. The end results are much more valuable insights which must yield far better long-term investment returns.

Of course, the local information is best gathered by informants who are living in the particular country and who have an intimate knowledge of the local environment. However, we have found at Templeton that this cannot replace frequent visits to each country in which investments are made, since we have found that local analysts need assistance and support in knowing which questions to ask. More importantly, the combination of local and foreign analysts leads to much more valuable insights. An analyst based in the country which he is analyzing will often overlook vital points of inquiry because he has been blinded by close interaction with the local management or other members of the community. Someone visiting from abroad is able to introduce an entirely different perspective and raise unique questions which could throw a different light on the subject matter.

This was brought home to me while I was in Istanbul interviewing executives at a copper-mining company. I noticed that our local consultant's questions centered on the firm's mining techniques and efficiencies. Accompanying us was one of our analysts who had studied similar mining companies elsewhere in the world. He entered into an entirely new line of questioning when he asked how this Turkish company was able to achieve profit margins above similar mining companies in the Philippines and Chile. He wondered whether it was because of the company's investments in copper futures and profits from currency trading. This question opened up an altogether different framework, and enabled us to lead the company's executives into a hitherto ignored but important facet of this firm's operations. As a result of our combined local and global approach in analyzing this company, we revised our entire assessment of the company and its prospects.

Can an investor be over-influenced by local factors and thus be better off assessing investments from a distance? Yes, you may be over-influenced by local factors, but globalists and generalists may also miss the important local details, particularly if a bottom-up style of investing is used. I have found that the best remedy for a view that is too local or too global is a synthesis of both. Good portfolio management requires a blend of all relevant information in order to achieve the best results. The best approach is to obtain the most detailed and accurate information, which can only come from local analysts aided and abetted by global analysts, and then digest that data from a global perspective.

Interestingly, mutual fund investors often feel more comfortable with a fund management firm that has an analyst or manager who is "on-site" and living in the area in which the investing takes place. Investors are often impressed when meeting local

> *Good portfolio management requires a blend of all relevant information in order to achieve the best results.*

experts, and well they should be, since such local experts provide invaluable information. However, sole reliance on such information can be dangerous without a global perspective. We have found that a heavy local bias can eventually lead to severe misinterpretations and give rise to unwise investment decisions.

When the Indonesian market was booming in 1989 and 1990, it was very difficult to find local analysts able to admit that the market was severely over-valued. They all seemed to feel that the rapidly rising market would continue indefinitely. Those outside the country, however, could see the danger clearly and thus refrained from aggressive buying. As much as 50 percent of one Indonesian fund was kept in cash, despite strong protestations from clients urging the fund manager to catch the bull run. The subsequent disastrous fall in the market vindicated his approach, but it is highly unlikely that he would have taken that stance if he had been caught up in the local feeding frenzy. An outside perspective at that time was invaluable, and subsequently resulted in out-performance of the other funds.

As an alternative to formal information sources, when visiting the countries in which I invest, I like to talk to working people and people who have to actually function in the economy we all analyze so theoretically. These people will tell me about their life and how the economic conditions are affecting them. In 1995, when visiting Brazil, there was a subdued feeling in the country as a result of the slowdown in the economy. Inflation was down substantially, but the economy itself had also been slowed. As a result, the business leaders we met with were not very optimistic. From their perspective alone, we would have developed a rather down-beat economic forecast for the country.

Talking to people on the street, however, changed the picture for us. One woman said: "For the first time in many years I now know how much money I am going to make at the end of the month. At the time when we had 2,000 percent inflation a year, each month I didn't know how much I was going to get paid, due to the indexation system for salaries. I had to rush to the bank and get in line to cash the check and then rush to the supermarket to buy anything I could get. Now, I can plan and I know how much I am going to get and what it will buy. Of course things are expensive, and I must be careful with my expenditures, but I think things are a lot better." From statements like this, our research teams formed much more accurate expectations of coming consumer attitudes and spending than we did from talking to the business people themselves!

It is important also not only to depend on a lot of respondents from different walks of life, but to use your own associates as sounding boards and sources of information. There are times when I travel with other Templeton analysts, with the intention of comparing notes and observations after the interviews and walk-abouts. At Templeton, we also assign analysts based in one country to cover other countries, so that they can develop well-rounded viewpoints. This cross-fertilization of analysts results in better research and more unique views.

Finally, and perhaps obviously, information regarding pricing is essential. This price information must be timely and available, while trading on the stock exchange floor is transacted or at least immediately after the close of trading. Fund management companies subscribe to a number of very expensive, electronic stock price information systems such as Reuters and Bloomberg. However, many emerging markets are not sufficiently covered by these services or may not even be covered at all. In some cases, this is because the host country stock exchange restricts the release of such information to independent information services. Without question, this is a severe impediment; emerging stock markets should freely make available such information and even subsidize its dissemination worldwide, since this will popularize their market and increase trading turnover.

Research at the country level

"There are three kinds of lies: lies, damned lies, and statistics."
Benjamin Disraeli

A controversy over the real state of Poland's trade in 1992 underlined the problems of making investment decisions on the basis of doubtful and often contradictory statistics. Questions were raised in March 1993 when Poland's Foreign Trade Ministry issued figures, based on customs data, which pointed to a US$2.5 billion deficit in 1992. These statistics contradicted earlier figures, collated by the central bank, which showed a surplus of US$512 million which had been widely publicized by the government as evidence of Poland's strong economic performance. It is easy for different agencies of the same government to differ over data. In August 1992 the Ministry of International Economic Relations (MIER) and the National Bank of Hungary (NBH) both published sharply contrasting figures. The MIER said that the country's trade deficit in the first half of the year was US$800 million, while the NBH said it was only about US$100 million. The bottom line is that national statistics, particularly in emerging markets, are much less reliable than most people think and should never be used as a proxy for real, on-the-spot research.

Statistics in emerging markets are to be taken with considerable caution for more reasons than just interagency rivalries. In some countries, as a direct consequence of earlier inappropriate economic policies, underground economies have sprung up. In these black markets and unreported exchanges of goods and services, a considerable portion of the nation's business may take place. But it is impossible to account for it factually in national economic statistics. This of course inhibits accurate economic estimations. Brazil has an excellent example of a pervasive underground economy. Official estimates put the number of informal workers in downtown Rio de Janeiro at more than 300,000 – in the whole of Brazil, there are said to be at least 28 million people obtaining their daily income from the underground economy. In a country of 156 million people, how can official agencies generate accurate data, when almost 20 percent of public's economic activity can't be captured in economic figures?

The risk of over-simplification when looking at emerging market economies also arises from an over-dependence on macroeconomic statistics. It becomes easy to think of countries as economic units. In fact, most countries are not homogeneous, and a conclusion drawn about a country as a whole is often wrong. Weakness in income growth may mask real changes in welfare for large parts of a poor population. Improvements in meeting the basic needs for food, education, health care, equality of opportunity, civil liberties and environmental protection are not captured by statistics on income growth, for example. Alternatively, pockets of successful business may exist in a country otherwise dismissed by international investors as a "basket case." Our research team had its eyes opened during a recent trip to Colombia. In the den of international cocaine smugglers in the eyes of the world Press, we found respectable, hard-working, sophisticated people, successfully getting on with the business of providing their countrymen with building materials, food, and consumer products on a daily basis.

Many investors have found that instead of relying on fancy international theories of investing, their best bet lies with a fundamental, company-oriented research approach. In applying such an investment philosophy to emerging markets, though, don't forget to make modifications to the usual analytical methodology where necessary. Analysis must be more flexible in terms of the selection of criteria used to evaluate companies. Principal criteria will probably differ between countries and industries. For example, the use of book value as a criterion may be flawed in some markets because of accounting idiosyncrasies, while in other markets it could be an excellent measure of value.

In February 1993, a former Soviet Prime Minister, Valentin S. Pavlov, boasted that he had been able to fool foreign bankers into believing that the Soviet Union possessed ample gold reserves. He is reported as saying: "We used to attract huge amounts of private banking capital. They brought us their money as if we were a savings bank." He said that the Soviet Union had squandered its gold reserves long before was commonly supposed, but concealed the fact in order to attract Western loans.

There is no question that there are some unscrupulous actors in some countries that are willing to consciously bend supposedly objective statistics to their purposes. At times, the interests of international investors and those of local actors are not the same, but local players will lure investment by pretending to act in a manner consistent with international standards. Later in the book, I've included an entire chapter on the "risks" of investing in emerging markets and lurking threats waiting to relieve you of your investment savings. Emerging markets are not the only place where one can be defrauded, but given their relative newness, and fluid regulatory structure, it pays to be on the look-out. This is another important aspect of thorough research.

Research at the company level

One of the key aspects of investing in emerging markets is the need to perform a careful analysis of companies. To meet this challenge, painstaking research is required, involving local analysis and extensive traveling. This involves examining individual shares on a five-year or longer view, paying particular attention to the potential for, and the stability of, earnings growth. Normally, the further back in time the analysis goes, the better it will be.

We maintain an emerging market database, used by all of our analysts, to record company information and monitoring. It now boasts 16,000 company reviews, from 48 countries. This database contains key information on all stock-exchange-listed companies for each country. Such figures include current price, highest and lowest price during last five years, number of shares outstanding, earnings per share, market capitalization, and market turnover. There are also key financial ratios such as price-to-earnings, price-to-book and debt-to-equity.

Factors such as a sound balance sheet, high return on equity, strong self-financing capability, good profit margins and good profit growth are some of the items sought when analysis is undertaken. This sort of analysis requires the investor to have reliable and timely access to audited accounts, which can present many problems when each country has different accounting standards. Improperly or falsely presented materials can make the difference between buying or avoiding a stock in the eyes of an international investor.

We also like to get a personal perspective on the company. Our frequent visits permit us to develop a personal sense of where the company is going and how management maintains the facilities and its employees. The appearance of the staff, operating environment, physical location, can all speak volumes about a company's success and priorities. Meeting with corporate representatives also helps us to develop an understanding of the company, giving us more sources of information than the annual company report.

Characteristically, there is only a limited amount of information available on emerging markets. In some countries companies listed on the stock exchange and companies planning initial public offerings, rights issues or privatization offers, do not offer the public timely, informative and detailed financial statements. In a number of emerging markets, there are no requirements or enforcement in this regard. There is often a lack of control regarding when or how financial information is released or distributed so that it will be accessible not only to major investors but also to the general public.

These problems have been compounded by the lack of incentives for many emerging market companies to reveal information about their operations. They are often closely controlled corporations, dominated by founding families or their heirs, where the majority of shares are held by family members. Their public listing is often made to obtain tax benefits and not to raise additional capital. Trading, settlement and regulatory systems are also evolving and differ between individual markets and from the standards typical in the developed world.

At Templeton, we use the time-tested strategy of identifying securities that stand at a low price in relation to the company's long-term value. We prepare what we call a "Country Scan" for every market, which shows all the listed companies in that market and their latest prices, most recent historical earnings, expected current year earnings, book value, etc. We identify companies that look undervalued from the Country Scan and prepare a Company Sheet for each company, which is a data sheet showing at least five years of historical performance or as many years back as we can go and five years of projections. This is usually followed by a company visit and if everything checks out, then we will put the company on our "Buy" list and buy it for all of the funds. In some countries, we have had to make adjustments because of different accounting treatments and other market peculiarities.

The stock must meet at least two of the following three requirements:

- It must be cheap relative to its price history, its P/E history, other stocks in the market, or other stock in its industry internationally.

- It must have good growth prospects, with at least a 20 percent average growth rate over the next five years.
- It must be cheap in relation to its net tangible assets.

Whenever you can buy a large amount of future earnings power for a low price, you have made a good investment.

Our estimates of the above are kept up-to-date with frequent reviews. Each day, the market price for each stock is compared with the estimated intrinsic value of that market. When the market prices for a particular stock rises above the intrinsic value to an unreasonable extent, we sell the stock. Conversely, when the market price falls below the intrinsic value for a particular stock to an unreasonable extent, we put that stock on a list of stocks which can be purchased. I liked it when one of my colleagues compared the process to a ladder – when one stock reaches the top, it gets knocked off, and a new one is added to the bottom rung to replace it.

The appraisal of value is complex and subject to numerous uncertainties. Some of these factors are management ability, growth trends, government control, assets per share, average past market prices for the shares, dividends, current earnings, average earnings in previous years, estimates of future earnings, etc. And don't forget that the fluctuation of share prices is roughly proportional to the square root of those prices. Thus, lower-priced securities are more volatile and thus have a greater potential reward.

ACCOUNTING IN EMERGING MARKETS AND ANALYSIS OF FINANCIAL STATEMENTS

Accounting standards differ from one country to another, so that treatment of accounting items varies significantly. These differences result not only from historical precedent but also because of changing taxation policies. Of course, differences in account-ing standards are not exclusive to the emerging markets.

Accounting policies are also not static, so the analyst must stay on top of changes. For example, in 1995 the Argentine govern-ment announced that companies would no longer be allowed to use inflation accounting when presenting their accounts. This of course resulted in some dramatic changes in companies' reported results. In a case like this, a company which previously had large earnings gains from "monetary adjustments" resulting from a depreciation of debt in real terms might now show a loss. At the time when Argentina was announcing this important change, Venezuela announced that companies would be required to start inflation accounting!

To show another way in which accounting changes can have a significant impact: in early 1996 we were visiting a Mexican retailer. That company showed a foreign exchange loss of pesos 837 million because they had US dollar-denominated debt and the Mexican peso had depreciated against the US dollar, increas-ing the value of the debt in peso terms. However, there was a gain in "monetary position" of pesos 1,301 million, because inflation accounting required that the accounts reflect the loss in purchasing power terms of the company's debt. Peso debt adjusted for inflation had declined in real terms, creating a gain in the company's monetary position. Ironically, this situation led those companies with the most debt to post the highest gains in monetary positions. (Of course the banks holding those debts had the highest losses!)

As is clear, accounts do not tell the whole story. It is therefore important to meet management face to face and to ensure that the company's operations are also inspected. Attention to detail is important. Henry Ford once said: "A handful of men have become very rich by paying attention to details that most others ignored."

Audited accounts are necessarily the starting place for the examination of any company in the emerging markets. Audited financial statements provide the first source of information an investor has about a particular company. These statements are supposed to show an unbiased account of the company's health and business. When analyzing accounts, keep an eye on the following areas:

- In manufacturing and sales organizations, monitor **inventory**, **accounts receivable** and **order backlog** trends. These are the strongest indicators of problems and are much more closely related to stock returns than reported earnings.
- More and more we must look at the impact of **inflation**. In high inflation countries, it is essential to adjust numbers for inflation or convert into US dollars to ensure a valid comparison from one year to the next.
- **Profit margin** trends are important.
- When looking at **volatility**, remember that the fluctuation of share prices is roughly proportional to the square root of the price. This means that lower prices shares will tend to be more volatile than higher priced shares. As an example, a $1 share that moves up 20 cents in a day (which is not uncommon) has moved 20 percent, while a $100 share that moves up 20 cents has gained only 0.2 percent. A $100 share is less likely to move up by $20 and match the gains of the lower-priced share.
- There are many ways to appraise financial statements, but one of the most common is the use of **ratio analysis**, whereby the various elements in financial statements are compared. When looking at the value of a firm, ratios such as price/earnings, dividend yield percentage, return on equity and price/book value are used. When assessing profitability, ratios such as profit margins, return on equity, and return on assets are used. When assessing safety or balance sheet strength, ratios such as debt to equity and current ratio can be meaningful indicators.

There are severe limitations caused by using only one ratio or relying too heavily on one type of analysis. For example, when analyzing banks, the capital adequacy ratio is often cited as an important factor when considering viability. However, the capital adequacy ratio as stated by the Bank for International Settlements only takes into account credit risks and excludes market risks that the banks are exposed to in their trading and investment portfolios in foreign currency, share and money markets. Supplement the capital adequacy ratio by looking at trends in the flow of funds, changes in various categories on the balance sheet and percentage changes in sales, assets, liabilities and cash flow.

Despite efforts on the part of various accounting organizations around the world to come together and agree on some basic accounting standards, the differences between countries are enormous, not necessarily because of a lack of agreement among accountants regarding how accounts should be handled but because of local laws and regulations which impose certain requirements different from what would be considered generally accepted accounting practices.

With regards to the demands on the analytical skills of the investor in evaluating those emerging market companies, most daunting are not only the varying accounting standards used in each country but the varying taxation regimes which affect how accounting standards are applied. It is essential, therefore, for the investor to ensure that he understands what methods the company's management and their accountants are using in their efforts to minimize their tax liability.

Regulatory officials around the world are deeply divided regarding questions such as what auditing standards should be required. The fact that auditing firms are constantly being sued by shareholders for large amounts indicates the degree of dispute regarding those standards and applications. Accounting and auditing differences between countries and regions have been with us for quite some time, and it doesn't look like we've seen the last of them.

For example, many emerging countries influenced by continental European accounting practices have a uniform chart of accounts. In countries influenced by British and American accounting, the chart of accounts is more flexible and, while not using an established format, tend to have more extensive information in the notes of the accounts. In continental European accounts, there is greater use of legal reserves and tax-based reserves, whereas in the United States the emphasis is on the concept of "fair presentation," and excessive arbitrary reserves are uncommon. In some countries, the process of accounting is very much the subject of government regulation, whereas in others, the main influence comes from accountancy bodies and professional associations.

Even in Europe, harmonization of financial reporting has a long way to go. Anglo-Saxon accounting systems tend to be more oriented toward shareholders and focused on disclosure, whereas continental accounts are rooted in Roman law and are more oriented towards creditors, guided by government rules and dominated by tax requirements. The International Accounting Standards Committee has embarked on a simplification program to reduce the number of options it judges acceptable in its standards. Many companies and countries are resistant to change, but with the globalization of emerging markets, and as companies seek funding and capital from outside their own country, they will feel the need to change their accounting systems. In the end, a lot will depend on the integrity and standards set by the international accounting profession. It appears that, gradually, under the threat of lawsuits on the part of disgruntled shareholders and the need to preserve their reputations, many international accountants are now resigning from assignments or avoiding firms which they deem do not meet their standards.

In developed markets, it is true that the very detailed rules and disclosure requirements are often viewed as a burden rather than as a boon to accountants. One accountant said: "I am a certified public accountant, but every time I read a pension footnote I have to refresh my understanding of what the various data mean. This is also true of the income tax information."

The main factors influencing disclosure of financial information in companies is the pattern of ownership and the scope of company operations. According to studies done by the Center for International Financial Analysis and Research, Inc., companies which have shareholders in more than one country or whose operations go beyond domestic borders tend to have greater disclosure regarding their company's operations since they must cater to international investors. Multi-national corporations thus have higher disclosure than purely domestic companies. In addition, companies which are closely controlled or whose major shareholders have a large proportion of shares tend to be less forthcoming in their disclosure.

The compilation of a company's accounts comes only after discussion and compromises between the company's directors, accountants, bankers and auditors about how the company's finances should be presented. If all those involved adhere strictly to the law and all accounting rules, it is still possible for accountants using identical basic facts to produce accounts that show a company is highly profitable or deep in debt. There are a variety of perfectly acceptable ways that income can be treated, depending upon circumstances, and there are similar variations in methods used to value a company's assets. However, the methodology used and the accounts produced must be consistent from one year to another, and the accounts must comply with the law.

China is perhaps the best example of how change is taking place in emerging market accounting. Currently much of the accounting is still done without the use of computers, and accounting varies from one area of the country to another. However, government rules are gradually changing to correct various discrepancies and computers are being introduced to speed up the process. One sign of the need for better accounting was recognized when a major international accounting firm won a US$2.6 million contract to develop accounting standards for China, awarded by the Chinese Ministry of Finance. The object of the World Bank financed contract was to bring accounting and auditing practices in China into harmony with international standards. As in other parts of the emerging world, the major accounting firms have established offices or joint ventures in China. Many of the big accounting firms have expanded rapidly and are training accountants in order to meet the ever-increasing demand.

In Brazil, the complications of inflation accounting and rapid changes in tax applications for accountants create substantial problems. For example, in 1993 many companies challenged in the Brazilian courts the validity of certain tax and regulatory changes decreed in prior years, which dealt with restatements of accounts, tax credits and social contribution provisions. Many companies received favorable decisions in the court and thus could defy regulatory changes.

High inflation and extreme currency fluctuations create a range of unique problems when emerging market investors try to analyze potential investments. For example, in economies such as Brazil and Argentina with a history of high inflation in the past, accounts need frequent adjustment for inflation. These adjustments require an entire set of rules which may differ from one country to another. Add in extreme currency fluctuations, and it is easy to appreciate why corporate comparisons become a time-consuming and difficult process.

One example of the degree to which revisions can affect accounts for emerging market companies, particularly those in countries emerging from socialist economies, can be seen in work required to revise and assess the accounts of Chinese company Brilliance China Automotive Company, which was listed on the New York Stock Exchange at the end of 1992. According to the underwriters, the accounting work took up 11,000 hours, with accounts for the past three years restated in line with American standards. A team of 20 experts from the accounting firm had to spend two months in China to complete the work.

A number of variations and accounting innovations can result in distorted accounts. In Singapore, the Singapore Bus Service and TIBS Holdings, another listed bus company, established a "fuel price equalization account" and showed it on the balance sheet as a current liability, which acted to smooth earnings results. At the beginning of each year a "standard fuel price" based on historical prices was determined. If the actual fuel price was below the standard fuel price, a fuel equalization reserve equal to the difference between the standard fuel price and the actual cost of fuel was charged against the profit and loss statement and transferred to the fuel price equalization account, thus giving the appearance of lower company earnings. If the actual fuel price was higher than the standard fuel price, a fuel equalization reserve was released from that equalization account and credited to the profit and loss account, thus helping to raise earnings.

Good news comes from Taiwan, though, where a major international auditing firm in Taiwan told us that with regard to auditing standards, Taiwan had moved more and more towards US accounting practices. Since 1987, there has been a move towards GAAP standards and a foundation has been set up including academics, government officials, businessmen and accountants to promulgate new accounting standards based on the US standards. They expect that within 6 to 7 years, accounting in Taiwan will be identical to that of the US.

A key problem is the timeliness of extraordinary events reporting. If important information is not reported in a timely manner it can lead to big problems. One example occurred in Hong Kong. The major shareholders knew that the financial conditions of their major customer in the United States had deteriorated. They therefore quietly sold their shares on the market. The share price was driven down from $2.40 in 1988 to $0.23 in 1989. However, in an announcement in April 1989, the Directors said: "The Directors of the Company have noted the recent decrease in the price of the Company's shares although the Company is not aware of any reason for such decreases ..." In May 1989 the company made another announcement: "... The Company's US customer announced on 17 April 1989 that it was carrying out a reorganization plan regarding its corporate structure. The Company does not believe that this will have any effect on its operations." Later in May 1989, another company announcement said: "The Chairman of the Company has informed the Board of the Company that his holding in the Company has been substantially reduced by sales in the open market throughout the last five months up to the present time and that he no longer has a significant shareholding in the company." The listing of the Company was suspended by the Stock Exchange of Hong Kong that same day.

In actuality, unannounced by the Directors, the company started to make losses in September 1988 and continued to make losses through to the end of the year. Meanwhile the Chairman started selling in November and continued until he had disposed of 99 percent of his holdings by May 1989. By speeding up the sale of his shares between March and May of 1989, the Chairman aimed to avoid a fall in the share price once the 1988 results were published. He was reported to have pocketed nearly $112 million from the share sales and saved himself from a loss of at least $22 million as the share price slipped down from $1.10 in February 1989 to $0.55 by May. Once the extent of his disposal became known, the shares collapsed to $0.24 in June, and prompted minority shareholders to force his resignation from the company.

Care must be taken when interpreting accounting terms since different terms are used in different ways by accountants around the world. The words may be in English but the meanings could differ substantially. In Sri Lanka, one set of accounts used the term "fictitious assets" to describe what were actually prepayments. In a case in China, a company used a term in the accounts which was translated by the Hong Kong Chinese as "pension fund liabilities." In fact, the Chinese characters used by the mainland Chinese had a different meaning from that assumed by the Hong Kong Chinese. The meaning was not "pension fund liabilities" but "development reserves." This difference in translation made a significant impact on analysis of the firm's balance sheet, since in one case the item was a liability while in the other case an asset (and a very significant one, at that).

Generally, differences in accounting practices are great and are too numerous to mention but some of the more common ones include the following.

Tax treatment

Each country has a different tax regime, and within countries different industries and geographical areas may have varying

tax requirements. Accountants will, of course, attempt to minimize taxes by their accounts presentation.

Off-balance-sheet items

The use of off-balance-sheet items could be rather significant in
a number of countries. For example, the balance sheets of companies in some countries may not reveal financing where controlled associated companies are not consolidated.

Treatment of intangibles

In some countries, items such as goodwill can be capitalized,
whereas in other countries they are not. For example, goodwill
arising from company mergers is inconsistently treated around
the world. Some countries allow the reduction of goodwill
directly from shareholders' equity, whereas others require it to
be amortized over varying time spans.

Reserves

There are different treatments for reserves, and in some countries reserves are provided, so that management can smooth
results between years. Discretionary or general reserves are
allowed in some countries and not in others. These reserves are
related to the revaluation of fixed assets. Earnings may be
reduced or increased by management decisions regarding the
adjustment of these reserves. Net income may thus be distorted,
making it difficult to evaluate the performance of companies.
Hidden reserves are often allowed for banks by some countries.
As a result, earnings are distorted and there is great allowance
for management to adjust reserves and distort income.

Currency exchange

The exchange rates used (and when they are used) differ from
country to country, thus having a significant influence on
accounts. Companies around the world differ in the foreign currency translation methods used, and sometimes the gains or
losses from transactions are not clearly segregated.

Valuation of assets or inventory

Some countries allow periodic revaluation of assets, whereas others do not. Marketable securities often are given a different value, so that in some cases they are given at cost or in other cases at market value. Different methods are used to value inventory, some at cost and some at realizable value, some at replacement costs and some by other methods.

Depreciation

This is one of the more common cost items which is used differently from one country to another. In some cases, governments give specific guidelines for depreciation timetables. In one country, an asset may be depreciated over ten years and in another country the same asset might be depreciated over 30 years. It is therefore difficult to compare accounting items such as the cost of goods sold, fixed assets, retained earnings and deferred income taxes between companies and countries.

Revenue recognition

The recognition of revenue and the timing of such recognition varies greatly from one country to another. For example, revenues in some countries are recognized when a contract is signed, whereas in other countries they are not recognized until delivery of the goods is made.

Consolidation of subsidiaries

There is great variation in the point at which subsidiaries will be consolidated. Although more and more companies around the world are consolidating subsidiaries where the parent company owns 50 percent or more, there still remain inconsistencies in this practice, with some companies consolidating when they own 20 percent of the company and others not until they own more than 50 percent.

Multiple classes of shares

In many countries there are different classes of shares for a particular company.

Inflation accounting

In high inflation countries, the treatment of inflation in the accounts varies considerably. More importantly, the inflation rates allowed for in the accounts varies.

Treatment of losses

In banks, for example, provisions for loan losses are often treated differently, and there are great disparities in the extent to which loan losses are allowed and charged.

Detailed and intensive research is critical in emerging markets. In the first instance the investor must focus on essential company performance characteristics, unfettered by macropolitical and macroeconomic considerations. Then gathering back-up material to support claims in the accounts is the next step. To illustrate how critical this is, one Thai bank we visited did not provide against property market losses, which were prevalent at the time and told us they had no exposure to this sector. Subsequent back-up checks revealed that in fact they had suffered a baht 200 million loss in a hotel project that was stalled due to the market down-turn. Back-up verification is critical in an environment where figures are questionable.

The bottom line, then, is that all information is useful, none should be discounted, but none should be the sole platform upon which to base an investment decision. Whether your company information is derived from local or global sources, wherever it comes from – brokers, the media, business executives, the man in the street, your associates – consider it all, and then make the most informed decision possible. Only after having lined up all of this company information do we reintroduce macroeconomic factors, to see if they are favorable in relation to the company's targets. If yes, then we buy.

*P*rogress, in fact, is being made all over the world as nations discover that in order to have a healthy economic climate, a healthy capital market system is essential.

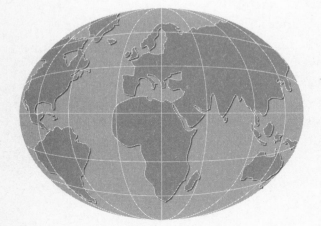

Chapter 8

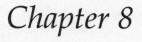

Stock Exchange Characteristics

Most investors in developed countries take for granted the market institutions that make equity investment possible. There is a lot of background infrastructure and legislation which goes into making smooth equity transactions possible. Emerging markets, by definition, are likely to be in different stages of the process of developing an effective infrastructure.

As an international investor, it is wise to know as much as possible about the context of the market in which you are investing. How safe are custodial arrangements? How long is the settlement process? What rules govern the provision of accurate and timely corporate financial information? What avenues of recourse exist for minority shareholders? These are fundamental questions and need to be answered before you plunk your money down in someone else's company.

Planning for the Templeton Emerging Markets Fund was an exciting and stimulating exercise filled with idealistic expectations and dreams. However, once the initial investments began in the familiar and already well-traveled markets where custodians were already at work, such as Hong Kong and Malaysia and Singapore, we were soon slammed against the harsh wall of reality.

⬤ TRADING CHARACTERISTICS

We found considerable differences in trading systems of many of the newer emerging markets. The unique nature of trading systems in each emerging market and the structure of tradition which dominates market practice results in considerable adjustments required by the global investor.

Foreign investors need to be very concerned about the absence or presence of quality regulation of capital markets. Absence of, or ineffective regulation, could lead to unfair market practices detrimental to the interests of fund managers and individual investors. Mutual fund managers sometimes have sufficient power to effectively seek improvements in regulation and suggest reforms. This demand for the effective regulation from mutual funds can make a country's economic leadership consider introducing regulatory reforms. The possibility of capital flight by large institutional investors such as mutual funds and the unwillingness of underwriters to raise additional capital act to spur governments to introduce regulatory reforms.

There are three areas of concern.

Market infrastructure

Institutional infrastructure provides the operational basis for the market: brokers, investment advisors, stock exchanges, currency exchanges, rating agencies, settlement systems, registration systems, custodial services, legal advisors, auditors and accountants.

Regulatory infrastructure

Regulatory infrastructure centers on the government body or bodies which have the power and responsibility to supervise the market but also includes self-regulatory organizations such as stock exchanges, accounting standards boards and accounting and auditing professional associations and similar organizations. It also includes their rules and regulatory procedures and facilities such as stock exchange listing and trading rules or accounting and auditing standards, plus the monitoring and, most important, enforcement of these rules.

Legal infrastructure

Legal infrastructure provides the underpinning to the operational and regulatory infrastructure. It establishes the framework of property rights, contractual relationships, forms of incorporation, and rights and responsibilities of participants in the market. It also specifies the powers and responsibilities of the government supervisory authority and self-regulatory organizations.

Infrastructure, then, is the underpinning body of rules, practices and redress mechanisms surrounding the conduct of financial transactions. As such, a sound infrastructure should provide four things. The first is certainty as to property rights and the inviolability of contracts. This means that an investor can be secure in the knowledge that the legal title they have purchased will be reinforced by the system surrounding the transaction, including enforcement bodies, the courts and administrators. Second, the overall infrastructure contributes to the transparency of trading and other transactions, reducing the potential for fraud or questionable conduct. It also sets the standards for public disclosure by companies of all information relevant to the value of their securities. Third, protection is provided by a sound infrastructure against unfair practices by intermediaries and insiders, via regulatory punishments and assured enforcement of any such provisions. Fourth, infrastructure bestows protection against the financial failure of intermediaries and market institutions such as clearing houses.

The Chinese market is a good example of how desperately a market needs infrastructure of all kinds. The list below describes areas that the Chinese government is still trying to address in their reform efforts.

- Listing rules and trading procedures between the Shanghai and Shenzhen exchanges need to be made uniform.
- Special classes of shares for foreigners, which were not fungible with local shares, with "A" shares for locals and "B" shares for foreign investors, and different prices for those types of shares all need to be consolidated.
- Poor investor communication: in China disclosures of corporate events are not timely or complete.
- Accounting standards have not reached acceptable levels.
- A lack of knowledge persists among the regulatory authorities regarding securities regulations. There is no clear line of authority or transparency in rules.

- New issue pricing problems, with many equity offerings issued at prices which are far below market acceptance or, in some cases, far above market acceptance.
- Lack of central depository, clearing and settlement systems for all classes of shares listed on all exchanges, thus obviating the possibility of a national market. (In early 1993, the Shanghai exchange established a central clearing and settlement and depository system, but it was not linked to the Shenzhen stock exchange.)

Reform

In an effort to codify the elements of a financial infrastructure that are necessary for secure financial dealings, the Group of Thirty was formed. A private, independent group of leading bankers and other financial leaders established in 1978, the Group of Thirty has paid particular attention to the global clearing and settlement issue. In 1988, a panel of experts from the Group of Thirty held a symposium in London to discuss the state of clearance and settlement practices in global markets. Concluding that these practices required significant improvement, a steering committee was assembled to propose a set of practices and standards that could be embraced by markets around the world.

The steering committee spawned a working committee of experts who, in March 1989, released a set of nine recommendations to remedy deficiencies such as delayed or extended settlement of securities transactions, lack of information dissemination to key participants in securities transactions and other problems in global securities transactions. It made the following key recommendations:

- The standard settlement period should be T+1 (trade date plus one day).
- Institutional investors and other indirect participants should be included in the trade comparison system.

- Central depositories for book entry transfer of securities should be established.
- Trade netting systems should be established so that debits and credits between participants can be netted, thereby avoiding excessive payment transfers.
- Simultaneous delivery versus payment in settlement should be ensured.
- All settlement payments should be on a same day basis.
- A rolling settlement system for all markets should be adopted.
- Securities lending and borrowing should be encouraged to expedite settlement.
- The ISO standards for securities messages and the ISIN numbering system for securities issues should be adopted.

Any effort to evaluate the safety of the infrastructure of a given market must make reference to the Group of Thirty's recommended standards. They set a standard which securities markets around the world should aim to achieve.

I evaluate the safety conferred by a given financial infrastructure in the area of securities trading, by applying the acronym "FELT." This is a simplified variation of the Group of Thirty's benchmarks, more easily quantifiable and readily analyzed. When investigating a market, I ask four standard questions:

- Is the market fair?
- Is the market efficient?
- How liquid is the market?
- How transparent are the activities and participants on the market?

In my analysis I define the above terms as follows (see Figure 8.1):

- **Fair:** Both small and large investors should have equal access to shares at comparable prices. Additionally, information flows and transaction execution should not favor insiders or outsiders.

- **Efficient:** The trading system must be established in such a way that paperwork is kept to a minimum, and operations are conducted in the most direct and simple way with the lowest cost. Time is also an important factor, including the capacity to settle a trade quickly, rather than being locked in while cumbersome settlement procedures are executed.

- **Liquid:** A trading system should foster high availability of shares on both the buy and sell sides. This also implies low transaction costs, generated by frequent turnover, which enable market participants to be active in the market. It helps if the market is not dominated by a small number of listings. Volume of trading should be high enough that all but the largest of market players are unable to move markets.

- **Transparent:** The true nature of supply and demand should be apparent to the investor so he is able to judge the parameters within which he must work when completing his trades. This transparency fosters liquidity, fairness and efficiency. Transparency also applied to corporate information disclosure, so as to foster accurate trading assessments.

F - fair

E - efficient

L - liquid

T - transparent

Fig 8.1   Capital market infrastructure: "FELT"

These are the FELT characteristics which we value when entering a new market. In some instances, we have found significant deviations from this desired state of affairs. Efficiency, which covers a broad range of issues, with perhaps the most important being settlement, can often be deficient. We do not, for example, consider trading to be efficient if settlement takes two weeks and registration takes two months, resulting in the buyer being locked into his position for a long period with no possibility of escape. Liquidity affects the investor both on the buy and the sell sides. In either case, an investor always wants to be able to deal in significant positions without affecting the market price. To achieve this, a healthy market in which a number of investors with different objectives are trading in a security, is needed. This is one reason why we are less likely to condemn investment "speculators," since they augment market liquidity and turnover.

I am convinced that the only way to meet the FELT requirements is through the introduction of two important innovations; computerized trading systems with an automatic computer matching of trades and a central registry which manages clearing and acts as a depository. These two requirements are mutually dependent and both must exist in order to ensure the accomplishment of FELT market conditions. The very nature of computerized operations where market participants may enter orders directly into the system enables a fair queuing system, the rapid display of information to participants, on-line operations so that investors may monitor execution of trades to ensure fair pricing, and swift trade execution. It seems obvious that the FELT-qualities can be best advanced through computerized trading, and a comprehensive central depository system. Because of the importance of these solutions to the achievement of FELT-compliant markets, I've reviewed them in greater detail below.

Computerization

In experience gathered around the world, the introduction of computerized trading operations has resulted in a quantum leap in improved trading operations. With the advent of computerized trading, advances in speed and accuracy are possible, and are being realized today in many markets around the world. The elimination of all kinds of fraudulent evils is also possible. Computerization makes a huge contribution to the attainment of FELT market conditions.

Trades conducted by computer are impersonal - the buyer puts up a request for bids on the screen, and sellers anonymously submit their sell prices. The buyer selects one of the bids on the screen, types "done" and the transaction is complete. This system totally eliminates double-dealing, favorable dealing, biased markets, cronyism, and all the other ills that beset trading when it is conducted on the basis of personal relationships. Additionally, computer trading is more time-effective, as reams of paperwork are eliminated. Computer trades are harder to "lose," as the documentation is not dependent on paper. Computer trades are also significantly faster, making the market capable of greater expansion. For all of these reasons, computerization of the stock exchange is an important step towards fairness for all users.

Many emerging markets are undergoing transformation from floor trading to computer-aided or screen-based trading. When I was managing the Taiwan R.O.C. Fund in 1987, the Taiwan market was, at that time being dramatically transformed. The impact was enormous not only in terms of the adjustments faced by brokers and other market participants but also in terms of the impact it had on price behavior and turnover.

But the computerization of trading operations is not solely an emerging market issue. It applies to stock exchanges around the world. Even markets which have existed for hundreds of years are not necessarily more advanced in their systemic infrastructure than those emerging markets we discuss in this book. For too long, stock exchanges have been permitted to remain little more than privileged clubs. Given how critical investment in corporate activities is to business development everywhere, this state of affairs must change.

In fact, today, changes and development of market infrastructure are in evidence. Germany, for example, has renamed its

Frankfurt Stock Exchange the "Deutsche Borse" and is computerizing its trading operations so as to gain a greater share of the total trading in all of Germany. Such changes are driving other exchanges in Germany, such as in Berlin and Bremen, to do likewise and remain competitive with Frankfurt. The presence of competition is increasingly real for stock exchanges around the world, who are gradually replacing systems which can only be characterized as cozy, monopolistic facilities run by club-like committees. Today, most exchanges acknowledge that they are operating under international conditions where there is competition between markets.

Nevertheless, resistance to reform and change runs very deep, particularly in those markets where traditions die hard. The efforts by the London Stock Exchange to introduce a computerized settlement "Taurus" system resulted in tremendous losses and the eventual abandonment of the project. Similar self-interest among players has resulted in Japanese efforts at computerization to face similar problems to those found in the United Kingdom.

The objective of this system was to dematerialize settlements, so that share certificates could be scrapped and share transfers handled by book entry on computer. However, the concept of having a central computer maintaining all records of all shareholdings was resisted by the registrars and banks, who were paid to maintain share registers for listed companies and who would have been put out of business by such a system. The resulting concessions made to rival interest groups resulted in the Taurus system turning into a highly complex and impracticable project.

Technically, the challenge is not insurmountable, since airlines and major banks have extensive experience of handling such systems. The Taurus efforts to meet all conflicting requirements, and thus agree to a distributed database system using the Stock Exchange as a hub, resulted in major complications. This project became even more complex when it was considered that dematerialization was a first step towards a rolling settlement system (where all transactions would be settled continuously rather than the prevailing London fixed-date settlement system). A delivery versus payment requirement (effectively "cash on delivery" of shares) would imply the integration of cash and transfer and clearing systems.

As with London, Japan continues to limp along with paper-based systems which basically have not changed for decades. JASDEC, Japan's depository center, was started in 1984 but didn't go into operation until

> *Perhaps the most exciting developments are taking place in emerging markets, since these markets are able to "leapfrog" into the newest and most advanced technology without going through the various stages of development that older markets experienced.*

1991, about five years behind schedule. As at 1992, only 2.6 percent of all shares issued in Japan were in the JASDEC system, because of the unattractive fee scale and limited settlement and custody services. Currently, JASDEC resembles a clearing house rather than a modern day depository. It does not distribute dividends, proxy or shareholder rights.

Interestingly, many emerging markets have the advantage of starting out anew in this field, and can find themselves in the position of being better able to install systems which would be resisted in some other developed markets. Perhaps the most exciting developments are taking place in emerging markets, since these markets are able to "leapfrog" into the newest and most advanced technology without going through the various stages of development that older markets experienced.

Central depository

The logical accompaniment to a computerized trading system is an interconnected central registration and depository system, which is also computer-operated and linked to the trading system. This enables book entry and central ownership allocation. In the face of such systems, a host of potential problems such as counterfeit share certificates, lost certificates and lost payments all become a thing of the past. Obviously, the impact of such changes on market confidence is inestimable.

There are those who continue to impede the progression towards central registries. In many countries, the firms themselves still maintain the share registry and this gives them a powerful weapon. In the case of Gazprom, a Russian gas company, there was an attempt to segment their domestic and international investors by controlling share registration. Foreign investors were to be charged US$5 per share, while local investors were able to obtain shares at US$0.25. What prevented the foreigner from buying on local bourses? Registration of their investment. Although foreign shareholders were able to register with the central depository, theoretically making the transaction arm's length, the company required all domestically bought shares to be registered with a group-affiliated bank. This enabled the firm to keep foreign and domestic shares separate, and therefore prices different. At the same time, the firm listed the foreign shares on the Vladivostok stock exchange in Russia's Pacific coast to separate trading from Moscow.

The growth of depository receipts is a clear example of what can happen when investors perceive differences in the security of their transactions between exchanges. Many investors prefer to purchase depository receipts of foreign issues, rather than trade the actual stocks in their home market, since the cost of trading and safekeeping depository receipts is often less than that applicable to the trading of the original securities. The expanding popularity of depository receipts and other similar products that allow investors to avoid markets with inadequate financial infrastructures should crystalize the problem in the minds of domestic regulators. I can see no clearer threat to domestic markets than continued resistance to the demand for FELT operating conditions.

STOCK EXCHANGES AS CLUBS

Where does the continued resistance to FELT conditions come from? Market participants such as banks, brokers, investors, custodians, and government regulatory officials can have a vested interest in maintaining the status quo – either because the current system provides employment, yields profits, or imparts power – causing change to come slowly. A number of institutional changes are required to satisfy FELT standards and if the participants in those institutions don't appreciate the greater gains to be had from a fair and unbiased market, the progress gets mired in bickering and conflict.

If we examine the development of stock exchanges around the world, it is clear that many, if not most, were started as very exclusive clubs of wealthy individuals whose involvement in the markets was hereditary. Some of these historical precedents are still in evidence today.

The Rio de Janeiro Stock Exchange dates back to the 18th century, when Brazil was a colony of Portugal. In 1945 the Imperial Government decided to place brokerage business under supervision and control. Brokers were thus classified according to their specialties, such as gold, coffee and securities broking. Originally, brokers were appointed by the government and held office for life. The tradition was perpetuated whereby the broker license was passed on to the brokers' descendants, so that brokerage houses grew into closed family enterprises. This situation existed until 1964 when the Brazil Banking Reform Act was passed and the National Monetary Council and the Central Bank of Brazil were created and assigned tasks to review the regulatory environment of the Stock Exchange and the security broker industry. The stock exchanges were reorganized under the Capital Markets Law where a number of new brokerage firms were allowed, but even then, long-standing brokers were given priority when seats within the new exchange were allocated, although they were required to reorganize from the family structure to corporate entities. In 1976 the Brazilian Securities Commission was established. This marked the beginning of a new era for the stock exchanges in Brazil. As of early 1993, there were about 330 brokerage houses registered in Brazil and nine regional stock exchanges in the major cities.

In Brazil, as in other countries, despite new regulatory structures, many of the old structures remain. These systems are difficult to transform not only because of long-standing traditions and habit, but also because of the threat of lost incomes. Having the right to operate as a broker, a custodial bank, a company registrar or other to provide some other service often means having a monopoly or exclusivity within a cartel which can guarantee a comfortable lifetime sinecure. Obviously, such entities have a stake in resisting systems which dismantle their monopoly, including innovations such as computerized trading, central depositories, book-entry registration systems and more efficient trade settlement procedures.

Rosario Lopes, the Philippines SEC Chairwoman, faced considerable opposition in her efforts to merge the two Philippine stock exchanges, the Manila and Makati Stock Exchanges. When she became the Chairwoman of the Philippine's SEC in 1989, Mrs Lopez argued that a single exchange would simplify listing procedures, strengthen enforcement of regulations and eliminate arbitrage between the two exchanges so that market manipulation could be minimized. But the rivalry between the two exchanges was difficult to rectify: the Manila exchange was established in 1927, making it one of Asia's oldest exchanges, while the Makati Exchange was established in 1963, when some brokers from the Manila exchange left to establish a rival exchange in the new Manila suburb of Makati and started charging lower commission rates. It was not until the intervention of President Fidel Ramos, who gave them a 1992 year-end deadline to unify, that things started to move.

Unfortunately, many stock exchanges around the world are still operated by the brokerage communities with little regard for the other participants in the market, listed companies, small shareholders, institutional shareholders and the general public. So long as the governments protect their narrow interests, the greater interests of the business community will go unserved.

SETTLEMENT AND CUSTODY

For the securities industry, the settlement of securities trades is a major efficiency hurdle. Investors generally expect a simultaneous exchange of securities for cash, termed "delivery versus payment" (DVP). If the DVP standard is not met, then the investor runs the risk of late delivery or failed delivery, and sometimes the loss of securities which were paid for, or loss of payment for securities which have already been sold or delivered. Inefficient clearance and settlement systems therefore present a great risk of capital losses, lost interest, and the possibility of fraud and malpractice. Emerging markets, along with some of the developed markets, have major problems in the clearing and settlement of securities. Capital flows into the emerging markets have been seriously impeded as a result of improper clearing and settlement systems. Inefficient and improper clearing and settlement systems have resulted in the perception by investors that such system failures could jeopardize their clients' investments.

Custodial services go hand in hand with settlement systems. These services include the provision of share safekeeping, share registration, accounting reports, and notice of corporate actions. Custodians usually collect dividends, take up rights issues, and remit back to the investor any sales proceeds less taxes generated by the investor's activities. When a trade is settled, it is the custodian which confirms the transaction and maintains records on the investor's behalf.

Interestingly, the whole idea of custodial services is still a foreign concept in many countries. It is often the case that companies keep the stocks themselves and maintain the shareholder's registry, a system ripe for manipulation. Where custodial services are a new phenomenon, they can be slow and inefficient.

In Bangladesh, we were told it would take seven to 10 days just to figure out the taxes applicable to a stock transaction, and then the custodian would need to get clearance to repatriate the funds. In another emerging market in which we have invest-ments, a local banker has recognized the business potential of custody services, and attempted to forge an alliance with an international bank in order to offer them to foreign investors. But so far only one bank has expressed interest, and even they are not willing to guarantee the validity of the certificates they hold on foreigners' behalf.

This underlines a major problem facing investors in emerging markets: the availability of custody facilities. Emerging markets fund managers usually work with a global custodian who is res-ponsible for establishing custodial facilities in each of the coun-tries where the fund is investing. This either means utilizing the local branch of the local custodian bank, or appointing a subcus-todian capable of undertaking that function. A great deal of work is required to evaluate the safekeeping system, procedures, insurance coverage, and other aspects, to ensure that the client's assets are safely kept.

The custodian is required to execute buy and sell orders, receive and deliver cash, receive or deliver securities, transmit information regarding corporate actions such as rights issues, collect dividend income, vote according to the instructions of the asset holder, and repatriate funds out of the country as instructed by the fund managers. In the global fund manage-ment business, there is a careful separation of power between the fund manager and the caretaker of the assets, the custodian. Thus the global custodian chooses the local custodian bank, and ensures that all concerns about trading, settlement safety, and efficiency are satisfied. If there are no local banks with the experience or ability to provide custodial services, international portfolio investors are effectively excluded from market partici-pation.

The process starts with market entry. Emerging markets spe-cialists are often the very first foreign equity investors to enter a market. But before the investor arrives, the custodian must first penetrate the market. Therefore we often find ourselves persuading reluctant custodians to enter markets which contain all kinds of risks and complications. The transformation in thinking by custodial banks has been gradual for a number of very good reasons.

(1) Assumption of responsibility for authenticity. A major responsibility of custodians around the world is to undertake that certificates in their safekeeping are genuine. However, custodians are reluctant to accept full responsibility in emerging markets because of the much greater likelihood of problems. If one approached a custodian in Tokyo and asked him to assume the risks for counterfeit securities in Japan, he would be likely to accept the risk, as the chances of counterfeit certificates are very low. However, counterfeits and all other manner of frauds are a real possibility in many emerging markets, and many potential custodians prefer simply to forgo the business rather than take the risk.

(2) Custodians customarily take on the responsibility for notifying clients about corporate actions such as meetings, new share issues, and dividend announcements. However, in emerging markets they may experience difficulty in even identifying the existence of those corporate actions, much less when they are taking place, or what are the "ex dates" and payment dates. Information flows about such matters are not ideal in emerging markets, so that the custodian's task necessitates an extra degree of care beyond what most custodians are called upon to provide.

And we have problems with custodial issues too. United States Securities and Exchange Commission (SEC) rules require that approved mutual funds meet a number of custodial requirements, among which is a requirement that any fund assets kept abroad be deposited in banks with at least US$200 million in capital. Some emerging markets do not have banks which meet that minimum requirement. Incidentally, I feel that such a restriction is misplaced since a bank's capital size is certainly not a good measure of its safety.

Some studies on the costs of maintaining and administering investment accounts indicate that administration, management and brokerage fees are considerable, contributing to the centrality of custodial and settlement issues to foreign investors. According to one study of a US$3 billion pension account, about US$1.5 million was for general management and administration, US$6.5 million for direct management fees or expenses, US$1.5 million for brokerage fees and US$10.5 million for stock and bond portfolio execution costs, excluding the brokerage fees. When considered as a percentage of the total portfolio, the US$20 million is only 0.7 percent of US$3 billion portfolio. This cost could be considered minimal in percentage terms but, as the size of the fund decreases, the percentage taken by various fees and expenses can be much higher because of numerous fixed costs. For the individual foreign investors, such costs are prohibitive.

Investors and their custodians are, of course, going to be faced with domestic market practices which do not conform to their expectations. For example, some emerging markets have adopted a "T+1 system," so that payment is required the day after a trade has been executed. While seemingly an efficient standard in the eyes of domestic regulators, the reality is that if a foreign investment manager want to invest locally, but works in a different time zone (while the global custodian is perhaps in still another time zone), the T+1 settlement condition demands considerable effort to achieve.

"Good delivery" is another area in which foreign and local investors often have differing expectations, and can result in substantial delays in entering markets. It is not unusual among emerging markets for the market practice to be to deliver securities several days after payment has been made.

In some countries, there is more than one system for settlement and custodial operations. Looking again at Brazil, the Rio de Janeiro Stock Exchange has a clearing and settlement system performed by the Camara de Liquidacao e Custodia SA, an independent profit-making corporation managed by an independent staff which undertakes registration, clearing, settlement and also operates a fully automated book-entry depository system for securities. However, in Sao Paulo, the largest exchange in Brazil, settlement and registration is carried out by Bovespa Registered Shares Fungible Custody, a service developed by the Sao Paulo Stock Exchange (Bovespa). That service consists of share transfer services, custody and settlement. With two systems operating for the same securities, an additional system is required to link the two.

One example of the problems of settlement and trading came when I visited Poland in 1992. When I met one of the bank officials whose bank also serves as a broker, and discussed the possibility of purchasing shares in Poland, I said: "I'd like to start trading. What should I do? How can we get things started?"

"Well, it's easy. Just open an account," he answered.

"Fine," I replied, "but the way we deal is we place an order first. You buy the stock, inform us by telex and then we transfer the money."

"Oh, no," he said, "I don't think that would work because I don't know whether we can trust you to pay up after we bought the stock."

I asked what trading system they used, and he told me it was T+1.

"Well," I said, "that might be a little tough, but we can do it because we're already doing it in Turkey. Are you a member of SWIFT, the transfer system that the banks have to transfer money by telegraphic transfer?"

"Oh, yes," he replied, "our bank is a member of that system. However, there is one problem. Although the bank can obtain instantaneous notification of payment, the department in charge of the SWIFT operations is in the next building and it takes them three days to notify us of the payment!"

● OVERSIGHT

In most of the emerging markets, regulation and surveillance of trading systems has not, in practical terms, been developed. More importantly the regulatory authorities have not developed a sophisticated and realistic legal framework for regulation of trading. The emerging markets are not alone in this respect, and much needs to be done in all markets around the world. On the one hand there are simply too many rules and regulations lacking a basis of accurately researched experience. On the other hand, those regulations are not properly or uniformly enforced. The consequence is that the fund manager must adopt a completely open-minded approach, not taking anything for granted and preparing to work with a variety of anomalies.

A lack of a company law describing how to create, operate and dissolve a company, no unified accounting principles, no strong disclosure system, and no detailed requirements for evaluating a company's assets are all problems that investors have to face in some emerging markets, along with a lack of insider trading regulations and potential conflicts of interest with regulators who are also participants in the market. Commingling of client accounts by custodial banks presents another challenge to emerging market investors. It is clear that in many accounts in emerging country subcustody banks, assets of different investors are commingled so that in the event of mishap, such as counterfeit securities, tracing the actual owner of the worthless securities becomes a major problem. Clients should demand separate accounts to ensure the viability of their holdings.

● TAXATION

It is common in emerging markets which have favored directed credit and State-ownership of commercial banks to find that tax rates discriminate in favor of savings and demand deposits, as opposed to securities investment, and in favor of borrowings from banks as opposed to capital raisings from the public. These policies have been used extensively in Communist and socialist countries to concentrate capital accumulation and allocation decisions into the sphere over which government could exercise the most direct policy control.

The starting point should be a taxation regime which is neutral in its impact on choices between different financial instruments, whether from the point of view of capital raiser or investor. This neutrality should also include any taxes which add to transaction costs. For example stamp duties and turnover taxes can be a disincentive to investment and should not be imposed without careful consideration of their impact. This applies as much to developed markets as it does to emerging markets.

GOVERNMENT INVOLVEMENT

I have not talked about government regulation of the stock market. This is not meant to diminish the importance of such a regulation: it does have a role but that role should be restricted to acting as a referee and not as a participant. For example, efforts by government regulators to fix "fair" prices to stocks are simply misdirected, since it is the market which is better able to determine the fair prices. The market boosting measures sometimes applied by the Governments in Korea and Japan are detrimental to fair and equitable capital markets. Such measures distort pricing and discourage rational investor decisions. While these efforts may benefit investors in the short term, in the long term they hamper a truly healthy capital market and damage investor confidence in the market.

THE FUTURE OF EMERGING MARKETS' TRADING, CUSTODY AND CLEARANCE INFRASTRUCTURE

Securities trading is entering a new era. With the advent of computerized trading, advances in speed and accuracy are possible and are being realized today in many markets around the world. I'm excited by the potential for emerging markets to "leap-frog" into the newest and most advanced technology, speeding the financial infrastructure development process considerably. Progress, in fact, is being made all over the world as nations discover that in order to have a healthy economic climate, a healthy capital market system is essential. We are entering a new era and I'm happy to be a part of this era of rapid change and improvement. Without sufficient market infrastructure, securities markets cannot prosper.

Of course risk exists, but that's what professional investors in emerging markets love to manage, and in fact, that's why mutual fund holders pay management fees: to get the most experienced and competent manager available to ensure the protection of their investment.

Chapter 9

Risks

"Moving forward necessitates risk. The important thing is being able to adapt and be sufficiently diversified so that a single mistake does not compromise your entire future." An Wang

● INTRODUCTION TO RISK

I was recently asked if I felt that "hoodwinking, flim-flammery, and bamboozling" were common practice in some emerging markets and if the local equivalent of the US's SEC were powerless to stop it. While it is easy to be taken in by some financial characters, my feeling is that such transgressions can occur whether there is a strong SEC or not. Some financial actors are simply in it as frauds. However, the frequency of such transgressions depends on the application of the law and effectiveness of the SEC-equivalent in each country. Generally speaking, our experiences have been quite good, and we find that most companies, working within the constraints of the country's tax code and competitive pressures, treat shareholders fairly and honorably.

However, the exceptions can be egregious. In this chapter, we focus on risk, which in emerging markets is fairly endemic and wider-ranging. People in frontier markets, without long-term established business norms, take advantage of the circumstances to make as much out of it for themselves as they can, and it behooves the neophyte (or not so neophyte) investor to be on guard.

Definitions

Modern portfolio theory gives a very technical definition of risk. It defines "risk" as the variance (as measured by the correlation coefficient) of a portfolio's historical returns. Therefore a portfolio which is yielding excellent returns to an investor may have a high-risk profile if these returns are volatile over the years. In emerging markets, due to the frontier-like nature of their financial markets, there are usually wide swings in returns, even over a short time period, making them high risk. We review below why big price changes can happen so readily in these countries, but at this point it is necessary just to make clear that a technical appreciation of risk is a function of market volatility.

To minimize portfolio volatility and thereby the risk (i.e., making your returns as close to constant as possible), one solution is to invest in countries which have a low correlation coefficient of market movements between each other. That is, select markets that are driven in the opposite direction by similar events. For example, an increase in world oil prices is likely to have a beneficial effect on Indonesian stock prices, as a net exporter of oil, but a possibly negative effect on Singapore's stock market, as Singapore is a net importer of oil. By investing in stocks of countries which have low correlation coefficients with each other, the volatility of your personal global portfolio is reduced, and by extension the risk to your investment, even though the big price swings on individual counters have not been eliminated.

> *In emerging markets, due to the frontier-like nature of their financial markets, there are usually wide swings in returns, even over a short time period, making them high risk.*

But this simple definition of risk and the relatively simple solution for reducing volatility does not explain the entire picture of risk in emerging markets investment. To fully understand risk, and why the big price swings occur, we will spend most of this chapter reviewing other aspects of risk. The real risks, the ones that you the investor perceive in the marketplace, are many.

Five categories of risk will be outlined in this chapter: political, financial, investment, transactional, and systemic (Figure 9.1). Effectively, these refer to the risks to your principal created by changes in political conditions in the country in which you invest, problems with the financial system in that country which may prevent you from recouping your original investment, failures of the individual companies or securities in which you've invested, the chance of losing your securities in a physical sense through broker or custodian error, and general risks which stem from entering into immature capital markets with insufficient infrastructure to effectively utilize and safekeep your investment.

Political risk

The risks arising from a political environment which might lead to an unfavorable or inadequate regulatory situation, political instability, expropriation or confiscation of assets, nationalization, such as government instability, assassination or a radical policy shift.

Financial risk

Risks resulting from a change in the value of a country's currency or to events such as exchange controls which make it impossible to remit capital, profits, interest and dividends out of the country.

Investment risk

Any risks arising from exposure to a particular company, such as the lack of information, incorrect information, a change in the company's management or ownership which could affect the operation of the business, or a change in the health of a business, depression in a particular industrial sector, or a sudden price panic.

Transactional risk

These are risks associated with exposure to a broker which would jeopardize the investment, such as loss of solvency or lack of efficiency resulting in share purchases in the market at unfair prices. Transactional risk also includes risks associated with problems in the settlement of transactions (such as long delays by registrars in registering shares, complicated and error-prone money transfers), problems in effecting delivery versus payment operations, or from exposure to local safekeeping agents (custodians who may not be operating properly, and may be unable to adequately secure the securities on behalf of their clients).

Systemic risk

We could consider this kind of risk to be any of the myriad risks which arise from an immature system, system bias, inadequate regulation or enforcement, loopholes or downright fraudulent manipulation which is much more prevalent in emerging markets. Risk also exists due to inadequate procedures or audit standards.

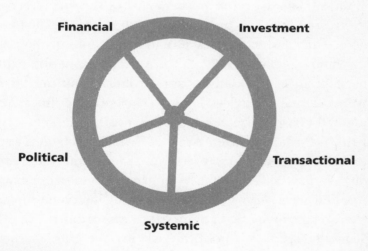

Fig 9.1   Risk wheel

One of the great things about mutual funds, is that they hide much of this behind-the-scenes risk from investors. It is enough to make any individual investor lay awake at nights, wondering what a politician, broker, manager or swindler is doing at that moment to undermine one's hard-earned savings. And yet, for the professional investor, the complexity and novelty of emerging markets is very engaging and often an opportunity for profit if he is able to take advantage of the market irregularities. It offers different challenges than are present in mature markets, and those challenges are often much more diverse than those encountered in traditional investment arenas. Of course risk exists, but that's what professional investors in emerging markets love to manage, and in fact, that's why mutual fund holders pay management fees: to get the most experienced and competent manager available to ensure the protection of their investment while enhancing investment returns.

POLITICAL RISK

The range of political risks is broad and covers the entire gamut of political behavior (or misbehavior!). This review covers sovereign risk, which is the risk of default by the State in the case of debt issuances or the risk of nationalization, in the case of equity holdings. Either way, this is a very blatant and extreme form of political risk. Other forms political risk can take are either accidental, when legislation to resolve one political matter incidentally has a negative impact on capital markets, or purposeful, as in the case where a piece of legislation targets a specific investor or specific kind of market transaction. And there are always circumstances in which politicians in emerging markets, like politicians everywhere, are driven to intervene in capital markets by the lobbying of domestic interest groups.

Generally speaking, political risk in emerging markets is much more endemic and often more severe in its consequences than is the case in developed countries. As a rule, there is a shorter history of institutionalized financial markets in emerging markets, and they are therefore subject to much more tinkering, change and challenge.

In fact, some of the wilder emerging markets have much less well-defined political regimes and systems overall, which are often the target of protest or contention. Some governments have little legitimacy, and elections are not often well entrenched as a system for change of government. Policy change of any kind, including financial, is directly influenced by non-legislative means, up to and including civil war or campaigns of terror. More often, political risk in the capital markets is less extreme, but it is still potentially costly. Below are three ways in which politics can effect your investment in emerging markets.

Political instability

For a long time, many emerging markets subscribed to radically different policy platforms, stemming from different religious or ideological philosophy. While governments are disavowing such policies today, many factions continue to harbor skepticism/resentment towards the new ways and hamper implementation of market friendly policies, making the reform process erratic or desperately slow, with occasional reversals. Combined with general electoral pressures, such as are evident in Turkey and a number of countries, the potential for political instability to extend to the stock market is real.

Yet the truth is that there is no statistical evidence to indicate that civil unrest in the emerging markets is significantly different than that found in the developed markets, particularly when we examine the amount of violence in the United States or severity of demonstrations in France.

Terrorists today are capable of bombing Paris or the World Trade Center as effectively as they are able to bomb downtown Karachi or assassinate the Israeli Prime Minister. The impact of such unrest on stock market investments is difficult to calculate, but the point I want to make here is that it is necessary to focus on the degree to which such unrest affects the on-going functioning of businesses and the stock exchanges. Under close examination, it is often surprising to find how well businesses can function under very severe conditions of civil unrest.

An interesting situation exists in Hong Kong as this book goes to print. The future of Hong Kong, the largest and most sophisticated emerging market, is soon to be reunified with China after years of British sovereignty. The transition worries many, especially those looking in from the outside. But I have lived there for almost 30 years and remember arriving in 1967 when the Red Guards were running rampant in China and most people in Hong Kong were peering nervously across the border and waiting for a horde of invaders. The future has looked bleak before for Hong Kong and it will again. In its history, many have denigrated Hong Kong and its potential. The greatgrandfather of the current Chairman of Swire Pacific, who established that company in 1869, wrote in 1874: "Nothing but loss is apparent." During the Korean War in 1951, there was a physical threat to Hong Kong and an American boycott which killed the entrepôt trade. In 1967 there were serious riots, and in 1973 there was the collapse of confidence in the markets. It happened again in 1983. Through it all, Hong Kong's stock market has survived and prospered. Yes, there were dramatic price crashes, but each was followed by equally dramatic new price highs. The point is that political development is never smooth, but that even in instances of extreme political transformation, markets can and do work.

The most threatening conditions are when governments or political factions decide to confiscate businesses and nationalize. It is at such times that investors, particularly foreign investors, are at great risk. The collision of many emerging economies with colonialism in the 19th century scarred the political landscape in these countries, turning the populace against ideas of internationalization, which they equated with domination. Out of fear and even revenge, many governments in newly independent countries nationalized critical industrial holdings, believing this to be the only way to harness business for the good of the domestic economy. After a decade of two of this, however, local opinion has swung around and local people feel better prepared to embrace international business interaction. On today's political horizon, it is difficult to see the likelihood of widespread nationalizations like those of the 1970s, but it is a fundamental political risk of which foreign investors must be aware.

Regulatory function

To be viable for the foreign investor, the entire regulatory and legal infrastructure of emerging markets must provide certainty as to property and contract rights, transparency of trading, public corporate disclosure of all relevant information, protection against unfair practices by intermediaries and insiders, as well as protection against the financial failure of intermediaries and market institutions such as clearing houses and registrars. In each nation, responsibility for this market infrastructure is divided among a number of different bodies including the stock exchanges, accounting standards boards, and other organizations in addition to the government bodies.

The way political figures perceive their regulatory function is not always consistent. There are conflicting mandates, variations in who they are trying to protect – politicians, minority shareholders, domestic interests, foreign participants – and end up often moving the market in unexpected ways. In emerging markets, where investors are less experienced, unexpected losses prompt them to contact politicians who tend to react to voter complaints, and when the complaint is about stock market losses, government officials are tempted to intervene. In some cases, governments try to manipulate stock market prices, or prop up the market with tactics such as asking government-controlled banks or mutual funds to purchase stocks on the market. Politicians may also use indirect means, such as legislative or regulatory control measures to move the markets in the direction of their choice.

There are instances in which regulators create an artificial environment which invites speculation or manipulation. In cases where rules have been established, determining the amount that prices may move within a certain trading period, excessive market manipulation and high volatility subsequently emerge. The artificial nature of the restriction makes it easy for market manipulators to push prices up to the limit price with a small trades and thus give the appearance of rapidly rising or rapidly falling share prices. They profit by selling out just short of the limit, safe in the knowledge that government won't allow trading beyond that artificial limit.

Although investors often complain of a lack of regulation, it is possible for Governments in emerging markets to go overboard in their regulatory fervor, and begin to interrupt the market system and functioning. For example, some Government regulators attempt to fix "fair" prices for stocks when they are initially being listed, rather than allowing the market to determine the best price. Or some Governments try to manipulate the market by directly boosting prices when the markets go down dramatically. There is an instance of this in Korea, where the Government "encouraged" equity market purchases by financial institutions. In some cases the "guidance" became quite explicit, and investment trusts and other financial entities were required to make daily reports on the amounts of stock purchased.

High inflation and extreme currency revaluations are each gigantic risks, that must be taken into account when estimating returns. If currency devaluation eats away your profits when you try to repatriate your capital, then there is nothing to be gained from the investment process. Large fluctuations in either inflation or exchange rates create a range of unique problems for domestic issuers as well, completely negating all business forecasts. The Brazilian and Argentinean economies particularly suffered through this, as high inflation ran rampant in the mid-1980s and required business records to be frequently adjusted to account for inflation. Evaluating the inflation and exchange rate impact on business fundamentals and financial portfolios is a serious headache for domestic and foreign investors alike.

Probably the most important task facing securities regulators in emerging markets is how to establish legal structures for investor protection. This is important as it means building the confidence of the general public, so that the securities market is seen as a safe place for savings, rather than a gambling den. One consequence of the gradual recognition of the importance of capital markets and stock markets is the growing tendency in emerging countries to establish more powerful and specialized securities regulatory organizations with the primary role of equity market development. This is a welcome decision from the point of view of the international investor.

Restrictions on foreign investment

Political restriction of foreign investment is a continuing problem in emerging markets. Xenophobic attitudes towards foreign investors are not uncommon and a number of countries have restrictions on such investments. Many developing nations cling to past fears of colonialism and foreign domination, shunning portfolio investments from abroad. In the majority of such nations, laws exist which discriminate against the foreign investor. This is particularly true of portfolio or passive investments. Even those countries not subject to colonialization will restrict foreign investment so that capital flows do not upset their normally small and weak markets.

It's true that foreign investors haven't helped themselves much either, as currency speculators with churn and burn strategies of investment have fostered a completely negative image of all portfolio investors. But as regulators gain experience, they will be able to distinguish more clearly between speculators and long-term foreign investors, leading to more sophisticated and targeted regulation. It is also true that as markets deepen and liquify, these kinds of concerns about foreign investors rocking the domestic market boat become outmoded and ultimately disappear.

A number of nations continue to welcome direct investments where the foreign partner brings in knowhow, management or capital, while prohibiting the entry of capital alone. Governments often do not adequately differentiate between direct investment and portfolio investment. Foreign direct investment exerts a great deal of control over the operation of an enterprise in the host country. Portfolio investment is much more passive and indeed prefers to stay that way. Portfolio investors, do not wish to exert management control over the enterprises in which they invest. Even where direct investment is not permitted, portfolio capital would bring local entrepreneurs the opportunity to obtain capital for worthwhile projects. Increasingly, emerging market governments are coming around to this position and gradually moving toward open capital markets. One way regulators can allow portfolio investment, while allaying local fears of foreign domination, might be by separating voting powers from ownership rights where necessary.

Market entry requirements evolve constantly. For example, when Brazil, Korea and Chile first opened to non-resident investment, they insisted that foreign investors employ local agents who were entirely distinct from the funds' custodians. Now, the agent's role there is carried out essentially pro forma as a part of the normal custody process. This shows that gatekeeping entry requirements, such as those outlined above, tend to fade over time, leaving only effective, open markets in their wake.

In the meantime, severe limits on portfolio investments persist in many countries. Examples of this are rife and the distortions they engender are easy to appreciate:

- In Thailand the limitations of what percentage of a company foreigners may purchase has led to a disparity between the price of locally registered and foreign-registered shares, with foreigners often having to pay hefty premiums for foreign-registered shares when demand is high. When the market declines, the foreigners then suffer a double loss, the stock price declines and the premium disappears. More importantly, the entire market liquidity is affected since the "local" shares are deprived of foreign purchases and sales, thus reducing liquidity. Under this system, pricing confusion also reigns.

- In China, the foreign reserved "B" shares have a history of selling at a discount to the local "A" shares. The local Chinese investors are thus deprived of shares which they obviously are demanding since they are paying higher prices for the "A" shares.
- In Mexico, foreign-owned shares are sequestered in the national trust NAFINSA, so that those shares may not be used for voting. As soon as the shares are sold to local investors their voting rights are then restored.

There are remedies other than an outright ban that Governments can employ to assuage domestic concerns. Countries which fear foreign control and ownership may consider the possibility of creating a single "golden share" in each listed company. This "golden share" has the power to prevent control of the company being acquired by foreigners. In this way, foreigners are free to purchase all but one of the shares of a company and thus contribute to the overall market liquidity.

To summarize, then, we can see that there is a variety of opportunities for Government to influence capital markets, either directly or indirectly. Government power ranges from outright nationalization, to limiting foreign investment, to legislating returns on investment. Political interference, which does not serve the purpose of refereeing a situation, but tilting the playing field in a manner to favor local players, effectively creates "waves," or higher volatility, than would naturally exist in the capital markets. That makes political developments an exogenous influence on the international investor's stock analysis, and one which must be considered before investing. Once an investment is made, monitoring political changes and the risk they may pose to investment returns requires a lot of time and understanding of local events, not to mention information sources.

● FINANCIAL RISK

Generally speaking in the emerging markets, the trend has been towards liberalization of international payments and transfers and, in fact, of the financial system overall. There is a growing recognition by governments that tampering with market-determined currency and interest rate movements, through restrictions on foreign exchange, fixing rates, discriminatory financial policies, etc., is an inefficient and counterproductive way of achieving the larger objective of financial stability. In earlier times, when currency devaluation was a problem for an economy, countries tended to simply fix the exchange rate, rather than deal with the underlying economic and trade factors that were causing the devaluation. This is no longer the case. Most countries recognize the long-term futility of restrictive financial policies. In some instances, countries continue to limit the outflows of foreign exchange, try to protect certain classes of imports or exports, or generate tax revenue by manipulating financial markets, but such behavior is increasingly on the wane.

Remittance

The most common problem when considering an emerging market is the problem of currency regulation and repatriation of profits and capital. There are myriad ways in which governments attempt to control foreign exchange movements. There are different varieties of complexities for various countries. In many countries, complicated sets of documents must be submitted, and each document must be authenticated by local notaries public and by the country's consulate overseas. Some markets require the use of local agents who act to approve payments and prepare reports for foreign investors. Of course, these services add to the cost.

In countries such as the Philippines, Greece and Israel, proof must be presented to authorities of when that initial hard currency was remitted into the country, prior to allowing capital and capital gains to be remitted out of the country. In some cases, records must show the complete chain from initial remittance to the ultimate sale of specific stocks. In Taiwan, Colombia, and India, investors must apply for prior approval and documents must be submitted from the investor's country of origin, authenticated by a local notary public, and then processed at the nearest consulate before being sent to the invested country. For long-term investors, keeping track of these records and ensuring that the local custodian also keeps track of such records provides substantial chances for error and involves high record-keeping costs.

In other markets, currency controls involve the creation of specially designated cash accounts with hard currency to fund settlements. At the next level of currency control are markets where investors must create special designated cash accounts with hard currency to settle trades. This is the case in Bangladesh and Sri Lanka, for example. On a more extreme currency control scale, currency movements in some countries must be licensed by a regulatory authority. In the most restricted countries, each movement of currency in and out of the country must be approved by the Government.

In other cases, investors must obtain unique identification numbers that are then used for tax accounting and final ownership controls. Venezuela has such a system, and the taxpayer's identification number must be used for every trade. In Korea, the pre-licensing system is in effect, and the investment identity card is used not only to track funds for tax and currency purposes but also to determine beneficial ownership.

The existence of any type of foreign exchange controls presents a considerable barrier to market entry by international fund managers. It adds another element of risk to what is already a risky undertaking. If there is a possibility that foreign exchange controls may result in our not being able to exit a country or, just as importantly, delay our exit, then we have a considerable problem. Delays may result in foreign exchange losses, unhappy fund shareholders, or not fulfilling our own contractual obligations.

The Central Bank of the Philippines once required considerable documentation from Templeton before money was allowed to leave the country. This resulted in delays, often as much as six months. During that time, the bank decreed that the money could not earn interest, thus compounding the risk. So we were sitting on deposits not earning interest with a steadily devaluing currency. Happily, the Philippines no longer has these restrictions and, not surprisingly, more foreign investment is entering the country.

Convertibility

In the area of exchange rate policy, there have also been major changes, particularly in policies regarding fixed exchange rates with periodic devaluations to more flexible exchange rate policies. It has been realized that exchange rate policies have only a limited effect on real exchange rates and that the real exchange rate is primarily determined by fundamental factors affecting the supply and demand for foreign exchange and is thus independent of exchange rate policy.

In the former centrally planned economies, particularly in Eastern Europe, payment restrictions have been significantly lifted, and currency convertibility has been established with bilateral payment arrangements broadly dismantled. In addition, there has been significant liberalization of capital movements in the developing countries. In Latin America, for example, these changes have been significant. Where external financial operations and capital flows were previously subjected to strict controls, these controls have now been liberalized and in some cases eliminated completely, thus hastening the integration of those countries into the international market.

As the liberalization movement gathers momentum, the tendency has been to allow more flexibility and even to have a floating rate within certain parameters. In the case of a "managed float," the central bank will set the rate, but will enter the market to ensure the currency trades within parameters it has set, based on various indicators such as the country's external payments position, central bank reserves, and "parallel" or black market developments. In other cases, an "independent float" or "free float" is used, where rates are fully determined by a free market.

When investing in emerging markets, it is important to understand how countries' governments try to influence exchange rates. In some cases, the government will try to peg its country's currency to a single currency such as the US dollar. According to some estimates, about one-third of developing countries have a single currency peg. In other cases, countries try to use a currency composite of the major trading partners, so as to make the pegged currency more stable than when just a single currency peg is used. In such cases, currency weights might reflect the geographical distribution of trade and capital flows. There are differences as regards the amount of flexibility allowed in a pegged system. In some cases the peg is rigidly enforced, whereas in other cases varying degrees of margins are allowed.

Devaluation

Probably the greatest fear of investors in the emerging markets is the fear of currency devaluation and the resultant possible loss. However, stocks and other passive investments such as real estate are naturally hedged against relative inflation and exchange rate devaluation. Local investors use investment in stock market equities as a means of escaping the effects of inflation and currency devaluation.

However, if an investor is investing in fixed-income securities, then the need for currency hedging could be vital, as fixed-income instruments do not adjust to currency devaluations because the returns are fixed. In some emerging markets such as Argentina and Brazil, many fixed-income instruments are adjusted for inflationary effects, thereby acquiring the characteristics of equities.

Currency transfer and foreign exchange transactions are issues international fund managers must carefully monitor. When placing money in emerging markets and when remitting payment, not only is it necessary to ensure that the bank is obtaining the very best and most competitive exchange rate, but transactions must also be timely. We had this experience during Brazil's hyperinflation period, when Brazil's high annual inflation rate of over 300 percent was reflected in equal multiples of devaluations, so that if a transfer of funds was even one day late, it meant considerable losses. Devaluations against the major currencies could run as high as 1 percent a day on a regular basis in those days.

Currency hedging

Recently, there has been a wider acceptance of currency hedging, with the argument that investors should fully hedge because currency hedges do not affect expected returns, while they substantially reduce the risks of international investment. The argument is that the currency aspect of international investment is a pure gamble and cannot be adequately predicted. More recently, studies have shown that hedging best applies to short horizons only, and that although short-term currency hedging reduces risks, over the long-term hedging would not reduce risks at all. Some studies have shown that currency hedging has had a spotty record when used in conjunction with equity investments. One study concluded: "Continuous hedging had the beneficial effect of reducing volatility. Unfortunately, return was also reduced."

The vagaries and dangers of playing the currency game are beautifully illustrated in the Chairman's Report of a New Zealand company, Agland Holdings Limited. In June 1990, the new Chairman of that company wrote what is perhaps the most candid and refreshing report ever written by a company Chairman. After stating that: "Since its birth Agland has been nothing short of a disaster," and that since its float the company had "merely lurched from one problem to another," Andrew Kroger reviewed his firm's introduction to the world of over-gearing and debt crisis management and the "ludicrous decision" to refinance itself with DM-denominated loans offset by zero coupon DM bonds.

DM11.3 million was borrowed, with DM7.5 being used to purchase assets in New Zealand and DM3.8 million used to buy zero coupon DM bonds expiring past the year 2000. The theory was that on maturity past the year 2000 the bonds would be worth 11.3 million DM, representing the total amount of the debt. It was fine in theory but fatal in reality.

"The inevitable naturally happened," Andrew Kroger wrote in his report to shareholders. The New Zealand dollar collapsed against the DM, resulting in Agland having massive debt serving charges, negative cash flow and effectively an unhedged DM position and a loan facility in default. The "experts" had ignored the fact that as the loan facility was expiring in 1993 and no bank would renew it, Agland's massive paper currency loss would be realized. The "theory" that there was no foreign exchange exposure to Agland was nonsense. Agland was, in addition to its massive interest bill, being forced to pay margin calls on its foreign exchange exposure.

"Little comfort could be taken from the fact that everything would be OK after the year 2000, particularly if the company went under in 1993!"

The vagaries and dangers of playing the currency markets are illustrated by a great number of examples. In early 1993, Malaysia's central bank, which was known as a major player in currency dealing and foreign exchange operations, announced that it had suffered a contingent liability of about US$1 billion on forward foreign exchange transactions. Up until that time, the bank had been known to do more than merely stabilize its currency, by speculating on foreign exchange movements. In 1989, for example, the bank was reportedly criticized by some Western monetary officials for speculating on the yen and the US dollar at a time when the Group of Seven industrialized countries were trying to stabilize currency markets.

INVESTMENT RISK

Perhaps the most essential and highly critical area for foreign investors, or any investor for that matter, is the area of company information disclosure. Many government officials in emerging markets around the world decry the "gambling" nature of stock market trading, but it is no wonder that investors' behavior resembles gambling when they have no information on which to base their investment decisions! If government regulatory authorities had only one task, that task would have to be ensuring that listed companies make full and fair disclosure of company information.

There is a natural antipathy created between the emerging market regulator and foreign investors, so long as reporting/disclosure standards are permitted to remain vague. The lack of trust on both sides drives the investor to play with the market, moving funds at the first sign of danger and causing frequent fluctuations in the indices. Were the regulators to put their energies into improving disclosure standards, little market fillips wouldn't cause foreign investors to divest so hastily. There will always be speculators, but the majority of investors would prefer to take long-term investment decisions, and would feel more secure in their investments during periodic crises if they had a surer sense of the true investment fundamentals evident in full disclosure.

Full disclosure requires all information relevant to a company's operations to be made available to investors on a timely basis, so that they may make an intelligent and informed assessment of that company's performance and prospects. A supplementary/ancillary concept, fair disclosure means that the information must be revealed to the entire market at the same time and in the same degree, not only to a few "insiders." It also means that auditors should be made responsible for preparing company accounts which are complete and contain enough detail to reflect fully the operations, problems, risks and performance as they have been experienced by the company.

Perhaps one reason for the lack of disclosure in some markets is a discrepancy between American-style corporate objectives, and those dominant in emerging markets. In the United States, a primary corporate goal in a public company is shareholder maximization. This is likely derived from the fact that many companies have now passed out of family hands and are full-fledged public companies, responsible ultimately only to their new owners – the shareholders. However, this is not a common structure for firms in emerging markets. They are much more likely to be closely associated with the founding family, and in fact, successive generations are likely to continue to hold majority ownership positions, even if the company has been publicly listed.

The origins of firms in lower-income countries are often relatively recent, and usually connected to a family's endeavors. Unlike more mature economies, where management is often effectively divorced from ownership, many companies in emerging markets, particularly in Asia, were founded and are still managed by individuals and/or family organizations. In many cases, these individuals and family organizations still own a substantial equity stake, frequently over 50 percent of the outstanding shares. This makes corporate management often more concerned with the interests of the family, rather than interests of the company. The well-being of minority shareholders usually comes very far down the list.

One area in which conflict can arise is between the public and private corporate holdings of a family conglomerate. Intra-firm transfers of assets and resources may occur which are not always in the best interests of the shareholders of the publicly owned arms of the conglomerate. If a private company gets into trouble, the family can use its majority ownership of the listed company to underpin the private company, even if such actions run counter to the interests of minority shareholders. There are myriad ways this can be done, some of which may even be illegal, but due to the nature of private company ownership and regulatory enforcement, accusations often go unsubstantiated.

In 1993, Indonesian-listed company Astra International got into trouble when the Soeryadjaya family, the company's founder and major shareholders, started selling shares to raise funds for their privately owned but bankrupt Bank Summa. As the country's second largest company and dominant player in the motor vehicle sector, Astra had a lot of resources at its command. The Soeryadjaya family owned 72 percent of the company's shares until November 1992, when they rapidly dumped Astra shares, in order to meet US$767 million in obligations stemming from the Bank Summa closure. This dumping of shares seriously undermined Astra's stock price and placed minority shareholders at a great disadvantage.

On the other hand, there are ways in which family participation in a public company can benefit the company. The substantial ownership positions held by the family, who act as managers of the company, bring their interests into alignment more closely with those of public shareholders. The family/managers will take care of the company because their family image is at stake. When chief executive officers of those companies are also senior family members, they are often more accessible and willing to talk about their company's plans and prospects than hired professional managers are likely to be.

Abuse of minority shareholders is also prevalent where strong individual personalities continue to dominate firms they started and built up. The culture of shareholder interest is not nearly as ingrained and management will often try to bully or overrun shareholder objections. In one instance, in an egregious display of disregard for the rights of minority shareholders, the lawyer acting on behalf of the president of Mah Boonkrong, a Thai agricultural processing firm, rejected proxies for large blocks of shares, and then ordered the lights and airconditioning in the meeting room to be switched off during the shareholders' representatives meeting. He was able to do this since he owned the hotel where the meeting was being held.

Just to demonstrate how contrary to minority shareholders some corporate management in emerging markets can be, the

following case study of Carrian Investments, a real estate development firm based in Hong Kong is outlined below.

In Hong Kong, the Carrian scandal rocked the stock market in
1981 and resulted in long-running investigations and court
cases. In 1979, George Tan had taken over a public company and
renamed it Carrian Investments. When the company made a
HK$900 million bid for the published net asset value of a listed
company, it shot into prominence. It then engaged in a widely
publicized deal to purchase an office building for HK$1 billion,
reselling it for HK$1.8 billion soon after. In a short period of time,
after a wild buying spree of all kinds of businesses, including an
insurance company, a shipping fleet, a hotel in California, a fleet
of taxis, restaurants, etc., the company was transformed from
one with a net asset value of HK$181 million to a conglomerate
worth HK$5 billion.

It was later discovered however that Tan had used a number
of dummy companies and associates to deal and purchase properties from himself, thereby ensuring ever-increasing prices and
profits. The complex intercompany transactions, cross-guaran-
tees and uncompleted sales were mindboggling to the authorities attempting to liquidate the company after the entire scheme
was unraveled. The scheme was discovered partly as a result of
the Hong Kong property market crash in 1982, during the Sino-
British negotiations on handing the Colony back to China.

Shattered confidence in the company meant that Carrian
could not sell assets to raise cash. Thousands of investors in Carrian shares lost their fortunes as the stock price crashed. The
company was then delisted and declared bankrupt. The result
was that 60 of Hong Kong's most respected banking institutions
were left with debts reaching US$1 billion. It was also later
revealed that Bank Bumiputra, a Malaysian bank established to
care for native Bumiputra Malaysian interests, had been lending
money illicitly through its Hong Kong finance company to the
Carrian Group.

Trials and investigations after the Carrian affair have continued until today. Two men involved in the case died unnatural

deaths. In 1993, a former Bank Bumiputra auditor, who was sent to Hong Kong as an assistant general manager of the bank's deposit-taking subsidiary, was found in a Hong Kong New Territories banana grove strangled with a four-foot-long belt. John Wimbush, a joint senior partner of Deacons, the law firm which handled some of Carrian's deals, was found at the bottom of his swimming pool with a concrete manhole cover tied around his neck.

There is no rule which says all crooks and swindlers live in emerging markets. There are plenty of similar stories in developed markets around the world. But these people thrive in an environment where the regulatory system is new and perhaps not tested, where loopholes are rife and enforcement is weak.

● TRANSACTIONAL RISK

There are all kinds of transactional risks that aren't generally considered when one decides to enter into equity investment in emerging markets. One faces the hazard of corrupt brokers, unfair or costly custodial services, delays in settling trades, etc. Transactional risk actually doesn't get as much attention in regulatory reform as it should, or in international press reviews of international investing. It's a dry topic and usually very technical. Much of the danger comes after the trade, so the investor's interest has often waned by the time the transactional risks emerge. But such risks are real, and you can end up with nothing to show for your investment, if you don't keep a close eye on transactional details.

This text of a letter from an investor tells a cautionary tale:

"I have visited the Republic of Slovakia at least 15 times over the last 10 years. I invested US$100,000 of my own money in a project and was defrauded by my lawyer. I have tried to recover these funds but have realized that the country's legal system is corrupt and in total chaos.

I do not intend to support a system that relies on bribery and corruption, where fraud is a normal business practice. In Slovakia they have a law which prevents the Press from reporting on legal cases still before the courts. In order to prevent me from going to the Press with my story, the officials are artificially keeping my case open! This prevents bad publicity from reaching the public. The recovery of stolen money and goods is impossible without resorting to violence."

Fundamental to transactional risk is the physical need to exchange stock certificates. In this process, it is necessary to use a broker, tell them what you want to buy or sell and in turn they find another party willing to trade. The broker charges a fee for this service. They may also have to collect stamp tax, exchanges' fees, what have you, depending on national regulations. Then the physical certificate must be collected from the seller, reviewed for authenticity and passed to a safekeeper named by the buyer.

Inherent to making this process efficient are (a) good computer systems and (b) trustworthy service providers. Without computer systems, the process of finding parties who wish engage in trades is tedious and slow, and creates opportunities for fraudulent activity. If the computer system can handle paper-free transactions, called scripless trading, lots of fraud (and fees) can be eliminated.

In order to demonstrate the efficacy of scripless trading, let me give you a quick rundown of the examples of fraud involving solely the physical exchange of certificates.

On the **Kuala Lumpur Stock Exchange** in 1992, 75,000 certificates, representing 75 million shares, were "mislaid." The confusion was a result of a rapidly expanding stock market and hectic trading.

In Greece in 1991, the stock exchange suspended trading in Titan Cement, a leading bluechip stock, following the discovery of several thousand forged certificates. Two Greek lawyers and a trader were arrested on charges of circulating the forged share certificates. The scandal exposed weaknesses in the stock market legal framework which did not spell out responsibilities for fraud and forgery.

In India during 1992, there was a major scandal involving millions of dollars. In early April of that year, officials from the State Bank of India discovered that security records for government securities transactions had been falsified, leaving the bank short of millions of dollars. A number of foreign banks, including international firms such as Citibank and Standard Chartered, were involved in the trading of Government-backed bonds, including those issued by State-owned companies. Trading rapidly expanded as price fluctuations and interest rates increased from 1990 to early 1992. However, because of the inefficient and sluggish transfer operations of the actual bonds, banks began to trade receipts for the bonds with promises to deliver the actual bonds later. Trading volumes became huge and some operators began issuing receipts without any supporting assets, using the money to play the booming stock market. The false receipts were traded as genuine receipts, meaning that in reality there were not enough bonds to redeem all the receipts. When the final denouement came, the gap was US$1.3 billion. According to investigators, much of the illegal money that had sent the stock market to record highs had been lent by banks on the collateral of bank receipts that could not be redeemed.

In March 1993, the Indonesian stock exchange regulatory body, Bapepam, suspended trading of five major stocks because fraudulent shares were discovered in four brokerage houses. Newspaper reports indicated that the extent of the fraudulent shares was approximately US$5 million. The criminals sold shares directly to brokers, including a number of foreign brokers. The counterfeit share certificates, according to Press reports, were of exceptional quality, passed ultraviolet tests for watermarks and carried seemingly authentic names and numbers. They also had a convincing history of past transactions on the reverse side, complete with brokers' stamps recording trades, indicating that brokers' stamps had been forged too. The stock exchange in Jakarta later admitted that, during a certain period, even genuine share certificates did not comply with the security printing standards set up by the Government. A market discussion was held regarding what should be done in the future and it was concluded that the best solution would be a shift to paperless settlement. One market observer said that the stock exchange management was slow to endorse such a move, since when everyone was required to register their shares it might expose the true scale of counterfeit or duplicate shares .

It is easy to see how weakness in any one area of the stock exchange system opens up opportunities for fraud or questionable practices.

Brokers

Without a trustworthy broker and custodian, there arises considerable scope for market fraud. In 1995, while a potential new broker was showing me around his office, he let slip that one major investor is a "market indicator" and many brokers traded for their own account off of news of our transactions. How did they get that info? Possibly via custodians, intimated the broker. He then explained in greater detail how brokers traded off the information. "They take the investor buy limit, wait for the stock to move below that limit, then scoop it up for their in-house accounts. Once the stock goes back up, they buy for the investor at the limit ordered."

The concept of trading fairness implies that each market participant will have equal access to shares at a given price. It means that when a seller offers stock at a given price, all buyers will have access to that offer, and when a buyer offers to purchase, all sellers will have access to that offer. This is almost impossible when there are conflicts of interest among brokers. If a broker is also acting as an underwriter, corporate financier or fund manager, and also operating a trading account for his own benefit, it is extremely difficult, if not impossible, for him to resist the temptation to take advantage of the situation, as described in the story above. It is not surprising that large brokerage houses often announce record profits – the bulk of it comes from trading on their own account!

Brokers often do not obtain the best available prices for customers. Also, prompt and timely execution suffers in a loose regulatory environment. In addition, many brokers are trading on their own account so that the customers' trades get short shrift. Insider dealing is rife in many markets and it is not unusual for firms to profit from material insider information. "Front running" is also a practice which is not unusual in many markets where there is no adequate regulation to prohibit such activity.

Unfortunately, many stock exchanges around the world are operated solely by the brokerage communities, with little regard for the other participants in the market such as listed companies, small shareholders, institutional shareholders and the general public.

Fees and charges

The costs involved in investment purchases are surprisingly numerous. Fund managers try to achieve the best possible returns for their clients, meaning that transactional charges must be kept to an absolute minimum. However, where trading commissions and fees are set by brokers, or influenced by regulation favoring domestic participants, these costs are often higher than necessary. Costs are also influenced by efficiency and volume in stock market settlement and custodial operations. The increased adoption of computers and the computerization of stock market operations is enhancing efficiency. And as trading efficiency improves and there are lower costs to enter the market, this leads to increased trading volume and improved market liquidity.

Computers

Emerging equity markets have opportunities to leapfrog into the most advanced techniques and systems, using the latest computer and communications technology. They are able to learn from the mistakes that have been made in the older, developed markets. This holds great promise, and has already borne fruit. For example, using the latest computer systems, the Taiwan Stock Exchange has been able to put in place perhaps the most advanced computer trading system in the world. By lowering the cost of trading, this dramatically widened the market for equity investments in Taiwan and created a more transparent market. When further market liberalization allows foreigners to make direct equity investments, the systems will be in place to attract and handle large capital inflows.

Because of the primitive nature of trading on the floor of many emerging market stock exchanges, it is often nearly impossible to obtain timely and accurate price and volume data. This has obvious implications for liquidity. The lack of transparency of pricing also leads to a lack of confidence in the market and inhibits active trading. For example, there are many cases where institutional investors have placed orders of as little as US$100,000 and it has taken weeks for the market to absorb this amount. Investors require a market which can handle orders in sizes of millions. To achieve such a market requires a modern, computerized trading system such as those found in Taiwan and Singapore.

Settlement

Gaining the initial efficiencies, however, isn't just a matter of installing computers. There is also the need to set rules which make foreign participation feasible. Foreign investors raised a hue and cry when a local stock exchange announced that it would institute a T+1 settlement system. This is because, in the global investment arena, fund managers are managing assets from places on all continents. Instructions for transfer of funds or receipt of securities must travel around the world, and may originate in time zones quite different from the zone in which the trade was conducted. Each country has a different set of holidays.

Delays are inevitable. Foreign investors therefore need a fair degree of time for settlement. We have found that a timeframe of T+3 is best, since it allows sufficient time for payments and transfers to be effected, while not being long enough to encourage speculation. I believe a fortnight, for example, is much too long.

Certificates

We demonstrated in the introduction to this section what can happen in a system before it moves to scripless trading. But you'd be amazed at the great resistance which can be marshaled against such a commonsense development in these markets.

Another way in which physical certificates can cause a problem is in their denominations. It's not something one would think of, but share denominations raise enormous barriers to trading. In 1992, for example, share certificates in Turkey could be in any denomination, at the whim of the issuer. This led to the issuance of share certificates of TL20,000,000, and others of TL1,000,000. Unfortunately, the buyer who accepted the TL20,000,000 denomination later found that the certificates were not in demand, and buyers wanted a discount on them as illiquid instruments. In addition, the buyer was unable to exchange the large denomination certificates for smaller and more marketable certificates.

Turkey offers many good examples of how not to structure physical issues. At one time, shares in Turkey, besides being in varying denominations, were not uniform in their voting or dividend rights. At any one point in time, a company may have both ordinary and preferred shares outstanding, which are divided into Class A, Class B, or Class C (that makes six types of shares). Shares could be further subdivided into old, new and new/new shares, depending on frequency of company dividend, bonus and rights issues.

Custodial services

More and more custodians are coming under scrutiny regarding their role as guardians of assets, and also as the record-keepers of stock movements and corporate actions. There is sometimes a debate about which method should be used for custodial responsibilities having an independent custodian, or having the fund manager provide custody services in-house as part of an integrated service. In the latter case, it must be ensured that the two activities are independently regulated, and separately contracted and managed. In the case of fraud, an independent custodian is an extra guarantee that the reasons for problems will be uncovered, unless, of course, the custodian is undertaking the fraudulent activities himself.

There is a lot to transactional risk, more than most investors bargain on in the beginning. We take for granted a strict legal environment and swift enforcement which curtails underhanded behaviour. Every stage of the stock purchase process must be monitored closely and even investigated in advance, to determine if returns from investment won't be undermined by insecure transactional systems.

SYSTEMIC RISK

In the ideal world, emerging countries should offer investors equity markets which have:

- an organizational structure, understandable to both the domestic and international investors;
- an efficient, transparent and low-cost trading system;
- a settlement and custodial system which enables simple and safe operations for the transfer of securities;
- the availability of timely and reliable company information, so that reasoned and informed investment decisions may be made.

In many of the emerging markets, regulation and surveillance of trading systems as well as the general regulatory framework have not been fully developed. A sophisticated and realistic legal framework for regulation of the markets is still in developmental stages. On the one hand, there are simply too many rules and regulations which were formed without a basis. On the other hand, those regulations which do exist, in effect, are not properly or uniformly enforced. In surveying the legal and regulatory problems in emerging markets, the following topics are most frequently encountered:

- shallowness of markets;
- weakness of regulation/enforcement;
- special interests prevail (change is blocked);
- irregular rules or hours of operation;
- transparency;
- distribution system (i.e., privatization or Initial Public Offering (IPO));
- organization/ownership of exchanges.

Securities regulatory systems have been implemented in many developed markets over a period of decades. In the case of emerging economies, governments are just beginning to tighten up regulatory structures surrounding financial transactions.

Some key considerations are

- disclosure of material information, fully and promptly;
- proxy solicitation, the right to vote and easily gain access to voting opportunities;
- take-over bids and related party transactions, protective mechanisms.

Investors need to be able to liquidate their holdings at short notice, and often quite frequently. The bulk of international portfolio investments are made on behalf of pension funds and open-ended mutual funds or unit trusts, where shareholder or pensioner redemption requests are constantly received, and where the fund manager is committed to honor such requests on demand. The portfolio turnover of some unit trusts has averaged about 50 percent per year. This means that the average holding period has been two years. But it would not be unusual for a fund manager to buy and sell investments in one country in as short a time period as a week, especially under conditions where redemption requests require such high turnover, or when the investment criteria demanded it.

This is where the lack of liquidity in many of the emerging stock markets is a source of major problems for foreign portfolio investors. To illustrate the point, let's imagine that an investor had about US$2 billion in emerging markets money under management, and let us assume that there were 200 companies in the portfolio, or an average of US$10 million per company. Liquidity becomes a concern when the manager tries to dispose of only one of those companies. How long would it take to do so without disturbing the price, especially if daily trading of that company amounted to only US$100,000, which is not an unusual occurrence in emerging markets?

Emerging markets can more often be distinguished by the lack of transparency in regulatory procedures, with the tendency for special personal connections to hold more weight than the written rule. Very often the rules are not clearly stated and thus difficult for foreigners to follow. This is compounded by insufficient coordination between different government agencies and the lack of explicit information on procedures:

- the quality of companies permitted to list on the stock exchange;
- exchange regulations and practices which tend to serve the interest of banks or brokers and not the investing community as a whole;
- the lack of government enforcement of regulations and the lack of initiative on the part of the government to make changes in the market structure;
- settlement and trading difficulties;
- difficulties with capital repatriation;
- discrimination against foreigners as regards to share owner-

ship and the establishment of complex security classes for foreigners and locals.

But many countries today recognize how systemic problems are holding back their market development and are actively resolving the conflicts.

The Malaysian government launched a commission to study the securities industry and insider trading. However, officials said that it would be difficult to enforce insider trading regulations since many large share transactions were done through nominee companies. One official was quoted as saying: "The Government is actually armed with wide powers to take action against insider trading. It is actually a question of implementing these powers to concerted action."

Conditions which once prevailed in Turkey are thankfully being changed. As late as 1992, the Turkish organizational structure for capital markets was confused and without clear lines of responsibility and authority. The Capital Markets Board and the Istanbul Stock Exchange both seemed to have overlapping authority and responsibilities while, at the same time, they were not covering some essential aspects of capital market operations at all. As a result of this, progress on the stock exchange's development suffered. Fast and efficient implementation of key matters such as trading and settlement computerization, formation of a central depository, and extension of trading hours and settlement dates were not resolved to the satisfaction of both domestic and international investors. For five years, there was no resolution and implementation in regard to establishing a central depository or computerization of trading which would make trading more transparent and efficient.

One example of the changes that take place in various emerging markets securities systems can be found in Israel. There were far-reaching reforms in the securities market after the collapse of the Israeli market in 1983. When the market collapsed, trading in the stock exchanges was suspended for two weeks until the government entered with a massive bail-out. Over the following years, monetary policy was liberalized and steps were taken to relax foreign currency limitations while the Government embarked on a program to reduce direct intervention in the capital market. A public commission which examined what went wrong in 1983 blamed the securities authority for surrendering to the demands of both internal and external pressure groups, thus leaving the public defenseless. In its 20 years of existence, the securities authority had filed only two indictments for alleged violations. The new regulations began requiring quarterly rather than semi-annual financial reports, and recommended establishing independent accounting boards modeled after the US Financial Standards Accounting Board. Most important of all were innovations where the securities authority was able to finance class action lawsuits initiated by minority shareholders, as well as equalizing the voting rights of shares issued by public corporations. Previously, managers could put up 10 percent of the equity of the firm and gain complete control.

The list of the investment risks in emerging markets is long and daunting. What is even more challenging is keeping up with the constantly changing status of these risks in emerging markets (Figure 9.2). Global custodial services are expanding, governments are getting serious about regulation, technical advancement is making computerization more achievable – the list of enhancements is long and getting longer. That's the nature of emerging – to be on a development course, and to be constantly moving towards the target of effective capital markets. To illustrate the combination of risk with an evolving regulatory environment, I've written up the case study of Cukurova Elektrik, a privatized power distribution utility in Turkey.

Political Risk

- instability
- reulation
- foreign investment restrictions

Financial Risk

- remittance/exchange control
- covertibility
- revaluation of currency

Investment Risk

- disclosure
- ownership
- minority shareholder culture

Transactional Risk

- brokers
- fees
- computerization
- settlement
- custody/certificate exchange

Systemic Risk

- liquidity
- regulatory enforcement
- transparency
- operational structure of stock exchange

Fig 9.2   Emerging markets risk summary

Cukurova Electric

Almost every kind of risk was evident in one of our worst investment experiences in emerging markets. This is the story of Cukurova Elektrik, here as an example of the abuse of minority shareholder rights, example of different classes of shares, example of scrip fraud, example of inadequate and confusing regulations. It demonstrates how important enforcement and legal backbone are, how politicized financial matters can become and how downright unscrupulous business people can continue to manipulate circumstances to their advantage without severe penalties.

This was a particularly complex case, in which we established precedents on the Turkish Stock Exchange as foreign investors wanting to attend and vote at a shareholder's meeting. The case itself was complicated by the fact that we were (a) portfolio investors, not direct investors, and (b) that we held shares in a special status company, a utility, which under Turkish law had only become available for foreign investment recently (Law 4046 respecting privatization).

In 1952, the Government wanted to establish the Seyhan Project for hydroelectric and irrigation purposes. They approached the World Bank, but the World Bank said that a private company should be used to finance the project. The eventual compromise reached was that electricity generation would be moved into the hands of a newly formed private company, while irrigation remained in the hands of the Government. Cukurova Elektrik AS, (CEAS) was formed to generate and distribute the electricity in Adana and Mersin.

Incorporation was completed in 1956 and the agreement with the Government states that the company will hold its franchise for 49 years.

After successfully managing the Seyhan projects, CEAS's customer base increased by 4.6 percent in 1993, while sales volume increased by 7 percent. On the back of this good performance, CEAS offered to take over and complete all projects in area on the condition that either ownership or operating rights were assigned to Cukurova Elektrik. With six hydroelectric power plants already under their control, and the possibility of being awarded government mandates to take over the management of others, Cukurova looked like a good buy.

We drove a half hour outside of Adana to reach the Cukurova Elektrik headquarters which is located near one of their small dams and reservoirs. After being shunted around a little bit, we ended up in Vakif Acunsal's office. He was a middle-aged gentleman who seemed to be quite diplomatic and knowledgeable but sharp. Initially he asked Mr Kutman's sister to translate, but later he moved into English which we found to be quite fluent. Yaman Akar, a younger man, later joined us, and he seemed to be even more fluent in English and used to dealing with foreigners.

We were impressed by the clean offices, good security and generally orderly way the company was operating. It's obvious that the World Bank and the multilateral institutions have been very influential in the company and have encouraged the use of more businesslike and efficient methods.

In 1981, the company had 60 megawatts of power, but demand was increasing. The construction of a fertilizer plant in Mersin resulted in demand from that plant alone being 25 megawatts. Therefore more power was needed and an oil-fired plant was subsequently built in Mersin. At that time, the plant was very attractive because oil prices were low in 1966. The plant went into operation in 1969.

In 1970, the Turkish Electric Authority (TEA) came into being. After 1974, the Authority restricted the construction of further power plants in Turkey. This hiatus lasted until 1984 and during that time, CEAS extended only its distribution and transmission network, purchasing the extra power it needed from the TEA.

After 1984, the ban was lifted and CEAS started building again. They completed the Sir project in 1991, effectively increasing their power generating capacity by 40 percent. A new project at Berke was initiated – its 510 megawatts capacity will practically double CEAS's output. The World Bank was brought in to finance the foreign currency portion of costs for the Berke project, with CEAS undertaking the local currency portion of the costs. Total project costs were budgeted at US$670 million, of which the World Bank was to arrange US$370 million.

The company has its problems with rates, as there is only one tariff structure for all areas of Turkey and it is dictated by the TEA. Despite the restrictions, CEAS's management claimed to be more efficient than TEA and were therefore able to turn a profit. The bigger problem in management's eyes, however, was that they could meet all of the demand for electricity through their own output. In fact, they could only generate about 50 percent of the electricity they sold. They said: "When we can cover all our demand with our own power supply then we will really be profitable."

Excerpt from call report after meeting with management, August 1992

The cause of all our problems emerged in 1993. The Uzan group of companies, a family-owned conglomerate in Turkey, was successful in talking the Government into selling an 18 percent stake to them during a privatization drive. By accumulating more shares on the open market, the family group found itself with a total of 37 percent and became the new majority shareholder. Before the end of this sorry saga, the Uzan family would be found to own over 67 percent of CEAS, much of which was bought up after the shares dropped to a pittance on the Turkish Stock Exchange as a result of corporate disarray.

After the Uzan takeover, initial irregularities were discovered through an audit, done by the Capital Markets Board, of Kepez Elektrik, a 30 percent-owned subsidiary of CEAS. The auditors uncovered evidence that money raised from a rights issue was used to speculate in foreign exchange markets instead of for capital expenditure. Additionally, Kepez failed to make provisions related to disputable receivables and was found to be holding large non-interest bearing cash deposits in a bank affiliated with the family.

We had ourselves noted that company performance had deteriorated markedly. Debt levels were up, and the share price fell to as low as $.018, from the US$1.25 per share paid by the Uzan family to acquire the company in the first place.

During the first year that the company was controlled by the Uzan Family, profits dropped 31 percent, from US$59 million in 1992 to US$41 million in 1993. By 1994, the company posted a US$18 million loss during the first nine months of the year, the first loss in the company's 34-year history. A pattern of layoffs and workplace strife also ensued, with the Uzan family locking out plant managers and hiring their own personal security officers to blockade the premises. No progress was made during this time in completing the earlier outlined expansion projects. In fact, a previously selected Italian contractor quit one project under development after working with the Uzans and claimed to be owed money by them. Rizas, a Uzan-controlled contractor replaced the Italian firm.

Concerned about the rapid deterioration in the conditions of the firm, we decided to attend the annual shareholders meeting, charge the family with corrupt practices and try to stall any changes they planned to make to the company's articles of association. In order to attend the meeting, we knew we had to register our shares. However, a message from Citibank Istanbul to our custodians, Morgan Stanley Luxembourg, regarding share registration, on 29 November 1994 gave us cause to hesitate.

"Share registration is not a requirement for custody and is not a market practice. If a foreign investor wishes to attend a meeting or vote by proxy, the investor should assign a power of Attorney to its Custodian to register the securities with the Undersecretary of Treasury and Foreign Trade as direct investors, as opposed to portfolio investors. Mutual funds may vote at company meetings only by registering as direct investors. Direct investors are subject to Turkish Capital Gains tax (48.3 percent for non-resident investors in equities) and all other taxes that apply and upon official approval of the registration from TFT, the custodian registers the shares with the company in the client's name. In most cases, the registration allows shareholders to attend the meeting or authorize the subcustodian to vote via proxy. If you do commence registration, you will not be able to sell the shares until the process is finalized, and the shares will no longer be under our custody."

Subsequent legal advice indicated that there would be no tax complications derived from registering the shares, as mutual funds (which are subject to the capital gains tax upon selling local shares) are legally exempted if they appoint a "representative" in Turkey to manage the shares. Ultimately, we did decide to register.

Our efforts to register our shares in order to obtain entry to the AGM were hampered by the need for FID (Foreign Investment Directorate of Turkey) approval, which was slow in coming. The process of a foreign portfolio investor registering shares was a legal precedent, causing the department to proceed with great caution. During this period, we were warned that by attending the meeting and accusing management of misconduct or wrongdoing, we were opening ourselves up to legal liability for slander if the accusations proved false.

When we finally received a response from the FID, it was negative, refusing to register our shares unless they were already registered and passed into the "safekeeping" of the company itself. Knowing full well how safe they'd be there, we felt that the FID's ruling was absurd and in a last ditch attempt, we wrote to the Office of the President, to President Ciller herself, to request intervention with the FID. We only wanted to register and gain an entry card to the meeting so we could vote. We didn't request any additional pressure on the company or protection of our interests over those of other shareholders. Ultimately, the President's office pressured the head of the FID and our shares were registered and an entry card provided.

The Extraordinary Shareholders' Meeting on 9 January 1995

Motions from management were:

- addition of clause to permit securities trading (and thus be able to buy their own shares without shareholders' approval);

- change shares to bearer format (to conceal number of shares held by major shareholders at any one time);

- reduce minimum number of directors to three from nine.

During the shareholders' meeting, our objections were officially noted for the record, but we were the only dissenters. The final vote was 2.8 million shares to 0.9 million shares, and the Uzan family was able to implement all the changes it had tabled. We were disappointed, but knew that at least we'd made a first strike.

The story doesn't end there, though. By early March 1995, the Capital Market Board in Ankara initiated a lawsuit against the Uzan group. It accused the Uzan group of violating Turkish Capital Market Laws as well as criminal law, all in relation to an alleged siphoning of funds from a listed company. They focused on received funds from the World Bank which were to have been applied to financing the Berke Dam project as well as the financial accounts, especially exchange differences and interest expenses. It was alleged that irregular loans were made to related companies, funds were held in low-interest rate deposits of affiliated banks and foreign currency transactions were undertaken at unreasonably high rates.

> "Our investigations covered the first nine months of 1994 when the problems actually began. We noticed sharp increases in foreign exchange losses and interest expenses. Although the company maintained a sizable amount of cash, it increased its borrowings. We were also amazed by the financial arrangement the Uzan group used to buy the cement companies from the Privatization Administration through their own private company and turn around and sell them later to CEAS: when the Uzan's sold the cement companies to CEAS, they received an advance payment! In other words, the deal had required very little upfront investment from the private company and had reaped a huge profit from CEAS. When we found such irregularities, our Legal Department suggested a lawsuit, but the Capital Market Board rejected the idea because we thought it was a free market. Therefore, we tried to leave it to the minority shareholders to take action. After a while, we were disappointed by how weak the minority shareholders were. We have now decided to take legal action ourselves."
>
> Audit Department of the Capital Market Board of Ankara, Mr. Aytekin, as quoted from a meeting on 7 March 1995.

Over this period, we maintained our correspondence with the President's office, and had a chance to meet with the Director General of the General Directorate of Foreign Investment, who was willing to assist us, though deferring to the Capital Market Board to press charges. The Capital Market Board did press its case, while at the same time, the Ministry of Energy came in on their side. The Ministry shut down CEAS, replaced its Uzan-family-dominated board of directors with one selected by the CMB, and initiated proceedings to withdraw CEAS's franchise/concession.

This was done on the pretext that the family hadn't paid TEA, the Turkish Electricity Authority the amount agreed on, and didn't pay installments on cement factories bought from the State during a privatization campaign. Six conditions were set for the Uzans to meet before regaining control of their company. The Uzans had also angered other public sector bodies. They cheated on the purchase of a license to enter the cellular phone business, which eventually resulted in the revocation of the license by Turk Telecom. CMB was also able to block all nine related group companies from securities trading, and shut down group-owned Adabank for perpetrating run-up trades on CEAS subsidiary, Kepek Elektrik.

These were major victories for the CMB and for capital markets regulation in general in Turkey. Unfortunately, the situation moved on to a new plane from this point. It ceased to be a public interest case, and moved into the private political arena. The Uzan family took off its gloves, lobbied for political supports in the opposition party, and even used their family-owned TV station to tarnish the reputation of the president's family.

The Uzan family settled its case with the Ministry of Energy, by agreeing to pay back debt owed to TEA and to withdraw from securities dealing. This satisfied the Ministry of Energy, and it was now up to CMB to wage the lonely battle of continued prosecution. The Ministry of Industry and

Commerce attempted to wade in on behalf of the Uzans, by appointing a special auditor with the powers to call a general meeting. Although a new general meeting was held in which the Uzans were brought back to power, that was declared null and void by the regional courts. The conflict, which used to be the Uzans against the State, appeared to have evolved into turning parts of the State against each other.

One observer (a Turkish broker, in early 1996) had the last word:

"The case gets more complicated every day with numerous lawsuits and politicians involved and it seems to me it will last for a long time."

Risks of every kind showed in this conflict; political, systemic, and transactional. What it makes clear is the need for very specific regulatory systems which take account of all shareholders. Below is a review of the bare minimum needed to keep the system honest and to make it safe for domestic and foreign investors alike.

Adequate minority shareholder protection

Developed countries generally provide specific rights to minority shareholders in the event of a takeover bid. Disclosure and other obligations are required of the majority shareholders seeking to alter the share arrangements. In the case of Cukurova, the Uzan group was permitted to acquire control without making an offer to all shareholders, without undertakings as to future operation of the company. In a most base disregard for basic standards of conduct, the Uzans were widely alleged to have solicited proxy votes in exchange for money.

Limitation of related-party transactions

There is clearly considerable scope for abuse in a system which permits intercompany transactions between public and private entities to go unreported. Using this gap in the regulatory system of Turkey, Cukurova's management was able to funnel cash out of the publicly traded firm and into the coffers of related companies by purchasing private issue shares. Cukurova funds were also used to bid for the State-owned cement companies being privatized.

Greater regulatory enforcement and penalties

Clearly, the case of Cukurova and the Uzan family could have been cleaned up considerably faster had the Capital Markets Board, the Treasury or any other ministry held enough enforcement authority to shut them down, cancel their contracts and have them arrested. The fact that the cases dragged on before the courts for so long and that in the end the Uzan family was not banned from public trading or sitting as board directors, much less convicted criminally, illustrates the challenges a weak authority faces when trying to remedy grossly illicit conduct. Clear jurisdiction between branches of authority is also necessary, to ensure the bad guys don't play one off against the other and stymie the legal process.

Recourse for minority shareholders

This condition is as much a state of mind among the investors themselves as it is a regulatory concern. Templeton Investment and its related parties were the only objectors during the January 1995 Extraordinary Shareholder's Meeting. It wasn't for lack of publicity in Turkey – rather a culture of minority shareholder defense didn't really exist. In the case of Templeton in Turkey, there were several steps in the procedure for registering shares and obtaining an "entry card" to the shareholder's meetings which, were they streamlined or done away with, would make shareholder participation much more feasible. Such a regulatory stance in favor of minority shareholders would also send the message to companies that they must be prepared to face questioning in the event of significant corporate modifications. There is also the need for a recourse mechanism which is both timely and cost-effective. If the only course of action is to lay criminal charges, this requires expensive court time, and can drag on for years.

Procedural norms

There are many practices in developed markets which have grown up over time, been codified and now stand as standard practice. However, in emerging markets, these norms are haphazard and incomplete at best. At worst, a management team bent on manipulative behavior has wide latitude to manipulate the system to their advantage. Procedural norms which are beneficial to shareholders include:

- the need for a trustee to count votes and confirm the validity of proxy votes;
- timely announcement of shareholders' meetings;
- clear differentiation of share classes;
- simple registration process of both shares, and votes.

All of the above points are aspects of the rules of incorporation and capital markets of which one should be aware when taking an equity stake in companies in emerging markets. It gives a flavor not only of the complexity of investment regulation, and the hassle of being invested here, but also of the pioneering spirit and determination required to pursue the issue.

This has been a long and perhaps somewhat disheartening chapter, both to write and to read. Focusing solely on the downside – the risks – of emerging markets is very one-sided and should by no means constitute a potential investor's entire view of the situation. However, a catalog in one place of all the latent perils associated with investing in immature financial markets does crystalize in the mind of the individual all that is involved in the under-

> *I think a recognition of political, financial, investment, transaction and systemic risk is vital to all those considering personal investments, whether in emerging markets or one's own backyard.*

taking. I think a recognition of political, financial, investment, transaction and systemic risk is vital to all those considering personal investments, whether in emerging markets or one's own backyard.

I've tried a number of investment systems and have found that a fundamental long-term commonsense investment approach is best.

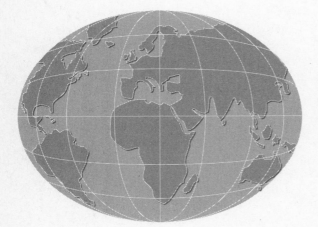

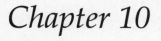

Chapter 10

My view of of Emerging Markets Investment

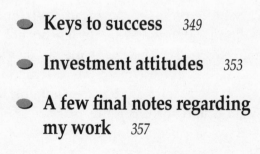

The development of emerging equity markets offers the future promise of outstanding benefits for developing nations' economic growth. Such markets will provide the means whereby these nations may distribute the owner-ship of privatized companies, provide a method where market forces may allocate financial assets, and most importantly, provide a stimulus for the attraction of new equity capital for growing emerging markets' companies. If these benefits are to be fully realized, the emerging nation governments must create favorable conditions through market liberalization as well as adequate infrastructures (such as computerized trading systems and central depos-itory schemes) which will allow for the smooth and effi-cient operation of equity markets.

In emerging markets investment, it is necessary to be optimistic since the world belongs to optimists; the pessimists are only spectators. The fact remains that there have always been prob-lems and there will continue to be so in the coming years throughout the world. But we are entering an era which is perhaps unparalleled in the history of mankind. With better communications, improved travel, more international com-merce and generally better relations between nations, the oppor-tunities for mankind and for emerging markets investors are better than they have ever been before.

There certainly are numerous problems in the world of emerg-ing markets and there are high risks in investing in such nations. But, as someone once said: "Problems are opportunities in work clothes." The demise of Communism and the coming together of nations around the world, combined with the emergence of China and India as free enterprise market economies, have cre-ated opportunities for the creation of wealth which are unparal-leled. Although some of the stock markets of the developing nations may sometimes seem to be "submerged," they are generally emerging into bigger and better things. The important thing is to keep an open mind and to diversify your global equity exposure.

In emerging markets investment, it is necessary to be optimistic since the world belongs to optimists; the pessimists are only spectators.

Studies have shown that stock market investments made in a patient and consistent manner will invariably grow, since there is a natural tendency for the value of equity investments to rise in order to keep up with inflation. In addition, independently managed businesses, competing successfully in the market place, are generally winners on the stock markets as there is a tendency for their sales, profits and assets to expand. However, it is not always possible to predict whether a company is going to be successful or unsuccessful, so it is necessary to diversify.

Everyone thinks that first and foremost, it takes an MBA to be a fund manager. That, and a head for numbers. But there is a lot more to it – personal integrity, flexibility, command, human insight, courage to go with your instincts, long hours – that people don't usually take into account when preparing themselves from a young age for the profession of their dreams.

KEYS TO SUCCESS

Frankly, while there are certainly numerous technical skills one can learn to aid in managing a fund, investing is still a large percentage psychological. Both buyers and sellers are acting on a combination of instinct, information and logic. It is important not to forget the key role that development of certain personal characteristics can contribute to your investment success.

I was recently asked to comment on leadership in finance. It was an odd set of questions, but I enjoyed the thought process it stimulated, because I hadn't approached some of the issues from that angle before. In particular, it brought back to my mind one of the key experiences in the life of the emerging market fund I help manage – the October 1987 crash of the markets around the world. The Templeton Emerging Markets Fund had only just started in early 1987, and it experienced a disastrous performance in its first year, with the loss in value of the Fund of about 20 percent. It was necessary for me and others in our team to demonstrate leadership by reassuring our investors that the crash was exactly not the time to pull out of the fund.

We at Templeton have been lucky to have sophisticated and disciplined investors who listened carefully to our reasoning, did their own analysis and stayed with us over that difficult period. By keeping their funds with us at that time, we were able to purchase stocks at very low price levels between October and December of 1987, so that in the following years we reaped the rewards with higher prices and excellent fund performance. Moreover, those investors who purchased additional shares in the fund while it was at its nadir, went on to make even greater returns. In the true nature of market cycles, by 1993, the same markets that bottomed in late 1987, hit their all-time highs, and we generated returns of over 100 percent at that time.

Hard work and discipline

Someone asked me once if I could condense the most important qualities needed for a good investor into five words and I replied: "Motivation, humility, hard work, discipline." It stands to reason that the more time and effort is put into researching investments, the more knowledge will be gained and wiser decisions will be made. Humility is needed so you are able and willing to ask questions. If you think you know all the answers you probably don't even know the questions.

Commonsense

I like to think that commonsense is most important when making investment decisions, since the word "commonsense" implies the clarity and simplification required to integrate successfully all the complex information with which investors are faced.

Creativity

A significant amount of creativity is required for successful investing, since it is necessary to look at investments from a multifaceted approach, considering all the variables that could negatively or positively affect an investment. Also, creative thinking is required to look forward to the future and forecast the outcome of current business plans.

Independence

A number of successful investors have commented on the importance of independence and individual decision-making. When making investments, it is very unlikely that committee decisions can be superior to a well thought out individual decision. If one buys the same securities as other people, one ends up with the same results as other people. When any method for selecting stocks becomes popular, it is time to switch to method which is not yet popular. Too many investors can spoil any share selection method or any market-timing formula. It is impossible to produce a superior performance unless one does something different from the majority.

Risk-taking

Investment decisions always require decisions based on insufficient information. There is never enough time to learn all there is to know about an investment and even if there were, equity investments are like living organisms undergoing continuous change. There always comes the time when a decision must be taken and a risk acquired. The ability to take that risk based on the best diligently gathered available information is the mark of a good investor.

Flexibility

It is important for investors to be flexible and not permanently adopt a particular type of asset or selection method. The best approach is to migrate from the popular to the unpopular securities, sectors or methods. It's also an attribute which keeps one from holding on to a stock out of loyalty – flexibility allows one to change as times change and new circumstances present themselves.

On a personal note, I know that a clear mind and well-rested body contribute significantly to my investment performance. Lots of people have the impression that people in the financial industry lead wild lives and behave in a cavalier fashion. If I were so arrogant and unbusinesslike, my sources of information would dry up and my capacity for making more informed investment choices would be undermined. Integrity and determination are much more likely to be rewarded with trust and information.

I eat healthily and drink minimally. It is also important to me to have access to a gym, so that after a long day in flight or sitting in a boardroom, I can stretch cramped muscles. Without this kind of discipline, I'm too distracted or tired to absorb the new information I'm picking up or to catch the nuances underlying the message. On the contrary, I get some of my best ideas during an exercise break, when I can mull over various inputs from the day's activities. Rapid travel through different time zones is also facilitated if one is healthy.

In emerging market investing, it is particularly important to be fresh, alert and calm, because dramatic curves can be thrown at you out in the field and one must be prepared to catch them.

On some occasions, I am expected to spend a long evening socializing with hosts after having flown 12 hours and after a long, dusty plantation visit. If I'm not in peak condition, I may be cranky or rude to the hosts and blow my chance to learn the inside scoop on the company's affairs. It's easy to see how personal preparation contributes to superior professional performance in circumstances such as these.

INVESTMENT ATTITUDES

So that's the personal preparation that goes into investing. On the professional side, it can't be stressed enough that reading, of a wide variety, contributes enormously to an investor's ability to make insightful decisions. There are also investment attitudes, on top of the personal attributes cited above, that will benefit your investment results.

Diversification

It is actually possible to have all your eggs in the wrong basket at the wrong time, especially in emerging market investment. To reduce one's vulnerability to this eventuality, every investor should diversify. This is particularly important in emerging markets where individual country or company risks can be extreme. Even given the risks, however, global investing is always superior to investing in only your home market or one market. If you search worldwide, you will find more bargains and better bargains than by studying only one nation.

Timing and staying invested

I love to reply to those who ask when they should invest in equities by using the provocative answer provided by Sir John Templeton: "The best time to invest is when you have money." The reality is that market timing is impossible, and since equity investing is the best way to preserve value, rather than leaving money in a bank account, it is best to just get going, rather than wait for the fabled perfect moment. A corollary to the question of when to buy is, of course, when to sell. My feeling on that issue is that investments should not be sold unless a much better investment has been found to replace it.

Long-term view

I know how unsatisfying it is for investors who invested in a fund only to see the net asset value turn sour, or not make the fast gains they were expecting, to hear that they should be in it for the "long-term." But it's the truth. As investment managers, we have a policy of looking to the long-term because experience has shown us that if we try to make short-term gains the results will work against outstanding performance. Since most investors look at the short term, then we certainly should not do that. By looking at the long-term growth and prospects of companies and countries, particularly those stocks which are out of favor or unpopular, the chances of obtaining a superior return are much greater. To minimize discomfort or disappointment, I advise fund representatives from the very start of their sales process to stress to their clients the importance of long-term investing and dollar averaging.

Investment averaging

Another point that should be remembered by investors is the importance of investment averaging by purchasing consistently in a measured and periodic pattern. Investors who establish a program from the very beginning to purchase shares over a set period of time have the opportunity to purchase at not only high prices, but also low prices, bringing their average cost down.

Accepting market cycles

Any study of stock markets around the world will show that bear or bull markets have always been temporary. It is clear that markets do have cyclical behavior with pessimistic, skeptical, optimistic, euphoric, panic and depressive phases. Investors should thus expect such variations and plan accordingly. We have all adopted the belief that the time of maximum pessimism is the best time to buy and conversely the best time to sell is the moment of maximum optimism. As often noted, if it's possible to see the light at the end of the tunnel then it is probably already too late to buy.

But don't just take my word for it, that these personal and professional attributes really help. According to conventional logic, historical performance is often the primary consideration in most investment manager selection decisions. However, a recent study conducted on fund managers concluded that there was a total absence of any predictive value in historical performance rankings of money managers. In fact, the research went on to identify the characteristics most helpful in identifying managers who achieve superior, long-term results. These characteristics included independent thinking, unencumbered decision-making, discipline, flexibility and last, but certainly not least, a true passion for investing. Successful investors do love what they do and see it as a personal occupation, not just a job or necessity.

The emerging market investor's creed
(or, maxims to invest by)

Here are some of the maxims inspired by John Templeton and other great investors:

- To buy when others are despondently selling, and to sell when others are greedily buying, requires the greatest fortitude but pays the highest reward.
- To avoid having all your eggs in the wrong basket at the wrong time, every investor should diversify.

- If you search worldwide you will find more bargains and better bargains than by studying only one country. Also, you will gain safety of diversification.
- The best values are available in those nations where economic problems are most obvious.
- If you buy the same securities as other people, you will get the same results as other people.
- Too many investors focus on outlook and trend, therefore profits are made by focusing on value.
- The time to sell an asset is when you have found a much better bargain. In the stock market, the only way to get a bargain is to buy what most investors are selling, because otherwise the price would never be pushed down to bargain levels.
- Share prices fluctuate more widely than share values.
- Achieving a good investment record is a lot harder than most people think. And believe me, that's important. There are so many people who buy investments because they hear something simple, for instance, this company has a new product, or this company is going to grow. That's just the beginning of what you need to know.
- When appraising the value of corporations, a good security analyst will be knowledgeable about more than one hundred yardsticks of value.
- Different yardsticks are more significant for some companies than others. In most cases the single greatest yardstick is how high is the price in relation to earnings; but of course it is more important to compare price not with present earnings, but with what the analyst estimates the corporation can earn five to ten years in the future.

  It is important to know that successful investing must be the reverse of the procedures for success in other professions. Very few investors and very few investment professionals fully understand that superior performance can be achieved only be doing the opposite of what is popular with the rest of the investment community.
- The best time to invest is when you have money. Of course this

assumes that you can find the bargains you should be looking for. Don't worry about market timing.

A FEW FINAL NOTES REGARDING MY WORK

Influences

I arrived at the present investment approach through experience and study. I've tried a number of investment systems and have found that a fundamental long-term common sense investment approach is best. But I tuned into that investment philosophy as a result of previous experience both negative and positive and also as a result of extensive reading on the subject such as Barnard Baruch's great book *"The Battle for Investment Survival"* and a number of other such books by veteran investors. Also the numerous experiences I have had around the world prepared me to adopt this investment philosophy. In the 1960s I conducted hundreds of industry studies all over Asia, I operated my own research consulting firm for a number of years, I've lived in a number of countries, and I've held a wide variety of jobs from playing pianos in Wisconsin bars (not recommended for the serious investor) to consulting on arms control and disarmament. All of these experiences are grist for the philosophical mill.

The Templeton organization presently manages many emerging market funds and private accounts. Our total emerging markets assets under management as at 1996 were over US$9 billion. The largest emerging market fund was the Templeton Developing Market Trust, a US open-ended fund with a value of assets under management of over US$2 billion.

Personal interests

A career in investment was a natural consequence of my interests and training. What I do now fits in beautifully with my interests

> *The more companies we visit, the more people we listen to, the more studies we read, the better will be our investment performance and the wiser our decisions.*

and psychological make-up; an optimistic nature with a skeptical slant, and interest in everything and anything, a desire to explore, a genuine desire to help people, a love of isolation and study, but also a joy in meeting new people and making new friends. My days are spent in study, observation and analysis, through meetings, faxes, telephone calls – I'm constantly in touch with people. A successful portfolio manager or investor must be infinitely curious and willing to continuously learn. This of course involves a considerable amount of humility, because you must be willing to allow your ego to be continuously attacked by new information which contradicts what you have learned previously.

Interestingly, what some might find to be distractions, I generally consider to be opportunities for observation. For example, going through the Shanghai airport would seem mundane and even annoying, as one passes through customs, loads luggage on the luggage cart, walks through the security X-ray, etc. But for me, even those activities provide observations and teach me about how the environment in a particular country has changed. In turn, these observations can be applied more generally to social and political developments in a given country. Sticking with the same example, I noticed that organization of the Shanghai airport had improved noticeably over my last visit, which suggests to me broader changes in activities in China.

Because I need to constantly switch gears, from country to country, company to company, it is important to be organized. To achieve this, I try to pare down the workload by delegating those items which are not directly connected to the investment process. The ideal day or series of days in investment management terms would be a day filled with visits to potential investment target companies where I meet the management, the owners and the actual company operations, whether it be a factory, department store or bank. The more companies we visit, the more people we listen to, the more studies we read, the better will be our investment performance and the wiser our decisions.

Personal investments

One question a lot of people ask me, or would like to ask me, is how I handle my own personal finances. I invest my own assets in the funds we manage, and the funds of other investment managers, as well as in real estate. As an investment manager, it is important to avoid conflicts of interest, so it's best if I detour individual share issues and try as much as possible to put my money into non-equity investments or the funds I manage.

Commitment

It's important to me that I have conveyed in the course of this book the message that investing and my personal philosophy are closely related. It wouldn't be possible to continue this kind of day in and day out commitment to the work if it didn't satisfy my personal as well as my professional objectives.

I believe in the course of development upon which the world has embarked. Free market enterprise enables people who want the chance to improve their lives to do so via hard work and thrift. Those are values I believe in, and as an investor, can feel I am contributing to when our fund invests in a well-managed company with a sound business plan in one of the emerging markets of the world. This is how the developed economies started, and this is how the emerging economies are going to succeed.

In an effort to draw these links, I've outlined the progress of social conditions which are enabling more and more people everyday around the world to participate in economic life. Then I reviewed the experience of several countries, all of them diverse in their cultures and language, but all with the common goal of implementing policies that ultimately lead to a better life for their citizens. And then I reviewed what is involved in investing in these countries, demonstrating along the way some areas in which national capital markets still need to mature.

This is an endlessly fascinating and meaningful process. It absorbs me completely. I plan to spend the rest of my life studying and working, finding investment bargains for my clients. I hope that some of the flavour of my investing experiences has been distilled for the reader, and that it entices you too to investigate these markets further and have an open mind towards their initiatives, their attempts and their dreams.

Index

....